SPORT AND SOCIETY

Series Editors

Benjamin G. Rader
Randy Roberts

TELEVISION AND
NATIONAL SPORT

TELEVISION AND NATIONAL SPORT
The United States and Britain

Joan M. Chandler

UNIVERSITY OF ILLINOIS PRESS

Urbana and Chicago

© 1988 by the Board of Trustees of the University of Illinois
Manufactured in the United States of America
C 5 4 3 2 1
This book is printed on acid-free paper.

Library of Congress Cataloging-in-Publication Data

Chandler, Joan M. (Joan Mary), 1930–
    Television and national sport.

    (Sport and society)
    Bibliography: p.
    Includes index.
    1. Television broadcasting of sports – United States.
2. Television broadcasting of sports – Great Britain.
I. Title. II. Series.
GV742.3.C43   1988   070.4'49796'0973   87-35709
ISBN 0-252-01516-9 (alk. paper)

CONTENTS

ACKNOWLEDGMENTS

I am grateful to a number of people who read all or part of this manuscript and commented most helpfully on it. Among them are William Baker, Marian Cole, Charles Harpole, Lawrence Malley, Patricia McClellan, Jane Russell, and David Voigt. The errors that remain are, of course, my own. Carol Saller's intelligent, perspicacious, and meticulous editing was very valuable.

I should also like to thank the many members of the North American Society for Sport History who have listened patiently to my attempts to work out these ideas at conferences and have discussed them afterward. I am particularly grateful to Melvin Adelman, Benjamin Rader, and Betty Spears. We have by no means always agreed, but their ideas have invariably caused me to think. I also owe a debt to Joseph Arbena, who organized the excellent Clemson University conferences on sport; the papers and discussion there, formal and informal, were always fruitful.

A graduate student at the University of Texas at Dallas, Margaret Hanson, did much of the work on which the research for chapter 9 was based. Undergraduates who took the Sport and U.S. Society course also helped considerably, whether they knew it or not. Many of them are experts in one sport or another, and their questions and common sense kept me from the common academic failing of believing six impossible things before breakfast. I thank them all.

INTRODUCTION

I love to watch sport on television. I have the best seat in the house, choose my own refreshments, and am told more about the game than I really want to know. Not for me the traffic jams, the hard benches, the chill or sweat of the stadium. And above all, TV takes me where I could never afford to go. Who could forget the extraordinary beauty and skill of Torvill and Dean at the Sarajevo Winter Olympics? Or fail to be moved by the quiet grace of Mrs. Kitty Godfree, Wimbledon Ladies' Champion in 1924 and 1926, eighty-eight years old and still playing tennis, as she received her 1984 centennial award? The marvelous moves of "The Juice" are treasured memories of thousands who have never been to Buffalo. TV begs me to see the best sport in the world.

This book, then, is not written by an unbiased observer. But it is not designed simply to eulogize televised sport. Rather, I hope to set TV sport in a historical context, and to demonstrate that TV sport represents cultural continuity rather than cultural change.

We now take it for granted that TV has altered sport in some fundamental ways. TV has allegedly spoiled professional athletes by making them rich and selfish; it has ripped franchises from their traditional moorings as owners reach frantically for the biggest buck; it has turned professional sport into nothing more than a facet of the entertainment industry, devoid of ideals and unworthy of our devotion.[1] My premise, on the contrary, is that the TV industry has not, per se, changed the essence of the sports televised, nor their conduct, although it has enormously enlarged the sporting audience. Far from seeking to alter the presentation of sport to paying customers, TV executives have simply built on the commercial foundations already laid by the sports industry. The new medium has not in some magical way transformed professional sport; it has only appeared to do so, because in seeking to maintain an illusion, TV has inadvertently exposed it.

For what TV has done is to rip away the packaging in which the professional sports mystique used to be delivered. In the first place, fans now see exactly what is going on.[2] The close-ups of television are merciless; the lapse of concentration, the hotdogging, the angry scowl and vicious jab are all starkly revealed and can be replayed again and again. As David Halberstam pointed out in *The Breaks of the Game,* professional basketball players in the seventies began to loaf. And "just as the camera had caught and transmitted the true intensity of the old fashioned rivalries in the earlier days of the league, so it now caught and transmitted with equal fidelity the increasing lethargy and indifference of many players in regular season games."[3]

In a televised game, we see with our own eyes. Sportswriters and radio commentators used to construct exciting games for us; if the great man or fabulous team did not quite meet our expectations when we got the chance to see them in the flesh, we knew that either we had missed something we should have been capable of seeing, or we had paid to watch an off day. A dull game on television remains dull, however frantically the commentators work "to create interest when none is there," as a student put it.

Certainly, television money has extended seasons, putting more pressure on tired athletes, but those athletes are now better fed, housed, conditioned, transported, and medically supervised than ever before,[4] thanks in part to that same money. Certainly, too, TV viewers' interests are likely to be capricious, because viewers have invested no time or money in going to an event and do not therefore have to persuade themselves that their investment has been worth it. But this merely means that televised sports must be of a consistently high standard if they are to keep their audience. Far from diminishing sport, TV has taught us to know what the best in sport is and to expect it.

It is however one thing to argue that TV has merely extended established sports traditions, another to demonstrate it. Accordingly, I have compared the handling of televised sport in the United States and Britain, both industrialized countries, but in which the TV and sports industries have different histories and are differently constituted. This comparison rests on the explicit assumption that there is·such a thing as "national character," however difficult it may be to define, and however easy to describe in facile generalizations. There are no doubt many British and American people who have more in common with each other than they do with their compatriots. But whatever distinctions may be made within nations (and the gulf between a WASP Boston attorney and a Hispanic migrant worker is wide and deep) differences between nations often outweigh them. Both the United States and Britain are now self-consciously and often bitterly multicultural; but sports fans have established their own traditions on each side of the Atlantic,[5] and these are continued on TV.

For however one inteprets the effects of the encoding that translation from stadium to living room requires, which I discuss in chapter 1, it is true that people living within a particular culture learn how to "read" TV. As Riochi Okabe puts it, "It is fair to assume that in an *intra*cultural setting a communicator and receiver invariably share some views, desires and values that can serve as the bases upon which a receiver-conscious communicator builds a receiver-centered case. This assumption, however, does not apply to *inter*cultural communications, where persons of diverse cultural backgrounds interact."[6] The "Dallas" series was watched avidly worldwide; what Americans made of it is not at all what foreigners made of it. What we "read" in a televised sports program therefore depends at least as much on what we bring to the program as on what the program actually shows.

Both in the United States and Britain thousands of hours of sports programs are broadcast each year, many of them live events. To keep my subject within manageable bounds, I have confined my discussion to the national sports of baseball, football, cricket, and soccer, as they are televised in the United States and Britain, and the international sport of tennis. All four national sports were commercialized, in that spectators were charged admission, by the end of the nineteenth century. If one considers professionalism to consist of paying cash to players, football was professionalized last; if one considers professionalism to consist of playing only to win, college football was professionalized very early. Lawn tennis was metamorphosed only in the late 1960s; its TV exposure provides a useful international case study.

What becomes evident from these sports, tennis included, is that what American and British spectators wanted from professional sport was established long before there were TV sets in every home, and that TV has worked within the context of those demands. TV, however, has revealed to sports fans on both sides of the Atlantic the business skeleton beneath the mythic clothing, and in so doing shattered the illusions on which professional promoters have long based their profits. We now know the truth; and if it has made us free, it has also made many of us bitter.

To try to do comparative work is not easy, because little has been written about the relationship of TV and sport in any connection. The only published monograph I have been able to find that deals with British sport and television, *Football on Television* is, perhaps significantly, the only British Film Institute Monograph presently out of print.[7] A good deal of material exists in article form, but very little of it is cross-cultural or historical in intent. I have therefore worked within clear and conscious limits. First, this book deals only with network TV, not because cable is unimportant or because cable services are undeveloped in Britain and so cannot be compared with those in the United States, but because I am concerned primarily with the televised event itself. If I am wrong in thinking that the essence of a professional game need not be changed simply because it is televised, and that television has simply built on established traditions, the difference between cable and network delivery is irrelevant to an argument that is wrongheaded. If, however, I am right, then the differences between the commercial requirements of cable and network TV deserve far more extended treatment than I can give them here.

Second, almost all my discussion concerns sporting events that are transmitted live and unedited. I have not, for instance, considered sports newscasts, kaleidoscopic sports programs that cover a number of different events, or edited versions of particular sports (except in the case of soccer for reasons I have explained in chapter 7). Viewers will almost certainly get some of their perceptions of football, for instance, from televised sources other than live games; but to examine properly the content and intent of edited sports programs requires considerably more comparative study than I have yet been able to give. My suspicion is that these programs demonstrate the same differences I have found in live broadcasts, but I cannot yet establish that.

Third, I have not examined here the broader context of a live televised event, but have concentrated on the telecast itself. In considering the coverage of the 1974 World Cup, a series of soccer matches broadcast by both the BBC and ITV, Edward Buscombe used three of the five papers in *Football on Television* to discuss the context in which the matches were set, rather than the televising of the matches themselves. He states, "The first chapter examines the ways in which both broadcasting organizations attempted through their programme guides to create a context for the matches, and shows that from well before the programmes began, there was never any question of viewers receiving an unmediated account of the events."[8] This is true; but it is not peculiar to television. TV executives were in this instance simply using print as it has always been used in connection with professional sport.[9]

For fans have always gone to the stadium with perceptions shaped by what they have read, heard, and said. Few people in history can have attended a professional sports event without preconceived notions about the teams, the star players, the importance of the game, and a host of other matters, much of it gleaned from newspapers and magazines, which helped shape what they thought they saw when they got to the game. The "Four Horsemen" of Notre Dame owe their places in football history not primarily to the quality of their play, but to the quality of Grantland Rice's prose. It is extremely interesting to examine the ways in which television executives seek to shape perception before the event itself through print, through advertisements in print and on TV, through pregame shows, and through introductory framing, but that is a subject separate from examinations of what is happening during the televising of the actual game. This framing of an event is also a slippery subject to handle, because the context of any sporting event that is not a one-of-a-kind spectacular goes far beyond the framing in print or on the screen that immediately precedes it, involving as it does all a viewer's past sporting experience. What I want to examine here is the essential nature of a live televised sporting event, setting it in a historical context. The question of framing seems to me to be a separate and intriguing issue, which requires separate historical treatment.

As Buscombe puts it, "Sport on television raises problems that are central to the study of the medium generally, and especially of its aesthetics and organizational structures."[10] Yet his monograph opens with a defense of the choice of sport as subject matter. Before and since the appearance of his monograph, the bulk of writing about television's coverage of the real world has been concerned with news and current events programs, which are considered important in a way sport is not. Indeed, to try to work in the area of the relationship between sport and television at all is probably to be grubbing about where angels fear to tread, because so many uncertainties exist. We do not know, for instance, why fans go to games or watch them on TV.[11] We have no agreed theory about how TV as a medium affects those who watch it; in spite of decades of research, we still do not know whether violent TV programs actually stimulate children to violence in real life. What "mass" culture really consists of is still a matter of debate. I address some of these problems in the course of the book.

Further, essential materials for a comparative study of sport, with or without TV, are still lacking. There is, for instance, no study of the evolution of the rules of baseball, football, soccer, or tennis comparable to R. S. Rait Kerr's book on the laws of cricket.[12] It is all too easy to announce that TV producers changed traditional rules and ruined the game, if one is happily ignorant of past rule manipulations. Apart from the rules, the history of baseball has been well researched; a good deal of work remains to be done on the social history of cricket and soccer. The histories of football (apart from the history of specific collegiate teams) and tennis have yet to be written. Much more analysis of the structure of the sports industry, on both sides of the Atlantic, needs to be undertaken.

Nevertheless, quite sufficient material exists for me to be able to suggest that we have hitherto regarded the relationship between television and sport in ways that are altogether too short-term. In chapter 1, I show how the stadium and televised versions of a sporting event mesh; the development of baseball and football is used in chapters 2 and 3 to illustrate chapter 1. These three chapters should be read together; several of the assertions made in chapter 1 are grounded on the evidence presented in chapters 2 and 3. Chapters 4 and 5 examine the different expectations British and American viewers are likely to bring to a sporting event, given their heritage and the structure of their television and sports industries. Cricket and soccer, which illustrate British conceptions of sport, are discussed in chapters 6 and 7. In chapter 8 the metamorphosis of lawn tennis is examined. In the last chapter, some of the technological, economic, and social changes that were taking place in the United States and Britain while sports telecasting was developing are noted; some of the criticisms of what TV has "done" to sport are also discussed. My conclusion is that if we do not like what we see when we watch televised sport, it is because we prefer illusion to reality.

As Daniel Snowman points out, the words *American* and *British* lack conceptual clarity. I have often used the term *British* when *English* would have been more precise, but to move back and forth between them was clumsy. So I have followed Snowman's lead in "adopt[ing] a looseness of language that, while no doubt technically incorrect, does correspond to popular perceptions and usages." Before I read his book, I was also uneasily aware of a point he expresses well: "The attempt to write comparatively about historical continuity and change in British and American social values flies in the face of aspects of the intellectual tradition of both cultures."[13] Only in recent years, however, has the study of sport itself become intellectually respectable; and life outside the pale can be quite exciting.

In short, this book is simply a beginning. J. A. Mangan, in his beautifully documented study of public-school sport, wrote, "Robert Merton has written of two species of academic investigator: the 'European and the American' . . . 'Europeans' interpret grandly from a short supply of material; 'Americans' interpret scantily from a mass of evidence."[14] This is a "European" book, a short voyage in largely uncharted waters. I hope it will stimulate some "Americans" to draw maps.

TELEVISION AND
NATIONAL SPORT

1

TELEVISED SPORT: A TRANSLATION

The film *Chariots of Fire* was celebrated as an exaltation of the amateur ideal, because its protagonists were not running for money. Yet both were using sport as a means to an end, one for the glory of God, the other to find a place in the sun for Jews. The only man who was truly competing for the fun of the thing surrendered his place in his second event, and thus the chance of competing at all. Nevertheless, all that was said and written about the film demonstrated that we long for sport to be transcendent, to be the vehicle for selfless aspirations.

Michael Novak has captured that yearning in his book *The Joy of Sports*. If he is right, the essence of a sporting event is not necessarily polluted because spectators pay to see it or players contract to play; that essence can disappear only if the games become mere entertainment. Like many others, Novak believes that television has cheapened sport, yet he also asserts, "The fault is not that of the technology involved. The fault lies in the conception of the sports directors, producers, and sportscasters. . . . Were television to govern its approach to sports by the nature of sports, rather than by the canons of entertainment, the technology available could do the job."[1]

Novak is by no means the only critic of television's treatment of sport; TV has been held responsible for most of the ills that afflict professional sport worldwide.[2] The arguments put forward by these critics are many and varied, but they have one strand in common: television, as a new medium, has taken over and revolutionized sport.

That premise appears to me quite wrong. In the pretelevision era we were encouraged to believe that sport exemplified certain "intrinsic values."[3] TV has dealt the deathblow to that illusion, demonstrating to the most witless of us that professional sport is a business, conducted in accordance with prevailing business practices. The crucial issue, however, is not whether TV has inadvertently revealed the body around which mythological clothing had been so painstakingly draped, but whether TV has tampered with the essentials of the game the fan experiences at the stadium itself. TV has taught millions to appreciate the best that the most talented athletes of their generation can achieve. Has it, nevertheless, somehow made that "best" less than it used to be?

I think not; but some of my students have written that they find it increasingly difficult to watch a live game, since they have become accustomed to the close-ups of TV. A few have complained that the incessant chatter in televised events and the plethora of screen statistics distract them. One wrote, "The producers seem to feel they have to manipulate the audience at all times." But other students have thought that watching televised sport has enhanced their understanding of stadium games and made them more interested in attending a variety of live events. Who is right? Little enough professional work has addressed these questions, but what has been done concerns three issues: the presentation of the mediated event, the effect of specific camera use, and the effect of commentary.

Many people still believe that "the media's coverage of sporting events, public ceremonies and news is unmediated, unadulterated, passed 'raw' to the audience through the 'eye' of the camera."[4] As the contributors to *Football on Television* so rightly point out, that is not and cannot be so, if only because three dimensions are not two. Is, however, the experience of the viewer in front of his set fundamentally different from that of the fan at the stadium? To my mind, the difference is one of degree, not kind, both because of the nature of the televised sporting event itself, and because of the way human beings interpret their perceptions.

What sports television producers actually do is to translate electronically the three-dimensional flesh-and-blood game onto a two-dimensional screen; they also lift the game out of its original cultural setting, the stadium, and set it in a new cultural context, the living room. In making their translation, the translators certainly exercise power over their original text, for they decide such things as which portion of the game the viewer will see, how often a segment of the game will be shown, whether it will be magnified by a close-up or left in its long-distance context. The translators can focus on the cheerleaders rather than on an injured player squirming on the turf; they can draw attention, through replay and commentary, to particular aspects of the game. They can impose statistics over the picture and use the medium's ability to shift time and space. But however hard they try, they cannot provide a wholly new text, although on occasion they clearly would love to have the opportunity; rather, they simply recast the original in terms that make it accessible to those sitting in electronic rather than stadium seats.

Indeed, to use the term *text* at all may be misleading. When I read, I move at my own pace; when I watch a game, I have to conform to the pace of the participants. Further, sport concerns itself with the present and future; a player who is brooding over a missed shot, a lost chance, is in no shape to make good his present opportunity. Text holds the moment in time; a game is always moving. In this respect, sport perhaps best epitomizes the nature of television itself, a medium composed technically of movement. Yet it is also true that videotape allows the recreation of what is past, at the speed at which it happened, or faster or slower. Television can therefore create its own text. But a viewer who switches on the set to watch the World Series expects to "see" the World Series. The event itself remains unique and unpredictable; the translators are working with living material.

And that living material has to consist of what takes place at the stadium. At the most elementary level, TV producers are bound by what actually happens on the field of play. They cannot, as producers of documentaries can, shoot a great deal of film and then drop a lot of the footage and rearrange much of the rest so as to create a compelling story line or arouse a particular emotion.[5] Nor can sports producers attend rehearsals to study the best camera angles, to decide when to shoot close-ups, or even to suggest how a stage play should be blocked, as was done for the PBS television production of the Ring opera cycle. Producers know in general terms how the game will be conducted, but they do not know how this particular game will unfold; they have no script.[6] Since the infamous "Heidi" episode (when a football game was chopped off so as to start the next scheduled program on time), producers are aware that they are working under time constraints determined by the event itself. A news item may be simplified, distorted, or even omitted altogether because it does not otherwise fit the preordained time slots of news programs; in televising a live sporting event, producers have to adapt their timing to the event, not the event to whatever conventions of time have been established by the networks.

As they are bound by what actually happens, so are TV producers of sport bound by those who actually play or control the game in progress. However much pregame interviewing they do, however well they know the actual players, all those connected with televising the event are in the same position as the viewers, in that they cannot dictate what occurs.

Political conventions make deadly TV fare, because they purport to be live events; we all know, however, that we are not watching a decision-making process, but a public ritual. In such cases, all the important things happen in places where the cameras are not; but at a sporting event, all that matters to a stadium fan goes on in full view of the TV audience. As viewers, we do not know what a coach is thinking when he sends in a particular play, although a commentator will often help us guess; but fans at the stadium do not know either. TV producers may halt play for a commercial, or, if the game administrators allow it, even require part of the game to be replayed; but they cannot dictate the process of the game itself.

Further, producers of TV sporting events are constrained by the experience of many of their viewers. When I see a documentary or news item, I have to suspend disbelief, because I have no means of checking what went on in the real world. When I watch a sporting event, I do know what is supposed to happen, and if, for instance, all the plays were to be shown in slow motion, I would turn away from my set in disgust. What I see on the screen must be faithful to what I know from experience if I am to believe that I am "seeing" a sporting event.

For this is the point. Whatever mechanisms or codes TV producers employ, these mechanisms and codes must correspond experientially for viewers with what is going on in the stadium. At the stadium, I can look where I choose, but if I want to "see," that is, to follow the game, there are certain places I am likely to look, at certain points in the game. I watch the server toss the ball in tennis; but I also notice where the receiver has positioned himself, and where he moves to if the first serve is a fault. TV producers are not bound to show a viewer these things, but if they do not they are translating the text badly or not at all.

Bad translations do undoubtedly occur. In 1967, Derek Morgan agonized over what TV producers were doing to soccer; in 1982, Richard O'Connor wrote in similar terms about basketball.[7] I shall examine what has happened to tennis in chapter 8. Bad translation occurs either when needed information is excluded from the screen or when the information given is redundant. Even though I can decode what is offered me in a much broader context than what is actually visible or audible, the better I understand the game the more impatient I am with imperfect renderings. But in any case, what I "see" goes far beyond what is "there," and a good translation offers me not necessarily the whole picture but all the elements of it I need to construct the whole.

When, for instance, I see the football spiraling along on a punt, I know that the "suicide squad" is rushing upfield, even though they are not shown on my screen; at the stadium or at home the focus of my interest is on the player who catches the ball, what he does with it given the space and blockers he has available, and consequently how far he gets. That is what the cameras show. To assert, as Brian Williams does in his content analysis of the third quarters of six NFL games, that "the effect of such a shooting pattern was to focus attention on the ball and ball-carriers to the exclusion of other players as well as of the overall geometry of the game,"[8] is to suggest that when I am at the stadium I do not focus primarily on the ball. We have very little evidence on this point; but our own experience tells us where we usually look.

I first became aware of this when I was trying to find out how much ground soccer players actually covered while they were playing. I prepared rough maps of the whole pitch and then drew in the path of a selected player for five minutes of play, marking a cross or dotted lines wherever the player actually touched the ball or dribbled it. I did this for a number of professional soccer games, at the ground. I quickly realized that while I was following the path of, say, No. 5, I had completely lost the sense of the game. So I then attempted to check on what I actually did look at when I thought I was watching the game, and found that I almost always followed the path of the ball, setting it in the larger context of the pitch according to the nature of the play. That is, a long pass moved my attention from a small to a large section of the field, but then I quickly focused again on the small spot where the ball landed, and on players in the vicinity.

The difficulties of reducing this kind of experiential activity to content analysis terms are formidable. But we cannot be satisfied to discuss televised sport simply in terms of its formal structures, necessary as it is to know what these are. Analogously, I can diagram a sentence from a Shakespearean sonnet or analyze it according to the rules of transformational grammar, but this will not tell me much about the sonnet's literary quality. Viewers of a televised sporting event set whatever they see on their screens in an experiential context that is not visible. Further, parts of that context are more salient than others. Even if the whole football field, for instance, is not often shown on the screen during one specific game, I know what it looks like, and provided the markings on it are visible during particular plays, I can orient myself without conscious effort. The mediating structures of the television cameras cannot, in short, determine my experience of the game unless producers so far forget themselves as to think it is their job to improve on the original rather than to translate it. Perhaps, as Berman suggests, most TV producers do hanker to put their personal stamp upon a sporting event.[9] If so, the volume of mistranslation is almost certain to increase. The problem again lies not with the mediating devices per se, but with the uses to which they have been put.

Williams also suggests that "ball-carriers were featured to a much greater extent throughout coverage than those players not normally in contact with the ball. Quarterbacks, running backs and receivers were most seen. Linemen and defensive tackles were least seen."[10] This is, however, no different from action at the stadium, nor has it ever been. As Percy Haughton wrote in *Football, and How to Watch It* in 1922, "The greatest failing of the average spectator is that he keeps his eyes glued to the ball, or the runner, during the progress of a play."[11] When the New York Jets needed charisma, they did not spend $400,000 on a center; and they were not thinking only of how Joe Namath would look on TV. Certainly, TV producers go to particular pains to make viewers aware of players as individuals, to personalize them; in doing so they are simply extending the star system newspapers had practiced decades before television ever got near football or any other sport.

As a viewer, I do have to look where the camera crews take my vision; but I am not confined to "seeing" what is at any given moment on the screen in front of me. Whether I am at the stadium or in front of my set, I constantly interpret what I see, whether I am aware of it or not; I do not even "see" everything that is on the screen, but interpret what I can follow of the sequence of events unfolding before me. Content analysis alone, therefore, cannot tell us what viewers make of a game, because we have no means of knowing in what particular context any viewer is placing it. So while it is true that a televised sporting event is a mediated event, such mediation can give a viewer the "real" game experientially, provided it is properly handled.

For it is also true that not everyone at the stadium experiences the event in the same way. "Did you see the game?" is usually taken to mean "Did you experience what I experienced?" Tom Ryall states that TV presents "*a view* of the football match (not *the view*) in addition to a view of football itself."[12] The problem is that there is no such thing as "the view" of football, even at the stadium. What I see depends on where I sit, how much I know about the game itself and these particular players, how closely I attend, and a host of other variables. To go to a sporting event and then read about it in the papers is often to receive a rude shock; one's own interpretation of it and the sportswriter's are simply not the same. Even friends sitting side by side may well differ about what they thought transpired. This need not alarm us; for what we think we see depends not only on the preconceptions with which we encounter the visual experience itself, but on the furniture of our memories that allow us to reconstruct it. Our minds are complicated; Rudolph Arnheim points out that as long ago as 1909 a pioneering psychologist, Edward Titchener, was already avoiding "the *thing-error* or *object-error,* that is, the assumption that the mind's account of a thing is identical with all or some of the thing's objective properties."[13] When the thing in question is a dynamic, complex situation like a professional sports event, it is no wonder that our eyes and our minds do not match.

If our minds affect our eyes, what do our minds do to our ears? Sports commentary has received little scholarly attention; but what is already clear is that what we hear may well affect what we think we see. Raters who saw taped segments of hockey games without commentary regarded the games as less violent than raters who saw the same segments with commentary.[14] Content analysis of football commentary on all three networks in 1976 demonstrated that much of the dialogue was used to heighten the drama of the games.[15] The original ABC team of Howard Cosell, Don Meredith, and Keith Jackson was deliberately hired to make "Monday Night Football" enthralling. In this, ABC was simply returning to a tradition of sportscasting pioneered by Graham McNamee in the 1920s. He wrote, "You must make each of your listeners, though miles away from the sport, feel that he or she, too, is there with you in that press stand." So McNamee described individuals in the crowd, the actions of the coach, the color and excitement, as well as the game itself. He left "the 'applause' microphones around the field . . . open," sometimes to allow "just a trickle of applause through my own mike . . . yet not enough to drown out or blur the voice," sometimes to broadcast "full throated the shrieks and roars from the stands and bleachers."[16] Stadium drama was not the invention of TV.

It is quite possible that experience of the stadium game is mediated more by what is heard than by what is seen. Much more work is needed in this area; but even when it is done, the fact remains that viewers will not all experience commentary in the same way. Some viewers turn off the TV sound and listen to the radio commentary; they may or may not be among the 21 percent of respondents in the *Miller Lite Report* who said they rarely or never listened to the commentator, or the 36 percent who said commentators had no effect on their enjoyment of the game. Yet 47 percent of respondents said they listened carefully, and 51 percent said commentators added to their enjoyment.[17] Again, controlled experimental work and content analysis will not necessarily tell us much about viewers' actual experience. Nor can such work tell us how individual experience changes over time; perhaps a sports novice listens carefully to begin with, but pays less and less attention as he or she learns how to decode the game without help, much as one's stadium conversation alters over the years.

As viewers, then, we set the mediated event in the context of our own experience and thereby transform it. The mediated event is, in fact, "real"; and significantly, the very people whose livelihood depends on dealing accurately with the stadium experience do not hesitate to use films for crucial parts of their work. Coaches and administrators have long since decided that game films that use the visual mediating devices TV audiences are accustomed to do not distort reality. Rather, the use of game films suggests that those who control sports events believe that a film may portray better what actually went on than the most careful attention paid at a game itself. Football coaches, for instance, use game films to scout players, to prepare game plans, and to grade players, as well as to demonstrate to them the error of their ways. The NFL uses game films to keep an eye on officiating and to pick up rule infractions that were not detected during games; players are fined for what they were seen to do only on film. The campaign for the use of instant replays by officials on difficult calls indicates that NFL officials and public alike believe that the camera can be more reliable than the human eye. Those who are paid to play, to coach, and to organize professional sport have no problems with the visual mediation game films contain.

What, therefore, is of paramount importance is the degree to which the differences between what I see and hear on my TV screen and what I see and hear at the stadium affect my experience of the game. At the stadium without electronic aids, I sit in one place and have a choice of using my binoculars or not using them. I see each play only once – or may miss it altogether if I sneeze. In Britain, no one directs my attention to specific parts of the field or explains the game to me unless I take along an informed and communicative friend. In the United States, stadium commentary may not give me a great deal of information. Yet in front of my TV screen, on both sides of the Atlantic, I am whisked about the stadium on a magic carpet, besides seeing plays and players in great detail or at a distance. I watch some plays over and over again, from different angles. If I listen to the commentators, I can learn a good deal about what went on, as well as imbibe a similar amount of trivia and some misinformation. Visually and auditorily the experience at the stadium and the experience at home are undoubtedly different.

What is not necessarily different is my own response. As Arnheim put it many years ago, "Visual representation must either reproduce its subject with mechanical accuracy or – in the higher aesthetic sense of the term – render its essentials faithfully."[18] When TV producers render both the essence and process of the game faithfully, I can experience the "real" thing; when TV producers by design or ignorance mistranslate the text, I can experience something very different. It is not the fact of mediation that determines my experience; it is the way in which that mediation is used that determines whether a live televised sporting event is real or spurious.

TV technology thus need not distort stadium reality. And even in the forms Novak so dislikes, live telecasts scrupulously refrain from tampering with his "seven seals [that] lock the inner life of sports."[19]

Novak's first seal is that of "sacred space," the arena set aside for special and sacred rituals. All televised sporting events are carefully located; the stadium, the ballpark, the golf course are identified and often set in their geographical and sporting context. If the event occurs where the "greats" have played, their names are recalled; players are asked in pre- and postgame interviews how they feel about playing on Wimbledon center court or whether they miss Forest Hills. Even a featureless college gymnasium is related to the university it symbolically represents. Our electronic seats do not debar us from the ritual of place.

Novak's second seal, "sacred time," is the lifeblood of a televised sporting event. His point that the game is never over until it has actually ended, however impossible the odds may seem, is something television commentators are paid to hammer home. Yankee ticket holders can begin to file out of the stadium in the sixth inning of the sixth game of the 1981 World Series; the television crews cannot. When the carefully structured unpredictability of the NFL breaks down, as it did on a "Monday Night" game in 1981 when the Rams trounced the Cowboys, Cosell can be relied on to produce sententious but heartwarming comments about the fact that the Cowboys will be back, and Frank Gifford to show statistically that what the viewer is seeing is an aberration. Meredith can play off both by sending up the Cowboys, saying after a play in which mistake after mistake occurs, "Well, the Cowboys always aimed for consistency." The cynical may say that a commentator's desperate efforts to hold the viewers' attention to a game whose outcome is not in doubt derive from the fact that sets turned off are not receiving commercials; but if by chance the unexpected should occur, the television crews, unlike fainthearted fans, will not have missed it.[20] Of course, "sacred time" is manipulated when edited games are shown; these, however, are in the nature of a commentary on an event, rather than the event itself, for the result is already known.

Charles Barr, for instance, compared edited British soccer coverage with German coverage of the 1974 World Cup, and discovered that the British cut to a close shot about twice as often as the Germans did. Barr maintains that these differences would hold even had he been able to compare unedited match tapes, yet he also admits that "Match of the Day" (the edited British program) "concentrates on goalmouth drama," because the whole ninety-minute match is compressed into twenty minutes.[21] Clips for news broadcasts, or even late-evening extended coverage events are similarly edited, on both sides of the Atlantic, to be "exciting." This kind of sports broadcasting, however, is a comment on the event, rather than an attempt to broadcast the event itself. TV producers will, therefore, treat such material according to whatever canons apply to magazine or news programs. A live TV broadcast does not tamper with the second seal.

The third seal, "the bond of brothers," is made clearer on the television screen than at the stadium. One of Hollywood Henderson's public sins against the Cowboys was that the camera caught him clowning after an unsuccessful play; he should have been keening. The bowed heads and dejected postures of the players on the losing team bench always provide a stark contrast to the lively attitudes of those who are winning. Cameras zoom in on the delighted crowd of hugging, patting, embracing players who surround the man who has just scored a touchdown or goal. The commentator points out who gave the runner a good block, or who passed the ball for the man who made the shot. Even in golf, an individual game, the "bond of brothers" may be stressed. ABC cameras moved back and forth among members of the 1983 Ryder Cup team who had finished their matches but who had come out again to cheer on the man who was still playing. Television viewers are constantly made aware that no one, however gifted, is an island in team sport.

"Rooting," the fourth seal, is closely tied to the first, the sense of place. As Novak puts it, "To have particular loyalties is not to be deficient in universality, but to be faithful to the laws of human finitude."[22] As a fan, I support my team or follow with concentration the career of a particular player in an individual sport like tennis. Television has enabled millions to adopt and care about teams they could never see in person. Few residents of New Mexico can ever visit the "half-Astrodome," but many follow the fortunes of the Cowboys. True, the Cowboys do not appear on television every week. I cannot, as a viewer, go week after week to watch my team, like a ticket holder. But to see my team sometimes and then to be able to keep up with it in the printed materials it and others circulate is much better than never being able to see it at all. Americans are mobile people. If I move, or the team moves, television can reunite us and rekindle the passions I first felt in the stadium.

It is true that football crowds at the stadium deliberately try to entertain viewers with placards; but college crowds were entertaining each other with flashcards in the nineteenth century. American football has always been a spectacle; we failed to notice it when we were caught up in the excitement at the stadium. We saw the cheerleaders, if we noticed them at all, at a distance; their frantic breasts, buttocks, and professional smiles were not thrust under our noses. Scoreboards showed us the score; they used not to exhort us. We did not see every detail of a mascot's costume or hide. U.S. television producers have chosen to heighten the elements of spectacle that have always been present in U.S. professional sport;[23] but viewers are always made aware of the stadium crowd's partisanship, and by seeing the game itself, can ally themselves with either side as they choose. Television does not necessarily tamper with the fourth seal; anyone who has found himself rooting for the "wrong" side in a group in front of a TV set will be in no doubt about the degree of commitment TV viewing can arouse.

Equally, "spirit," the fifth seal, the triumph over odds or simply the courageous and joyous battle against them, is caught by the cameras. The urgency of the stance in the huddle, the fierceness of the grip on the racket, are more clearly seen on the screen than at the stadium. Similarly, the team or player who gives up or, worse, desperately seeks an advantage by illegal play, is writ large on the screen; and the replay can catch the cruel thump, the unnecessary late hit or tackle, that is so easily missed in the stadium. Television underscores rather than destroys the fifth seal.

The sixth seal, "competing," and being forced to lift one's game to a higher level by the skill of one's opponent, is the seal linked with "sacred time" for TV producers. Electronic seats are not worth sitting in, if what is going on is not a quality performance. It is one of the jobs of a commentator to help me recognize quality when I see it; but if a succession of games is televised in which neither side forces the other to new levels of excellence, viewers can readily find other sources of satisfaction. A walkover is dull at the stadium; on TV it is a disaster.

Nor does television interfere with the seal of "self-discovery." We know very little about who watches sport on TV, but the work of Ronald Frank and Marshall Greenberg suggests that women do not watch sports as much as men.[24] Not only do women have less disposable time and money than men, but until the last decade American women were actively discouraged from participating in sports. They never found their own limits; why should they now exult in watching athletes who are still testing themselves, still seeking perfection? Although it is likely to be a slow process, as more girls take part in competitive sport while they grow up it is possible that their interest in televised sport will increase.[25]

TV has not only kept Novak's seven seals intact, but while doing so has allowed people to see the best professional sport the world can offer. The money that TV has poured into sport, and the exposure it provides, have drawn the most athletically talented members of their generation into competition. Millions of spectators have the opportunity to become fans because commentators have undertaken not only to announce but to instruct and inform. If we care to do so, we can learn to appreciate and love a game by watching it at home to the point where we may decide to look at the original text for ourselves.

If then, TV can produce such wonders for us, why does it not always do so? Why are some games, like football, translated so well, and others, like soccer, so miserably? This is partly because producers and camera crews have their own background of experience; Americans understand football in a way in which they do not understand soccer. Far more important, however, is the cultural context within which the television industry on both sides of the Atlantic operates. Many of us suppose that the very use of television has changed our perception of the world; but what is striking about the way in which television has treated particular sports is the degree of continuity that exists in the attempts made to attract people to watch a sporting event. Perhaps sport is unique; but most of the calumnies directed against television as a medium do not appear to stand close scrutiny when they are placed in the context of televised sport.

Sports telecasting has been examined very little; but in neither Britain nor the United States do writers expect TV to enhance what it shows. We have all been taught to denigrate television. On both sides of the Atlantic, critics, scholarly and otherwise, have deplored the effect of television on public attitudes and values. The "cultural wasteland" in the United States is the "goggle-box" in the United Kingdom; in both countries fear of TV's effect on children has led to extensive studies, particularly of the relationship between viewing and violence.[26] Both in the United States and Britain television has been used for educational purposes; but critics have devoted their energies largely to the examination of prime-time programming[27] and to the nature of the relationship between the medium and its audience. Many of these critics regard television as a device that represents the apotheosis of the industrial revolution in its domination of human by machine. For such critics, public taste, already debased by earlier forms of mass communication, has been further assaulted by a medium that by its very nature tends to captivate and enslave.

This is not the place to explore the huge corpus of literature concerning the changes that the industrial revolution is asserted to have wrought in human habits, perceptions, and aspirations. Jacques Ellul expresses most clearly the revulsion of many intellectuals for what he calls "technological determinants." In *The Technological Society,* Ellul postulates that industrialized societies are ruled by "technique," which is "the translation into action of man's concern to master things by means of reason, to account for what is subconscious, make quantitative what is qualitative, make clear and precise the outlines of nature, take hold of chaos and put order into it." Efficiency becomes our only goal; morality relates not to principle but to effect. Each of us must become a specialist, united to others not by empathy and shared experience, but by the necessity of filling our own niche to get the job done. Law no longer represents justice, but a code of rules that attempts to ensure that human relationships are efficiently organized. Even sport has been transformed by "technique," because "training in sports makes of the individual an efficient piece of apparatus which is henceforth unacquainted with anything but the harsh joy of exploiting his body and winning."[28] This is an interesting perception; what Ellul sees as exploitation can also be interpreted as the acceptance of a discipline that will allow one to reach levels of perfection that provide personal ecstasy. Ellul, however, does not regard it in this fashion.

If Ellul is a most thoroughgoing critic of industrialization, other critics have similarly deplored the effects of mass communication. The spread of literacy and of broadcasting has led, according to writers such as F. R. Leavis and Denys Thompson, Bernard Rosenberg and David White, and Richard Hoggart, to a progressive deterioration of popular taste.[29] Such writers set "high culture" against "popular culture"; the latter always, for them, represents a falling away from acceptable standards. Erik Barnouw takes this argument a step further. He believes that even high culture, as purveyed by commercial television, is pernicious, because sponsors deliberately direct discriminating viewers' attention away from present problems to those of the past. Whether TV deals with high or popular culture is therefore to Barnouw irrelevant, because both are simply a conduit for commercials.[30]

Whatever its content, the very nature of television makes it suspect to some. To writers such as R. K. Goldsen and Marie Winn, TV is sensually overwhelming and renders its viewers helpless by substituting vicarious for real experience, thereby making viewers incapable of distinguishing between them.[31] To critics of this persuasion, television viewers are watching the shadows in Plato's cave.

Gaye Tuchmann puts this helplessness of viewers into a political context. She asserts that the American television industry operates to legitimize the status quo. Viewers have little or no influence over what is shown because "the programming activities of all networks and stations are dominated by the search for corporate profits realized by selling audiences to advertisers."[32] Changes are made in program content not in response to the demands of an enlightened audience, but in order to coopt viewers so that economic, political, and social power will remain with the powerful.

For such critics, television is by definition an alienating invention. People are linked together by a machine, which can operate only if thousands of workers each perform their own isolated and specific tasks. The experience of watching is addictive, making the watchers ever more dependent on a mode of existence that is essentially passive, manipulating them without their being aware of it.[33]

Now, it is by no means certain that this fundamentally pessimistic view of television is accurate. In the first place, intellectuals have no right to assume that what they like represents what everyone else ought to like, or would like, if only they were exposed to it. When Everyman became able to read print, he did not choose to come to grips with Shakespeare.

That, to me, has nothing to do with industrialization or technology; it is a fact of the human condition. To believe otherwise is to transform the noble savage myth into the noble peasant myth; we have no evidence that aesthetic sensibilities are or were more highly developed in cultures without mass communications than in our own.

Herbert Gans goes further. He has suggested that both high and popular cultures are in fact "taste cultures," which reflect "the class and particularly educational attributes of their publics."[34] Moreover, there are many more than two such taste cultures in America, and each is valid for its own particular audience. Alan Swingewood points out that no one has demonstrated "a causal link between popular culture and popular consciousness."[35] He also shows that the "upper classes" as well as the "masses" thoroughly enjoy cultural products designed for the hoi polloi. I suppose it is only in Dallas that football scores are announced during the intermissions at the opera, but it is obvious that there is considerable overlap between participants of different taste cultures.

Nor are the effects of television as a medium wholly different from those of its predecessors. Intellectuals who study television naturally attend to it closely; on the other hand, most viewers have got into the habit of regarding the box as a part of the living room furniture. In a twelve-nation study of adult activities, the investigators found it necessary to categorize TV viewing as either a "primary" or "secondary" activity because viewers were so often busy with something besides the broadcast.[36] In an American study in which actual watching behavior was filmed, investigators found that "for much of the time the sets were on, no one was watching." Sometimes the room was empty; sometimes no one in the room was attending to the screen. Movies were watched 76.0 percent of the time they were on; sports events, 58.7 percent; and news, 55.2 percent; commercials fared worst. What Nielsen ratings mean when for 45.2 percent of the time advertisers are at best attracting the attention of the cat,[37] is another question;[38] but it is clear that TV viewing is not necessarily a reverential activity. As George Comstock puts it, " 'Television viewing' is correctly thought of as a discontinuous, often interrupted and frequently non-exclusive activity for which a measure in hours and minutes serves only as the outer boundary of possible attention."[39]

Even when viewers attend closely to a TV set, as James Halloran points out, "different people can perceive and use the same media content in different ways."[40] For television is only one aspect of any human being's cultural world. In 1986, viewers in both Britain and America can switch channels if they choose; although fewer Americans have access to PBS than to network TV, most of those who can watch noncommercial television choose not to do so. Executives like Fred Friendly who have agonized about the responsibilities of TV seem to have forgotten that it is not the networks who have substituted "escapism for insight,"[41] but viewers. CBS Cable and the Entertainment Channel, both of which offered "high culture" programs, failed. When the BBC in the late 1950s wanted to prove that it could draw mass audiences if it put its mind to the matter, programs like the "Black and White Minstrel Show" were deliberately concocted. To complain that viewers have to put up with whatever they are offered is to suppose not only that they are incapable of switching off the set, but also that TV is the only medium of entertainment over which individuals have no power. Books, magazines, newspapers, plays, concerts, and all other cultural products that require an audience are organized by middlemen. Art and music history are the story of patrons. Playwrights must find agents to persuade managements to find the financing to put on their plays; members of the public do not have input into the process until tickets are on sale.

Certainly viewers of sport do seem to be able to choose between programs. However inaccurate the ratings figures may be, if we can assume that there is usually the same proportion of homes in which someone is actually watching the set when it is on, we can also assume that changes in the figures may indicate more or less interest on the part of viewers in particular programs. What these figures show is that Americans are perfectly capable of distinguishing between sports and other programs and of ceasing to watch sports programs they do not find satisfactory.

It is surprising to discover how low the ratings actually are for regularly scheduled sporting events.[42] Over several decades to the seventies the audience of prime-time general drama, suspense and mystery, situation comedy, variety, feature films, and evening news outdrew weekend sports programming.[43] In the week ending September 28, 1980, "Monday Night Football" was number 24 on the Nielsen rating list, behind such shows as "Little House on the Prairie" (4), "The Jeffersons" (13), and "Lou Grant" (22).[44] For the week ending April 5, 1981, the "NCAA Championship Basketball" game was number 15 behind "Dallas" (2), "Masada, part 1" (7), and "Lou Grant" (10).[45] "Monday Night Football" had moved up to 15 in the week ending October 18, 1981, but was still outranked by "Dallas" (1), "M*A*S*H" (7), and the "Country Music Association Awards" (13). In the same week, the first game of the American League Championship was number 16, and the third game, 25.[46] Overall, prime time or not, regularly scheduled weekend sports shows in the first three months of 1982 had miserable ratings: "Saturday Wide World of Sports," the top sports show, garnered an average of 11.0, the "Pro-Bowlers Tour" (ranked 3) 8.4, "Superstars" (9) 6.3, and NCAA Basketball (10) 5.3.[47]

The sports events or programs that gain high ratings are not the regularly scheduled season's games or programs, but special events such as the Super Bowl, the World Series, and the Bobby Riggs–Billie Jean King "Battle of the Sexes" 1973 tennis match. The ten top-rated live sports telecasts in 1983 were all bowl games or some sort of playoff; the ratings ranged from 48.6 for the Super Bowl to 24.4 for the Sugar Bowl.[48] One of the reasons is that everyone knows exactly what the events stand for; they mean something, because of their historic significance and because they represent the culmination of a season's effort, because they seem culturally symbolic, or because they involve a great deal of money for the protagonists. We all know who is playing; the events are advertised far enough ahead in newspapers, magazines, on radio, and on television itself for us to have time to savor the special event. This is something worth planning for, worth attending to seriously.

Moreover, the ratings figures suggest that viewers can and do distinguish between sports. In spite of the baseball strike in 1981, a typical "Monday Night Baseball" game got a 12.6 rating;[49] from January to March in 1981, the Professional Bowlers Association got a rating of 8.5, while college basketball in the regular season could muster only 6.5, and the regular season NBA games 5.9.[50] In May 1983, the final round of the Atlanta Golf Classic got a rating of 5.5.[51] If, in fact, viewers are such passive creatures that they accept whatever is offered them, one would expect sports events to secure ratings that are more nearly comparable to one another. In fact, although the ratings vary somewhat from year to year, some sports are always distinctly more popular than others.

Yet even a popular sport will not be watched unless it is set in a context that has meaning. During the 1982 football strike, the networks made desperate efforts to provide a substitute for NFL football. Typically, NFL Sunday afternoon football drew combined ratings of somewhere around 30; on the first strike Sunday, all sports programs together could draw only 22 points. Two Canadian Football League games drew ratings of 5.1 and 5.0; that is, about two-thirds of those who normally watched NFL football decided they would rather not look at a substitute.[52] On October 3, NBC tried another Canadian Football League game and was rewarded for their pains with a 2.4 rating. CBS tried televising two Division 3 college games, the only ones they could get on short notice; they got 4.9 and 3.6 ratings.[53] On October 17, viewers got a chance to see NFL players in a game arranged by the Players Association; they didn't think much of that either, and the game drew ratings ranging from 5.1 in Philadelphia to 2.4 in Los Angeles.[54] It is not football per se that viewers tune in to see, but football that they believe will be worth watching. The sad tale of the United States Football League ratings supports this point. Beginning with a rating of 14.2 in 1983, the slide downward was almost steady; in ten weeks the ratings went from that high point through 7.4, 6.6, 6.4, 7.7, 6.6, 6.4, 5.8, 5.0, and 4.2.[55]

From the networks' point of view, of course, it does not matter very much if the regular games do not do spectacularly well, because it costs considerably less to televise a contest that has already been arranged than to put on a studio show, and demographically, the audience that watches sport is an appealing one for advertisers.[56] The point is that if these figures mean anything, they appear to show that viewers are not mindless, but that at least in respect to sports programs they know what they want to see, and refuse to watch substitutes for it.

Nor is watching televised sport necessarily a solitary, alienating activity, as critics have alleged. We know almost nothing about why people watch sport, and so far as I know no one has investigated fan behavior at home.[57] What we do know is that thousands, perhaps millions, of people regularly watch televised sports events together; newspapers even publish food guides for "tailgate" parties to be held at home. The stereotyped image of a spaced-out, manipulated, inert creature, passively attending to whatever sports event corporate conspirators care to purvey, does not seem to fit what we each know about the sports viewing habits of ourselves and our friends.[58]

Nor are all sports promoters mesmerized by TV. During the 1982 football strike, the University of Minnesota lost $42,000 it could have gained from a TV contract had it been willing to change the starting time of the game at short notice.[59] This was a business as much as an ethical decision; but it underlines the point that television is a means to an end, not an end in itself. In October 1982, six New England colleges declined to move their games from Saturday to Sunday for TV's benefit; eight others were happy to do so.[60] The use of television in sport requires consenting adults.

Television has also freed us to decide how violent we want our professional sport to be. At the stadium, we may miss the cheap shot, a player's surliness. Television replays are remorseless. We are forced to accept the fact that to play to win may involve tactics and attributes we would prefer to be able to overlook; and while we see more clearly the godlike quality of the best athletes and best plays, we also have revealed to us the sordidness of the "winning is the only thing" ethic. Televised sport forces us to choose; do we want our team or our player to win whatever it takes, or do we want to enjoy the aesthetic satisfaction of a battle fought within the spirit as well as the letter of the law? Televised hockey ratings slumped, I suggest, not merely because hockey is a regional sport, but because viewers did not find the violence (which was officially encouraged on and off the ice) pleasing over the long haul; one brawl looks very like another.[61] The very excesses that threaten to destroy the essence of professional sport are forerunners of their own destruction. In creating the largest and most sophisticated audience for sport ever known, television producers have also ensured that substitutes for excellence will not long be accepted.

TV producers operating in a commercial system on either side of the Atlantic are therefore on the horns of a dilemma. They want to buy into the prestige and continuity of sports industries that attract demographically acceptable fans, but they also want to fill the electronic seats with more of the "right" people, even to draw in those who have never thought of buying a stadium ticket. They are therefore bound to work within culturally conditioned notions of what any sport ought to be like. Americans, for instance, expect a game to end with a winner and loser; the British are quite prepared to accept a tie. Americans expect spectacle, the British, an unadorned contest. Much mistranslation occurs because particular professional sports do not readily fit such predetermined patterns; a faithful translation must go beyond Novak's concern with the nature of sports as such and deal with the nature of each particular sport. This, as I shall show in chapter 8, is far from easy to do.

TV producers are also constrained by cultural traditions of sports viewing. People in any culture are clearly disposed to care about specific sports because these are part of their national culture. These sports are played formally in school and informally outside it, are discussed constantly at work and in newspapers and magazines, and are a source of local and national pride. Americans know about football as Canadians know about hockey and the British know about cricket. Some sports also attract large numbers of adult participants; some of these people will be drawn to watch professionals on television. But these factors alone are not sufficient to guarantee a sizable television audience for sports events; nor can a television industry dedicated to garnering the largest number of viewers for all of its programs afford to rely on them.

For in translating the game to the living room, television producers are constantly battling the everyday business of living. Stadium viewers have bought their tickets, parked their cars, fought their way to their seats, and are rarely alone, and so cannot conveniently leave when they decide to go. They have invested time, money, and energy in a social event. Many TV viewers have also set aside time, invited friends in, and prepared to enjoy the game. But should the event prove disappointing, there are other activities immediately available; and in any case, the ratings will not improve unless people who hitherto have shown little interest in sport can be lured to the set.

Any sporting event that is to be shown regularly on the screen must therefore possess the qualities of good theater. When we go to see a play with which we are familiar, we know how the story will end; yet we are still gripped by the contrast between what might have been and what is. In a sporting event, the outcome must be unpredictable; as Geertz says of

Balinese cockfighting, "The Balinese attempt to create an interesting, . . . 'deep' match, by making the center bet as large as possible, and the outcome, thus as unpredictable as possible."[62] No sport is going to last long on commercial television if steps are not taken by its governing authority to equalize the teams and players so that the contest requires each to play to the limit of capacity.

Further, tension must be maintained throughout. This means that recognizable crisis points must occur throughout the game; to save match points, or to make first down from third down and twelve, is to have faced disaster and overcome it. We must all be aware of the crisis; we must all know how it was resolved. The more tension that can be built into the game the better, and if the crisis can be resolved through specific, conscious choice, as when a coach decides whether to gamble on a touchdown or settle for a field-goal attempt, our emotions are still more deeply stirred.

In the theater, timing is all. So it is in a sporting event. One reason football translates so well to the screen is that part of the game's tension is derived from the characteristic fight against time. The huge electronic clock is frequently shown; the seconds tick off digitally on a screen insert. The game is divided into four quarters, not two halves; the two-minute warning is publicly given. Teams are battling not simply each other, but an inexorable enemy, the clock. The clock plays no part in baseball, but the number of times a batter may swing is limited; he battles not time, but a fixed number of opportunities. He has just so many chances; and so does the pitcher. Limited-over cricket matches, in which the number of balls either team can receive is so few that batsmen must try to score off virtually all of them, instead of hanging about for balls they think they could comfortably hit, have introduced a wholly new sense of tension to what used to be a game that could apparently last forever. Soccer lacks both inevitable crisis points and a tension-ridden relation to time or opportunity; as a result it is not good theater.

Drama also depends on change of pace and visual variety. If what happens during the course of the event, such as bull riding or bowling, is visually repetitious, we must see different bulls and riders and different bowlers, if our attention is to be held for long. The variety of action that occurs on the football field, and our uncertainty as to when the ball will fly through the air and when it will disappear into a mound of writhing bodies, keeps us alert. We must also be able to follow the action; a hockey puck is small and moves incredibly fast, usually on one level. Unless one has grown up with hockey, it is hard to become committed to it.

We are not likely to watch a game on television unless we know what is going on. Television producers in search of an audience take enormous trouble to inform and instruct their viewers and to provide this instruction in so many different ways that the process is virtually painless. Profiles of team players, normally shown whenever the player has excelled himself, help us to believe we know the team. Statistics on the game, explained by the commentators, help us to understand its rhythm. Close-ups of the officials, and their use of microphones to tell us precisely what infraction incurred, keep us posted on the reasons why the point was lost, the touchdown called back. We can practice the legendary art of official-baiting rather better in our living rooms than at the stadium, because the camera takes us right to the call itself, often from several angles. Not only do replays help us to savor again the supremely satisfying moments of the games, but their analysis by commentators can teach us how to look at the game for ourselves. Before the days of television, we had to learn the game gradually. We went to enough games, watched and listened, asked questions of aficionados, remembered our own playing days, and found ourselves understanding what was going on. Television commentators are now paid to induct us into the mysteries, if we choose to be initiated; and if we do not always agree with what they say, we enjoy a pleasant sense of knowing more than the so-called expert.

Commentators are indispensable to televised sports events, as anyone who saw the football game televised experimentally without them can testify.[63] My own analysis of tapes shows not only that the amount of talk varies among sports (from 87 percent of the game time in football to 30 percent in tennis) but that its content differs.[64] While football commentators spend almost a third of their time describing the game, they may give another 25 percent to matters that have nothing to do with the players or event being watched. Baseball commentators give less than a third of their time to description of the game and more than a third to talk that has nothing whatever to do with the particular game or players being watched. One reason for this discrepancy is that football players are constantly being moved on and off the field and are not always readily identifiable; each baseball player spends much of his time on the screen in close-up, and who he is and what he is doing does not require explanatory comment. Beyond the regular season, there are up to seven games to decide the World Series, so the importance of the first three is porportionally diminished. It is therefore imperative for commentators to demonstrate that each game has a context and a heritage, if viewers are to be convinced that what they are seeing is worth attending to. There is, however, only one Super Bowl; it is not necessary to anchor it to per-suade viewers to keep watching.

Tennis commentators operate differently. While there is little to be said about the competitors after we have been reminded of their previous encounters, prize money, and strategies, there is much work to do in helping viewers understand the game. Professional tennis has no history to speak of, and has never been a game for the masses in the United States. If the attention of viewers used to team sports is to be held, viewers must be helped to understand the scheming and planning that is taking place on the court, and must learn that a winning shot has to be set up, rather than simply made. So the commentators must explain the game, not simply describe it; they must help viewers cultivate the expertise in watching that they themselves possess, rather than draw attention to the purely spectacular nature of a few shots.

Much more work needs to be done to examine sports commentary; we have barely begun to scratch the surface. But it is clear that commentary can, like notes in a text translation, enlighten and even help captivate a viewer. When John Madden tells us on a replay that Ron Springs was able to score a touchdown against the Minnesota Vikings on October 2, 1983, because the defense moved to the right as Tony Dorsett started in motion, we learn more about the chess game that is football. When Madden uses his chalkboard and then shows us the replay again, we are learning how and where to look to get the most out of what we see. Good commentators can also give viewers a sense of a sports continuity and structure; they can draw attention to the elements of transcendence in any particular game that make it worthwhile to watch every week, not merely to wait for the meretricious excitement of the playoffs. Poor commentators, equally, can misinform and simply gabble.[65] How they do their job will depend on their own skill and a network's conception of their function.

Nevertheless, however good the commentators, however skilled the conversation, some sports texts are either not worth translating for commercial networks because too few people are interested in them, or extremely difficult to translate, because they lack the inherent qualities of good theater. Golf is played by millions, but its dramatic qualities are few. The game itself, the text, cannot be changed, and it would tax the endurance of the most dedicated viewer of golf to follow players on TV around the course, hole after endless hole. So producers ensure visual variety by switching back and forth between holes, using videotape if necessary. More variety is assured by showing tee and bunker shots, but the cameras concentrate overwhelmingly on putts, the one feature of a golf game that is both predictable and represents a crisis situation easily perceived by the viewer.

For the Colonial National Invitational tournament in May 1977, the cameras were positioned at the last three or four holes; a scoreboard was superimposed on the screen to show exactly how close the leaders were. Until Ben Crenshaw and John Schroeder showed up, viewers were told where tee shots should be placed to the best advantage; some "no-hopers" were shown driving and putting. Both Crenshaw and Schroeder were driving, then attention was focused on the putt. The viewer watched Schroeder remove invisible detritus between his ball and the cup, and the camera stayed with him while he read the green. When he took too long about it, the viewer was switched to another hole where there was some action, but the screen was then split, so that the viewer could see Crenshaw, one hole ahead, and Schroeder putt simultaneously. At hole after hole, the camera zoomed in on the position of the golfer's hand on the putter and then followed the ball right to the hole; every viewer agonized with Schroeder as the ball that would have given him a $40,000 play-off chance jumped across the edge of the cup.

The commentators never allowed the viewer to forget the relative positions of Crenshaw, Schroeder, Tom Watson, and Lyn Lott. And they knew their duty in a potentially disastrous TV situation. Schroeder, who had led Crenshaw by five strokes coming into the last nine holes but on the eighteenth was one stroke behind, was playing with Butch Baird. Baird hit a drive into the trees. The commentators had to "fill in" while the ball was traced, while Baird decided how to hit it, and then while he took his third stroke. Baird was not about to be hurried; with at least a thousand dollars hanging on each swing of his club, he proposed to exercise his prerogatives and take all the time he required. There was no other action the camera could be shifted to; so viewers were given shots of the crowd, of Crenshaw and his wife, of the fairway, and of Pat Summerall. All this was done very deliberately, but the quiet and mounting desperation behind it was finally revealed in the blurted remark, "We don't want to hurry Butch Baird; he's been playing this course since the 1950s. He's played a good round here today, and he can take all the time he wants."

However golf is televised, it will not set the pulse of a casual viewer racing. The sponsors have no mass market here, but provided the parts of the game that are shown can hold the attention of golfers themselves, a demographically appealing advertising market is assured. What is significant is that such aspects of the game that can be given dramatic force are emphasized and heightened. But the text itself is not changed; it is almost as hard for the fan at the course to follow the flight of the ball from the tee as it is for the fan at home.

Other sports also lack inherent dramatic qualities. ABC made a great fuss about televising the 1981 New York Marathon, but running is not likely to become a weekly program. Professional football became America's winter national game not only because its structure makes it easy to translate, but because the NFL until the mid-1980s was able to convince spectators that they were watching a product carefully controlled for quality. But football was not adapted wholesale to suit TV; the NFL simply built on the process that had been begun in the days before TV to draw crowds from the college to the professional game (see chapter 3). The NFL owners chose to use television in ways baseball and basketball owners did not. Similarly, whatever they may do now, American promoters of lawn tennis metamorphosed the game to attract spectators first to live games, not primarily to garner TV contracts.

Drama is much less important to TV producers whose success is not tied to the delivery of a demographically acceptable audience. Many British people have now lost interest in cricket; but the BBC, conscious of its claim to represent the nation, will broadcast every ball of a test (international) match. Channel 4, a commercial channel that is legally required to serve minority interests, could show a bowls contest in June 1983 that was the most funereal sports event I have ever watched. Nor does commentary have to be entertaining. Toby Charles, the PBS soccer commentator, reflects his British background. Broadcasting on a noncommercial network, he assumes that his viewers are soccer fans who would be insulted by being given instruction about a game they thoroughly understand. His function is not to describe, entertain, or inform, but to provide company for the viewer who cannot, poor soul, be at the stadium. This electronic seat has been provided for the fan, not the spectator.

The "success" or "failure" of a sport on television thus depends not simply on the sport's structure, but on the significance the viewing public attaches to it, its cultural symbolism, the core values its viewers share, and the habits of attention they have acquired in growing up as members of a particular cultural group. If a sport is to be watched consistently on TV it must *matter;* it must be more than a game. The roots of such experience lie deep.

Baseball, football, cricket, and soccer have all been translated to the screen in ways that meet the expectations of viewers nourished on customs developed long before TV was invented. TV producers have concentrated on some aspects of this "cake of custom" to the exclusion of others, but they have made few innovations. Compared with the radical experimenters of the past, TV producers have been a cautious lot, as the histories of baseball and football both demonstrate. These sports, then, are the subject of the next two chapters.

2

BASEBALL

Baseball did not begin as an American game; it was mythologized into one. In 1907, the major-league owners who had initiated an inquiry into baseball's origin were delighted to accept a report that baseball had been miraculously invented by Abner Doubleday at Cooperstown in 1839. The report was quite spurious, but it told Americans what they wanted to hear; America's national game was no immigrant upstart, but native-born, conceived and nourished only by peculiarly American ideals, and epitomizing peculiarly American values. Albert Spalding made the matter crystal clear in 1911. He pointed out that he had played cricket, and he liked cricket, but that it was "a gentle pastime. Base Ball is War! Cricket is an Athletic Sociable, played and applauded in a conventional, decorous and English manner. Base Ball is an Athletic Turmoil played and applauded in an unconventional, enthusiastic and American manner."[1] By 1911, to play or watch cricket was to identify oneself with Europeanism and elitism; to play or watch baseball was to be all-American.

Spalding's instincts were sound, however faulty his historical scholarship. Virginia Woolf, delighted by Ring Lardner's *You know Me Al,* published in 1916, commented perceptively on baseball's importance. She wrote: "It is no coincidence that the best of Mr. Lardner's stories are about games, for one may guess that Mr. Lardner's interest in games has solved one of the most difficult problems of the American writer; it has given him a clue, a centre, a meeting place for the divers activities of people whom a vast continent isolates, whom no tradition controls. Games give him what society gives his English brother."[2] By 1916, baseball epitomized national self-consciousness.

It is easy to forget that before the Civil War cricket was firmly established on the East Coast and showed every sign of prosperity. In the first place, whatever needs the actual game of cricket met, baseball could in most cases also meet, because it so closely resembles cricket in structure. Both baseball and cricket are slow, subtle, summer games and no one has to be a behemoth to play. Positions are specialized, but every player (until the invention of the designated hitter) has to bat and to field. One whole team fields, while the other provides the batters or batsmen.

The ball is hard, and the crux of each game is the continuous duel between the pitcher and batter, or bowler and batsman; yet in both games the player who delivers the ball is dependent on his teammates, who can win or lose the game by their fielding. Until 1864, cricket bowling resembled early baseball pitching, because the ball had to be delivered underarm.[3] In both games, there has been constant dispute about the legality of the thrown ball. In baseball, pitchers have been accused of tampering with the ball itself;[4] in cricket bowlers have been accused of throwing.[5] In both games, attempts have been made to prevent pitchers and bowlers from delivering the ball so that it would injure a hitter; by 1983, in both games batting players wore protective headgear.

Both games are full of statistics, all of which are fundamentally meaningless, because the conditions of the grounds, the pitch, and differently designed equipment over the years make true comparison impossible. Ballparks are not all the same size and shape; players are affected differently by prevailing weather conditions. Atlanta Stadium was altered in 1974, "apparently to slow things down a bit" because of the "inordinately high" number of home runs hit there. In contrast, at Arlington Stadium the prairie wind defeats power hitters; Richie Zisk, Jeff Burroughs, and Jim Spencer are only three players to have suffered from it.[6] Similarly, cricket scores are often determined by the state of the wicket. Rain on the grass can produce a "sticky wicket" on which even mediocre bowlers can have a field day. As Neville Cardus put it, "Bradman, when he is batting on a dry smooth lawn, and Bradman on a 'sticky pitch,' are only distantly related. One day he is the greatest run-maker ever known; tomorrow, possibly, he seems to go into bat only [so] that the scorers, like official receivers, may be supplied for accountancy's sake with the current details of his bankruptcy."[7]

Efforts to put baseball statistics on a more scientific footing are now being made by people who practice *sabermetrics,* a term coined from the name of the Society for Baseball Research. Using computers, researchers are taking into account the climate, the ballpark, and the relationship between a player's activities. That is, instead of simply looking at a player's batting average, they combine in a formula a range of activities such as home runs, singles, and outs, which they claim gives a more accurate assessment of a player's contribution at bat to his team.[8] Their work is not yet widely known, but it is immensely promising. Nevertheless, the apparent certainty of numbers, a plethora of numbers, endlessly discussed by players and fans alike, memorized by small boys on both sides of the Atlantic, conditions attitudes to both games. Yet in spite of such concern with precision, both games are still linked to pastoral images. Played in urban ballparks or grounds, baseball and cricket are nostalgically linked to the sweet-smelling green fields of a rural community.

In its early days in the United States, cricket was not regarded as an alien game. The *New York Clipper* in 1857 suggested that cricket would become "one of our national sports, and form one of the connecting links of that bond of brotherhood which ought to exist between the sons of old England and young America."[9] But as Melvin Adelman points out, cricket was rooted in an English tradition that allowed adults to spend whole days playing what was regarded by most Americans as a children's game. Its rules were standardized, and it was tainted with wagering, socially acceptable in England, but regarded as gambling in the United States. Between 1855 and 1865 the popularity of cricket waned, while that of baseball waxed, primarily because cricket lacked the crisis points that studded baseball.

It is not merely that cricket is a slow game. So is baseball. Ian Tyrell has suggested that cricket and baseball matches in the 1850s both took about the same length of time to play because baseball rules at that time allowed the batter to decide which balls, if any, he wanted to hit.[10] Length of play alone, however, does not determine whether or not a game is perceived to be slow. In 1845 the Knickerbockers organized themselves, the first baseball club about which very much is on record. Even though their baseball rules specified that the pitcher had to toss the ball underhand in such a way that the batter had the best chance of hitting it, and the batter could, even then, choose his ball, the fielding team had to get only three batters out to end the inning.[11] A cricket team had to dismiss ten batsmen before the inning was over. Further, under Knickerbocker rules the first team to get twenty-one runs won, regardless of the number of innings; but because only three batters had to be dismissed before the teams changed over, the game could seesaw. In cricket during the same period, only two innings were ever played, and there was no possibility of knowing what the result might be until the whole of one team and most of the other team had batted at least once. That is, nothing much appears to happen until the game is well advanced. Also, a cricket match can very easily end in a draw (tie); whereas even under Knickerbocker rules, one team had to win. The actual time a match took was therefore of less importance than what went on during that time; and from its inception, baseball was "faster" than cricket.

Adelman argues that structurally the rotation of batters in baseball encourages participation because each batter knows he will have another chance.[12] Yet in amateur cricket, participation is also encouraged, because the skill level of the best batsmen is usually not very high, so almost everyone will have a chance to bat at least once. An amateur cricketer trades frequent opportunities to bat for the chance, of which even the worst batsman dreams, of shining over a long period of time by using his judgment as well as his quickness of eye and hand. For spectators, however, there is no contest between the games; only connoisseurs can enjoy a cricket match. As Dick Tyldesley once remarked to Neville Cardus, "There's nowt wrong wi' t'game, it's pooblic needs eddicating oop to it."[13] Americans had no intention of undergoing the necessary tutelage.

Nor could cricket be easily altered for the benefit of an American audience. Tyrell quite rightly suggests that even had cricketers desired to speed up their game, they would have been hard put to do so.[14] The "laws" of cricket, evolved over a long period, were standardized by 1835 and were designed for the benefit of players, not spectators. When baseball began to spread across the United States its rules were still embryonic and could be readily altered to meet the needs of spectators as well as players. By 1863, baseball umpires were to "call balls or strikes against pitchers or batters who delayed the game or showed poor 'form.' "[15] No one worried much about delays in cricket; indeed the game was always delayed after four balls, because the bowling had to begin again from the other end of the pitch and the fielders had to change their positions.[16] After the Civil War, as entrepreneurs got hold of baseball, the rules were further altered to increase spectator interest. In 1881, pitchers were moved five yards further from the batter to a distance of fifty feet; in 1884, overhand pitching was legalized.[17] Until 1887, batters were allowed to choose a high or low strike zone; when that was abolished, they were allowed four strikes. As David Voigt points out, in the 1880s "hardly a year passed without some change in rules regarding balls and strikes." Stadium owners knew that the pitcher/batter duel was the heart of the game, and wanted to adjust it to generate the greatest possible tension. Not until 1889 was the now standard three strikes and four balls accepted.[18]

Baseball also contains more visual variety than cricket. In cricket, two batsmen play one at each end of the pitch. To score a run, the batsmen must each run to the other end of the pitch at the same time, thus passing each other en route. A spectator therefore has to watch only the ball and the batsmen, who always cover the same ground. Only one batsman can be dismissed by one ball. In baseball, up to three men can be on base, and more than one batter can be put out at a time. More possibilities are therefore open to the pitcher and fielders, and spectators have to keep a sharp eye on several different places. With the bases loaded, the whole complexion of the game can turn on one pitch. In cricket, the most extreme events that can occur are that one batsman hits a six or is out, and only at the end of a game will either of these be likely to have much immediate significance. Consider the psychological impact of a home run with the bases loaded; there is nothing in cricket that remotely compares to it. Cricket is essentially a game of process, not of result; and as the English captain of a touring 1872 team remarked, Americans "will not give the time necessary for the game . . . they are not charmed by monotony, even if it be High Art."[19]

Even had it not been so monotonous, cricket might not have been acceptable to Americans. In contrast with other more international statements, a writer in the *Brooklyn Eagle* in 1862 made the point that as cricket "is not an *American* game but purely an English game, it never will be in much vogue with the Americans."[20] Certainly the members of cricket clubs on the East Coast did their best to keep cricket to themselves, in that they laid out grounds from which nonclub members were excluded and played long matches, which only those who could afford it could take part in or watch. In these circumstances, it was easy to perceive cricket as an ethnic, exclusive game, antithetical to democratic values. The cricketers played for their own enjoyment, not for that of spectators; they did not care that by 1869 the Red Stocking Club of Cincinnati had contracted all players' services for a full season. The cricket clubs declined, while pro and amateur baseball took over the hearts and pocketbooks of the American public.

Quite apart, moreover, from the structure and values of the game, baseball could be played in a space and with equipment far less costly than that required by cricket. I have seen cricket played on wretched surfaces, but the ball normally has to bounce before it gets to the batsman, and often has to be hit along the ground. British missionaries laid down matting or had the ground trampled flat in parts of the world where grass is hard to come by; baseball needs no such preparation. Given the different kinds of grass that grow in England and the United States and the problems of getting it to stay alive at all in extreme cold or heat, a game in which the ball travels through the air most of the time is easier to play. Cricket bats and balls were usually imported; in the early days not even gloves were used in baseball. As specialized equipment was developed, American manufacturers (of whom, of course, Spalding was one) made and distributed equipment for an American game.

Baseball may have supplanted cricket; but why did it become America's "national" game? As Allen Guttmann so clearly points out, the usual explanations of "ease of access, the technological impetus, the presence of folk heroes, the occasion for nostalgia," will not do.[21] It seems to me that baseball became America's national game because it was marketed to be so. It had, of course, to possess characteristics that would make it possible for anyone to play and understand it; "ease of access" is a necessary but not sufficient condition for its symbolic significance. But the fact remains that Americans were looking for a way to express their uniqueness; as Porter's *Spirit of the Times* remarked in 1857, there ought to be "one game peculiar to the citizens of the United States." The editor supported the idea of the New York baseball clubs forming an association, because it was time to develop "a Native American Sport."[22] When the National Association of Base Ball Players was formed, the *New York Clipper* criticized its composition on the grounds that it was confined to New York. The *Clipper*'s editor wanted the association to be a national, not a local and exclusive, one. The association did extend its membership, and very quickly state and regional associations were formed.[23] In 1867, representatives of more than seventy individual clubs and eight state associations attended the association's convention.[24]

The association originally had strict rules against players being paid, but as the game spread, local rivalries ensured that these rules would be more honored in the breach than the observance. In 1871, the National Association of Professional Base Ball Players was formed. Yet even while the game was being turned into a business, some people recognized that it needed proper merchandising.[25] Harry Wright, called the "Father of the Game" in the early 1870s, objected when the Philadelphia Athletics displayed the pennant they had won for the 1871 championship in a bar. Wright wanted the pennant in the clubhouse, because "to elevate the National Game we must earn the respect of all." This came from the man who refused a player's request to be late for spring training, on the grounds that "professional ball playing is a business."[26] Wright understood very well that an unsavory sport does not draw large numbers of spectators for long; and if baseball was to tap into the emotions attached to nationalism, it had to conform, outwardly at least, to the values Americans believed the United States ought to represent. There was money to be made from mythology; Wright anticipated what it would take to make professional baseball synonymous with national virtue.

Wright was equally clearheaded about the need for proper business organization of the baseball industry. In a letter he wrote, "Professional clubs, to keep in existence, must have gate money, to receive gate money they must play games, and to enable them to play games, their opponents must have faith that such games will prove remunerative."[27] Wright's grasp of essentials made him perfectly ready to act as the secretary of the 1876 meeting called to form the National League of Professional Base Ball Clubs.[28] He was willing to see the managing and playing functions of baseball separated and a monopoly established, because he believed there was no other way of ensuring the consistently high level of competition, free of fixed games and corrupt officials and players, that spectators would pay to see. A disciplinarian himself, Wright was among those who gave management power over players to improve the game's image and thus increase its profit-making capacity.[29]

What Wright understood, in short, was that any professional sports franchise must operate on two levels at once. It must possess the characteristics of any successful business enterprise; but because what it is marketing is illusion, the business scaffolding must not be visible to the public. Ostensibly, professional baseball furthered the cause of democracy, because any player, from any background, if he were not black, could become a hero. The fact that he could do it only on management's terms was not something the public needed to know or much cared about. In September 1879, Arthur Soden, who owned the Boston National League Club, got his fellow owners to agree that five players in each club would be reserved to that club.[30] Not many years later, the reserve clause was part of every baseball player's contract. That is, the player had no opportunity of selling his services to any other club, although the club could decide at any time to get rid of him.

This fact, however, was conveniently overlooked by the public. Further, National League players were expected to behave in acceptable ways, on and off the field; sportswriters drew nationwide attention to players such as Mike Kelly and Jim McCormick, who were alleged to drink. In the 1880s, club rules forbade players to hang about bars, to stay out late, to game, or to make friends with gamblers.[31] So while players had little or no voice in the conditions under which they were employed, baseball could be marketed as an institution that represented the best of American middle-class values and that was fundamentally democratic. John Tener, president of the National League during World War I, was not being hypocritical when he stated, "There is no other sport or business or anything under heaven which exerts the levelling influence that baseball does . . . England is a democratic country, but it lacks the finishing touch of baseball."[32]

Mythology is extraordinarily powerful; baseball's was no exception. If baseball was to be America's national game, it clearly must represent overtly the best of American official aspirations. As Tyrell states, "Business shaped the game of baseball into a money-making concern, yet it is equally significant that the coming of professional ball should be justified not as a commercial concern alone, but that press and promoters should feel it necessary to invest the coming of the cash nexus with enormous moral significance."[33] The success of this marketing strategy can be gauged by the shock and sense of betrayal felt throughout the United

States when it was revealed in 1920 that eight members of the Chicago White Sox had thrown the 1919 World Series for money.[34] Given baseball players' limited salaries, held down by the reserve clause, it is not hard to understand why some should have succumbed to temptation. But they were given no quarter by the baseball commissioner, Judge Kenesaw Mountain Landis. Although seven players who went to trial in 1921 were acquitted, they were banned for life from the game by Landis, who intended to see that professional baseball would continue to be marketed as epitomizing the virtues of "the city set on a hill."

Landis's strategy succeeded; during the 1920s and 1930s the baseball establishment and sportswriters sang the same song. Baseball was an American sport because it was highly competitive and an activity in which individual success could be achieved only by virtue combined with hard work and hustle. There was no place in it for weaklings, cheaters, or those who gave up before the last ball was thrown. A professional player had to be, publicly at least, above reproach, because he was the hero of America's youth; his ethical and moral standards would become theirs. In 1923, for instance, when it was rumored that boxing matches were to be staged in baseball stadiums, the president of the American League promptly banned boxing in its baseball parks on the grounds that baseball should not be contaminated by association with so grubby a commercialized activity as boxing.[35] Professional baseball's early history of drunkenness and gambling had been erased from public memory; the game now was to stand as a monument to public morality.

Vestiges of that attitude remain today; in 1981, it was reported that baseball's commissioner, Bowie Kuhn, had rejected the suggestion that James Cagney should throw out the first ball for the World Series' second game, because Kuhn believed no politician or entertainer should be accorded such an honor.[36] James Cagney did in fact throw out the first ball, and given the results of the 1980 presidential election, Kuhn's stance seems even more outlandish than it need have been. But in baseball, mythologic traditions die hard.

Yet during the years when baseball was being marketed as a repository of eternal values, the style of play was changing beyond recognition, partly because changes were made in equipment. During the early 1900s, runs became a rarity; Elmer Flick's batting average of .306 was sufficient in 1905 to win him the American League batting championship, and in the same year the White Sox managed only three home runs among them. Spectators began to complain; in 1909 James Lovitt wrote, "Every fan can testify to the lackadaisical quality displayed . . . in a thirteen inning game with neither side scoring. Some will say that even though no runs are made, such a game is exciting. To him, I say, you are not a true sport!"[37] Some blamed the use of large fielding gloves, which cut off potential runs;

but what changed the batters' efforts to "push, poke, shove and chop" at the ball was both the introduction of a new sort of ball and a change in tactics. First used in the World Series in 1910, the ball with a cork center traveled far better than the old "deadball," and by 1926 had been officially adopted.[38] Fans by then expected to see high-scoring games and home runs.

Changes in the ball had occurred before 1910. In the 1870s the National League had sought to encourage a shorter game so that working men could afford the time to attend games.[39] The slow ball adopted during the period was harder to hit very far and had a more predictable bounce than the lively ball of the 1860s; games, therefore, were over more quickly. By 1910, the businessmen who ran baseball were beginning to think that fans preferred high scores to low ones, regardless of the time the game took; therefore, they were ready to change the ball again. These tactics were deliberately employed to increase spectator interest, long before the advent of television; they merely reflect one way in which the game has been adapted over the years to make it marketable.

But it was not the ball alone that changed baseball's style. Babe Ruth demonstrated to owners the drawing power of long, powerful hitting. The prewar "scientific" baseball was a game in which teams bunted, sacrificed, stole bases, and tried to keep the ball in the infield except for the single run that was properly protected and therefore sufficient to win the game. After the war, newly affluent crowds began to come to the ballparks; in 1919, Babe Ruth's home runs, powerful, obvious, and thrilling, changed the style of baseball. To strike out was no longer a disgrace, to protect the plate no longer a batter's aim. As fans poured into the ballparks to wait and watch for the big hits, owners hastened to instruct their managers; as Robert Creamer points out, baseball "changed more between 1917 and 1921 than it did in the next forty years." Before 1919, the earned run average was around 2.85 each year; in the decade after 1920, pitchers could not keep the ERA much below 4.00. Excitement was what pulled in the crowds; so excitement was what they got.[40]

The new style offended some old fans. Purists had always disliked home runs. As early as 1890, Henry Chadwick, the sportswriter who popularized baseball, fulminated against them; in 1915, when Babe Ruth hit his first major-league home run, home runs were not reported separately in the newspapers' batting statistics. In 1916, the National League issued new directives about the distance of the outfield fences from home plate to cut down on home runs. Yet in June 1918, Babe Ruth was first called the "Home Run King," and in August 1919, his pursuit of home runs counted for more than the race for the pennant.[41]

There is no means of knowing how many oldtimers shared Ring Lardner's distaste, forcibly expressed in 1921 in his weekly syndicated column, but he probably stood for a sizable group of fans who had shared his early passionate devotion to baseball. He wrote

> It ain't the old game which I have lost interest in it, but it is the game which the magnates has fixed up to please the public with their usual good judgment.
>
> A couple yrs. ago a ball player named Baby Ruth that was a pitcher by birth was made into an outfielder on acct. of how he could bust them and he begins breaking records for long distance hits and etc. and he become a big drawing card and the master minds that controls baseball says to themselfs that if it is home runs that the public wants to see, why leave us give them home runs, so they fixed up a ball that if you don't miss it entirely it will clear the fence, and the result is that ball players which use to specialize in hump back liners to the pitcher is now amongst our leading sluggers when by rights they couldn't take a ball in their hands and knock it past the base umpire.[42]

But if Lardner did not care for the "new" game, his place at the stadium and many more besides were taken by fans of the Lovitt persuasion.

Yet if style and tactics changed, not even television has altered the fundamental structure of baseball. As Harold Seymour points out, "Baseball's rules have been refined and polished over the years, but the hard Knickerbocker core has remained central. The four-base diamond, 90-foot base paths; three out, all out; batting in rotation; throwing out runners or touching them; nine-man teams, with each player covering a definite position; the location of the pitcher's box in relation to the diamond as a whole – these are still fundamental in baseball."[43] What television has altered is baseball's mythology.

In the days before television, it was relatively easy to conceal the skeletons in professional baseball's closet. Large numbers of boys played baseball, and adults who loved the game rarely saw major league players in the flesh; the national game was sustained by sportswriters who were not anxious to bite the hand that fed them. As radio swept the land in the 1920s it took baseball with it, but again, fans could not see what the players were doing. Instead, they made up their own fantasies, as the announcers made up theirs. As baseball was, in essence, a game of the imagination, Babe Ruth, for instance, could be regarded as a "character," rather than a bum.

Babe Ruth epitomized baseball. Perhaps he still does. He made his name in the decade when Judge Landis took charge of baseball and set it back on its pedestal. Ruth was America's Hero. In a letter Judge Emil Fuchs wrote in 1935 to tempt Ruth to help him salvage the Boston Braves, he told Ruth he was "a source of consolation to the children, as well as to the needy, who look up to you as a shining example of what the great athletes and public figures of America should be."[44] The letter is full of such hyperbole and need not be taken seriously. The point is that no one could possibly have written such words to Joe Namath, Reggie Jackson, or any other highly publicized sports figure of the 1970s and 1980s. Ruth was, and was known by sportswriters to be, a crude, drunken, lecherous, vulgar, generous but self-centered peasant. He was also a superb baseball player, with a gargantuan appetite for everything, who had enormous charisma. He would have been as popular with fans in the television era as he was before it; but he could no longer have been marketed as a repository of American values. It is true, as Creamer points out, that everywhere Ruth went he was known and noticed;[45] but what individual fans knew of his behavior was submerged in the rhetoric of the public image, nurtured nationwide. Babe Ruth was not the subject of investigative reporting.

Even when writers did criticize Ruth, their criticisms could not dent the hero's armor because Ruth's superhuman feats on the field had been carefully crafted into an off-field image of superman. In 1933, after an avalanche of publicity critical of Ruth's refusal to accept a $50,000 salary at a time when millions were unemployed, Ruth was mobbed by enthusiastic fans on the first day of spring training – after he had signed for $52,000.[46] Other players turned baseball's mythology to their own advantage; Dizzy Dean, for instance, marketed his rural roots. In 1934, he cashed in on "'Me and Paul' sweatshirts and toothbrushes, a 'Me and Paul' vaudeville tour, Dizzy Dean caps, shirts and booklets – all promoted by radio and personal appearances." But the *Sporting News* was quick to criticize him when he had contract problems in 1936;[47] he and other ballplayers were supposed to play not for money, but for love of the game. In the age of television, such fantasies cannot be sustained.

Baseball's owners were deeply suspicious of radio at first, because they feared it would cut into attendance at the ballparks. When they found stadium audiences increasing and radio rights bringing cash into their depression-depleted coffers, they welcomed broadcasting.[48] In 1936, Gillette paid over $100,000 to sponsor the World Series; individual clubs negotiated broadcasting rights to their home games. By 1939, the least any major-league club got for those rights was $33,000; many clubs made much more.[49]

The fact that they had become used to radio meant that the owners were considerably less suspicious of TV when it developed after World War II. What they did not realize was that while radio commentators were content to describe the game (or transform it into something much more exciting if it suited them), TV coverage would inadvertently rip away the packaging in which baseball had been so successfully marketed.

Baseball was marketed as America's national game when there was no major-league franchise on the West Coast. It was marketed as a game with its roots in the country's rural (and therefore "most worthy") past when it was played at its best in urban ballparks. It was marketed as a game presenting stability when major-league franchises had in reality been tied to their locations by their fireproof stadiums. After World War II, cracks began to appear in the marketing facade.

Between 1901 and 1953 major-league franchises had remained in the same cities. This was not because the owners were providing a public service or cared about their fans; it was because ballparks were located in profitable places. As Steven Riess has shown, the professional club in Chicago moved five times between 1871 and 1893, seeking a location that was affordable, best served by mass transportation, and in a desirable neighborhood. Teams in New York and Atlanta also moved about in the late nineteenth century.[50] Because they were not settled, and baseball was not yet a mature industry, owners built cheaply; in 1894, major-league ballparks in Baltimore, Philadelphia, Boston, and Chicago caught fire.[51] The first fireproof ballpark was built in 1909 in response to new laws and new demands from the spectators.[52] But these concrete and steel ballparks were very expensive to construct; once located, no franchise owner could afford to move. Television was not responsible for the determination of municipal authorities to get into the stadium-building business after World War II; nor was it television that made the Dodgers and Giants leave New York. Owners could no longer afford to build their own ballparks; nor was it worth renovating their crumbling facilities, which urban demographic changes had relegated to parts of town that were no longer desirable. But the desertion of hallowed ground by major-league franchises ripped the fans' world apart. Baseball was not supposed to change; it had been marketed for seventy years as an expression of the eternal American verities. It was all very bewildering.

Yet whether fans realized it or not, baseball promoters had always provided more than the verities. From Christopher Von der Ahe's efforts in St. Louis in the 1880s to Larry MacPhail's in the 1930s, those who made money from baseball set the game firmly in the context of entertainment. First, they attended to fans' physical comfort and enticed whole families, not just men, to come to the ballpark. Von der Ahe built "a ladies' toilet room" at Sportman's Park; West Side Park in Chicago was provided with rooftop boxes for the affluent.[53] Charles Ebbets put in "opera chairs with curved backs that were two inches roomier than standard seats because they had just one armrest." As Ebbets Field was finished in 1913, it included a parking lot opposite the main entrance.[54] Promoters also supplied food and drink; in Von der Ahe's case, fans got beer.[55]

Then sideshows were added; Von der Ahe provided horseracing and fireworks, MacPhail, "red uniforms, usherettes, [and] cigarette girls in bright-colored satin pants."[56] The *Sporting News* endorsed "night games, field days, special days and drum and bugle corps," but in 1937 suggested that "such things as 'fan dancers, hog-calling contests, donkey ball' and other activities not even remotely related to baseball should be avoided."[57] It was not television that surrounded baseball with commercial gimmickry; that show was well on the road before World War II began. A fan attending a professional ball game in 1986 does not necessarily expect to see a fan dancer, but assumes there will be an announcer, an electronic organ playing ritual motifs, a plentiful supply of beer and snack food, roaming vendors, a mascot, and an electronic scoreboard capable by itself of diverting attention from the game, even to the extent of talking to the crowd. In a National League Championship game between the Astros and the Phillies on October 10, 1980, the scoreboard typically exhorted Dave Smith to "Strike Him Out"; and then announced happily "He Did!" To attend a baseball game is not simply to watch professional sport; it is to take part in a peculiarly American commercialized ritual.

Efforts to get people to the ballpark did not merely involve razzle-dazzle. One of the most fundamental changes to the game involved shifting it from day to night. The first night game was played in Massachusetts as early as 1880; but the first regular-season night game was played on April 28, 1930.[58] Not until 1935 did major-league baseball move to night games; the motive, as always, was financial. The same complaints were made in a *Literary Digest* report about the first night game in Cincinnati as were to be made about a World Series staged for television. The night was cold. The real fans disliked night baseball. Players were "bitter" about disrupted training routines and not being able to follow line drives in the glare. The game itself suffered. "The game became a strangely colorless, synthetic affair. Like the lights it was artificial, mechanical. Personal characteristics and facial expressions on the players became vague in the haze which hung over the field." As Dan Taylor, a Dodger, complained, "The major leagues, supposed to represent the top of the business, are being turned into a five-and-ten-cent racket by night baseball."[59] The pundits and the purists, however, were overwhelmed by the gate receipts; 130,337 people came to the seven night games in Cincinnati, which was more than the total attendance for some teams at home for the year. By 1940, only five teams did not play night games at home.[60] Whatever the myth, professional baseball had embraced a technological development that made of each game an artificial, staged event, simply in order to increase the gate receipts. All this was done before television had begun. To move the World Series to the night is but an extension of normal business practice; to expect players to play in the cold is no more of an assault on their skills than to expect them to play in the enervating heat and dust major-league baseball has always known.

TV coverage, however, put an end to several sorts of baseball fantasy. In the first place, commentators could no longer make up what was going on, because viewers could see it for themselves. The players were brought right into the living room and what they were doing was remorselessly revealed; distance no longer lent enchantment. Sportswriters could create "characters"; now players were interviewed and followed on camera, and what had once been in the control of the writer slid out from under him. It is no coincidence that the style of sportswriting changed in the 1960s; it was not merely that the world had changed, but that it was no longer possible to peddle sentiment in the press when cameras were so candid.[61]

Another fantasy that rapidly disappeared was that people went to watch minor-league baseball because the team was a part of the community. When fans could see top-class baseball on TV, rather than third-class baseball in the flesh, they chose the better product. This also had been foreshadowed. When Jackie Robinson was signed to the Brooklyn Dodgers in April 1947 it signaled the demise of the Negro National League; although the Negro American League lingered on until 1960, its prestige had gone by the early 1950s. Black fans could by then watch black players in the hitherto segregated major leagues (where they often outplayed whites); community support for the black leagues vanished.[62]

TV also laid to rest forever the notion that ball players were playing chiefly because they loved the game. Some of the vastly increased revenue that accrued to the industry from television found its way to the players; their increased salaries coincided with and helped produce a publicly recognized change in attitudes to their job. Baseball, from its inception, was marketed as a game; so successful was the marketing that when the Baltimore Federals owners filed suit under the Sherman Antitrust Act, the Supreme Court in 1922 declared that baseball was not trade or commerce and was therefore exempt from antitrust proceedings. The court also declared that baseball games were intrastate matters, because players traveled across state lines incidentally to the actual games themselves, and that baseball rules such as the reserve clause did not directly affect what interstate aspects of baseball there actually were.[63] Mythology thus gave a sports industry exemption from prosecution enjoyed by no other industry in the United States; the players suffered as a result.

In the early days of baseball, players jumped freely from club to club. In September 1879, National League owners agreed to reserve five players on each team for the 1880 season. By 1883, the number of such players that other teams agreed not to bid for increased to eleven, and to fourteen in 1887; very shortly all players were reserved. Players hated the reserve clause, and in 1890 formed their own league. Both the National and Players leagues lost money during the season, and they merged at the end of it; but the reserve clause remained. When the American League was formed, players eagerly jumped to it; when the National League recognized their new rival officially in 1903, the reserve clause again operated throughout baseball. The Federal League was formed in 1914 and offered brief hopes for better conditions for players, but it died in 1915.[64]

Players' unions were formed in 1885, 1900, and 1912, but none was successful in forcing owners to bargain collectively. The American Baseball Guild was formed in 1946; although players could take advantage of the National Labor Relations Act (1935), tactical errors left the owners still firmly in control of the players. Nevertheless, the guild's formation led owners to organize formal representation of the players on the executive council. In 1954, the Major League Baseball Players Association was formed; in 1966 Marvin Miller became its executive director.[65]

By this time, players' salaries were no small beer. But players could not market themselves, because the club for which they first signed had contractual rights to their services. In 1953, the Supreme Court confirmed baseball's antitrust status, in a case brought by George Toolson; in 1972, Curt Flood's case was similarly disposed of. Curt Flood, however, had been offered $100,000 for the 1970 season, in which he did not play, and $110,000 for the 1971 season.[66] The stakes for which baseball players were now playing were high, and players were well aware of their market value. Agents had begun to negotiate for and educate players as soon as the percentage of the gross made it worth their while; baseball had become a game one played not because it was pleasanter than alternative employment, but because it could well be the pathway to a lifetime of financial security.

It was the union, not the courts, that finally gave baseball players their passport to free agency, and this was achieved through the grievance and arbitration procedure. The one neutral arbitrator in a free agency case brought in 1975 ruled that the reserve clause held only for one year. Subsequent collective bargaining has brought to baseball more stability than such contracts would provide; but no longer are baseball players bound by what the founder of baseball's first union, John Montgomery Ward, called "a fugitive slave law."[67]

To my mind, it is extremely doubtful that the reserve clause would have been overturned had not the human rights movement made the public aware that ball players were humans too. But higher salaries also allowed the players' union to employ first-class lawyers. TV revenues undoubtedly helped to pay those salaries. Yet free agency has not led to increased salaries for football players, although huge sums of television money have been poured into that sport. Baseball and football owners have adopted different marketing strategies and reached different formal and informal agreements. The presence of TV money is a necessary but not sufficient condition for giving professional athletes the leverage they need to make the most money they can during their brief careers. Whether they actually get that leverage depends on a number of factors that are at best tangentially related to TV revenues.

All the salary bargaining, however, is reported at length in the press. Fans can no longer watch the "boys of summer" and envy simply their athletic prowess and the fame it brings. What separates baseball players from their audience is not only skill but money. A baseball player could be forgiven an off day when this salary was thought to be relatively small; now, if he does not perform, fans assume it must be because money has spoiled him, he is able to indulge an expensive drug habit, or because he bamboozled stupid owners into giving him a long-term contract that offers him so much security he doesn't care whether he plays or not. As television has provided much of this largesse, it is held responsible for the deterioration of what was assumed to have been a game. Few fans can imagine the kind of pressures major-league players are subjected to because of their celebrity status; it is easy to say that they are paid for it. If television has released players from penury, the money it has provided for them has raised spectators' expectations. Players are not now simply godlike; they must be as gods if we are to continue to care about them.

Contrary to what many jaundiced fans believe, far from debasing the game, TV has in many ways improved it. Umpires whose every move is watched by millions and recorded for expert reexamination later must be at least moderately efficient. While it can be argued that hungry players will give their all, it is equally true that the more a man stands to lose, the greater will be his incentive to retain what he has. TV is remorseless in revealing stupidity, carelessness, lack of concentration, and poor play, just as it underscores brilliance. Our expectations have risen; we see players in the flesh, not in fantasy.

We can now examine our gods more closely than ever before, because those who translate baseball understand it very well. Even before a game begins it is set in context. The singing of the national anthem is televised; America's national game must be introduced by America's national anthem. The sense of "sacred space" here is extended beyond the stadium; symbolically, viewers are reminded of their allegiance not simply to a game but to their country. Shots of the ballpark identify it, and baseball's historic tradition is called upon whenever possible. In the first game of the 1980 World Series at Veterans Stadium in Philadelphia, viewers were reminded that the last time a World Series was played there was in 1950; viewers were then told that the manager of that team would throw out the first ball. Thus it is made clear that the game the viewer is seeing matters not simply because of its present significance, but because it represents continuity and stability in an uncertain world. The symbols used both conform to and strengthen tradition.

Rain or shine, the television crew will remain at their posts and on the air until the last ball of the game has been accounted for. "Sacred time" will not be tampered with. Shots of the dugout remind viewers that this is a team game. The "bond of brothers" is highlighted whenever a runner scores, or a batter hits a home run; the viewer is taken to the dugout where the successful player is greeted with hand slaps and congratulations. Mutual congratulations at the end of successful defensive innings by the fielding team are also shown; whatever backbiting and dissension is going on behind the scenes, the viewer is presented with the public face of baseball, a group of men working for each other's good. This posture is maintained even when a player's moves from team to team are catalogued; it is assumed that he is, by definition, playing for an entity larger than himself, and that whatever the circumstances of his trade, he is now playing wholeheartedly for the team in whose uniform the viewers are now watching him.

Crowd shots are shown not just to provide visual variety, but to demonstrate the power of "rooting." In the sixth game of the 1980 World Series, the atmosphere at the top of the ninth inning was electric. The Phillies were well on their way to the championship; the camera moved from behind the pitcher, Tug McGraw, on ball 2, strike 1, to show the crowd on its feet, then back to show the pitch. Strike 2. Immediately, there was another crowd shot, followed by a close-up of McGraw, a close-up of the batter, Amos Otis, then from behind the pitcher the pitch was followed to the strikeout. Again the crowd was shown, wildly enthusiastic. Viewers were being drawn into the tension created not merely by the game itself, but by its context; what was being translated was another baseball ritual, the response of fans to the activities of the teams they had chosen to call theirs.

No television viewer of a baseball game can miss "spirit"; in fact, it is all the more obvious to home viewers because they are as close to the player as his sweat. In the fifth game of the National League playoffs between the Phillies and the Astros in 1980, Craig Reynolds's determination to give every ounce of himself to the play was obvious. The tension showed in his face, in his hands, in his arm as he rubbed it across his forehead; what, one wondered, could possibly drive a man to put himself voluntarily in this position? Yet here was no panic, no craven yielding to fear; rather, there was the determination to, as Novak puts it, "grab greatness as it passes by."[68] And how can one grab greatness if one does not measure oneself against the best, cost what it may? Even with binoculars, it is sometimes hard to catch such evidence of "spirit"; television close-ups make it impossible for the viewer to ignore it.

Similarly, television reveals the sheer professionalism of ball players. Who can forget the marvelous athleticism of U. L. Washington's leap in the second game of the 1980 World Series, as he scraped the ball from the turf and hurled himself into a turn so that he could get the ball to first base? The play was stunning as it happened, but it was burned into the memory by the replays. There, even with the grace of God, I do not go; these men belong to a different world of movement from mine. Yet they are not content with what they can already do; the search for excellence persists.

The process of "self-discovery" is marked by television. A player's statistics are printed on the screen, and commentators analyze them; whether a man is improving, keeping up his past level of performance, or slipping over the hill is remorselessly examined. A player is measured, exactly and continually, not only against his present opponents, but against himself. Keith Jackson reminds viewers of the 1981 World Series, "Here's the man that homered for the Dodgers last night." Cosell points out that "he never has gotten back to that 31 game hitting streak form that he had with Minnesota." Jim Palmer explains that any player switching leagues has to adjust to new pitchers. Listeners are made aware that baseball batting is a complicated, awesome skill; it is no mere matter of striding to the plate and mindlessly doing what one has done thousands of times before.

But even as the text is translated, every conceivable device is used to attract not only the fan, but the spectator to the game. Immense pains are taken to secure visual variety by using different camera angles in varying order, by focusing on different subject matters, by splitting the screen, by printing information over a picture, and by fitting pretaped photographs and interviews into the context of the game itself. A typical sequence of shots is represented in the first game of the 1980 World Series.

The viewer sees the batter, George Brett, close up, and then is whisked behind the pitcher, Bob Walk, to see the pitcher, the batter, the catcher, and the umpire through the pitch; the camera then follows the pop-up to the catch, and a section of the crowd is shown responding to the play. The viewer is taken back behind Walk; then the batter, Willie Aikens, is followed to the plate and seen in close-up. While Aikens paws himself a place in his batter's box, the viewer is taken behind the catcher for the pitch, then back behind Walk; a close-up of Aikens is shown, then the camera switches to first base where Hal McRae is waiting to take off. The viewer moves back behind Walk, then close up to first as Walk fires the ball to hold McRae; the camera moves back behind Walk for the pitch.

One of the reasons for this constant change of focus is obvious. The heart of baseball is the duel between pitcher and batter; each pitch must be televised. But after a couple of innings, no viewer can ever forget the pitcher's face; concentration on the movement of the ball from the mound would be stupefying to the hardiest fan. Accordingly, a different pattern must appear on the screen whenever possible.

Sometimes (not as often as the camera crew would like) a man is on base. The screen can then be split to show both the pitch and the actions of the base runner as he tries to get the jump on the ball. Viewers can keep an eye on two things at once, as they would at the stadium; the tension can be increased by a close-up of the pitcher's face as he dares the runner to leave the base. His concentration is matched by that of the runner; no viewer had any doubt of what was in Willie Wilson's mind in the 1980 World Series as he stood poised on first, his head and shoulders filling the screen as he stared straight out at the viewer, who was thus enabled to be Steve Carlton by proxy.

Shots of the field can also be introduced to provide variety and to indicate crucial fielding placement. When it is hit, the ball can be followed close up across the turf, or from a distance as it goes through the air or down a line. But field shots present a real translation problem. The fan knows where the fielders are and how they should be moving, even if the camera is following the flight of the ball in close-up. Spectators are suddenly disoriented; they have no idea where they are in the ballpark. This situation is momentary, but it is crucial because baseball is a game of placement. The translators can only do their best while producers and commentators use replays to instruct the ignorant so that they will know better next time.

Home viewers are also given something akin to a magic carpet, because they can be wafted about the stadium. They go into the dugout and bullpen, they travel to the top of the Astrodome; they sit next to the players' wives and children and in different sections of the stadium crowd. And as they travel, they are constantly reminded that they are watching a wholesome, family sport; cute toddlers are always included in the crowd close-ups.

Baseball games are not usually dramatic. Accordingly, great pains are taken to ensure that the continuity of the game is not lost during the commercial breaks. At the end of the inning, the photos of the next three players up may be shown as well as their names; when play resumes, the players' names are placed on a shot of the field, in their positions. The numbers of balls, strikes, and outs are frequently printed on the screen; the score is always shown at the end of each inning.

It is, however, the commentators who are primarily responsible for making sure that spectators stay with the game. In the first place, commentators make explicit both the fundamentals and subtleties of the game. They identify specific pitches and draw attention to fielding positions, particularly to ways in which outfielders move in anticipation of various batters, and to the state of an inning. Some of this instruction also provides visual variety; in the 1980 National League Championship game between Houston and the Phillies, viewers were instructed to "look at the gap in right center field," an instruction that evidently took the camera crew by surprise. But to understand the possibilities, we did need to look there. Further, what is the right move in one context is hopelessly ill judged in another; the commentators make clear the particular context of a game and the aim of both pitcher and batter. Some of the notes and statistics printed on the screen are interpreted; that helps viewers interpret the rest. Commentators teach, and in so doing may enlarge their viewers' interest in the game.

After a play is over, particularly if it merits a replay, commentators can explain why the play worked or where and how a mistake was made. In sharing their own admiration for a particularly dogged or skillful play, even if it is not always spectacular, commentators can help viewers become more sophisticated about the game. Howard Cosell's device of asking questions, "What do you think, Jim?", irritating as it may be to the cognoscenti, often elicits explanatory information on the present situation, game techniques in general, or reminiscence that would not otherwise have been forthcoming. If one commentator complains about a play, another can correct him by remarking that the play was simply part of normal baseball: "He was going to take a chance right there – he gambled and they got 'im."

The function of the manager is also explicated, partly by means of pretaped interviews, partly by guesswork as the game proceeds. The choices open to each manager and the reasoning behind decisions he makes can be conveyed to viewers, who may begin to apprehend the complexity of any manager's calculations and the stress of his position. Many viewers may not care; for others, it adds an element of tension to the unfolding tale. Yet in discussing a manager's decisions, TV commentators retain the ambivalence that has always been present in games where the player must suspend his own judgment and do what he is told. As fans or spectators we come primarily to watch the performance of athletes; we do not want to be made too much aware of the fact that a player is a man under authority. When Yankee Reggie Jackson bunted instead of swinging away in the tenth inning of a game with the Royals, he was suspended, because as Billy Martin put it, "I'm the manager. He does what I say."[69] The lineup, the rotation, the pitching are all under the manager's control; but while he can stop a player from performing, he cannot make a player play well. TV commentators continue to walk the fine line sportswriters have followed; it is the manager's job to arrange matters so that players can capitivate their fans by giving of their best. He has the control; they have the limelight. As fans, we do not want to see the strings being pulled.

Commentators also personalize the game by ensuring that viewers can identify, and identify with, each player. Eccentricities of dress and behavior are remarked upon; players' relatives in the stands are shown in close-up, and details of their private lives discussed. Handicaps and injuries are noticed, whether or not they have bearing on the actual game the viewer is watching. Such remarks serve not only to fill in time, but to differentiate between players and to underscore the notion that a true athlete never accepts defeat.

Were the function of the commentator simply to keep the viewer informed as to the state of play, one man could do the job quite adequately. Conversation between several commentators not only provides audible variety, but company for the viewer who is invited to join by proxy a circle of friends at the stadium. At the same time, the commentators draw the crowd, as well as the players, into the living room, not merely by commenting on particular people in it, but by referring to the crowd's enthusiasm and interest.

Each game is also set in its historical context. Players' performances are compared not only with their own past, but with similar great feats of others; past teams and games are recalled. Cosell compared the 1981 World Series second game with the first game of the 1949 series, also between the Yankees and the Dodgers, because the 1981 game was scoreless in the fourth inning and the 1949 game was won by one run in the ninth. By implication, viewers were reminded that in the best baseball games very little ostensibly happens; baseball is a cerebral as well as a physical game. Some commentators can, of course, be stupid, dreary, and insensitive, while others are far too fond of their own voices. But whatever they may do in practice, commentators are simply working within the established tradition of marketing baseball as an entertainment, a spectacle, not simply as a pastime or game.

Long before the advent of television, baseball was marketed as America's game. Viewers are still kept aware that in attending to a baseball game they are attending to a part of their national heritage. The ballpark may have moved, equipment may have altered beyond recognition, players may now be millionaires, but televised baseball is even now an exercise in nostalgia.

Similarly, ball players were marketed as men worthy of emulation. TV viewers are not now given sordid details of a player's private life, or of his peripatetic existence, or of his almost total dependence on decisions taken by owners and managers; that kind of thing is left to the print media. Rather, a player is praised because he is "a man of character. He throws a knuckle curve, but he will never knuckle under." It is left to sportswriters to show us the seamy side of the game; television executives, like all their predecessors with a financial stake in baseball, want the paying public to suspend disbelief and enter into the game itself – then to come back for more.

In translating the text, every effort is made on the part of TV producers to entertain the viewers, to draw them to their electronic seats, and keep them there. The stakes for the entrepreneurs are higher now than they ever were; but professional baseball's purpose and means are fundamentally the same as they have been ever since the game became a business after the Civil War.

Ostensibly, all Americans can compete to excel in baseball; the way to the top is open to all who hustle, work, and persevere. Upward mobility is apparently secured by merit alone. Franchises exist to make money, as they always have done; and if the market to be exploited is now that of television, that market is the one to be cultivated. Yet it is the substance of baseball, its tradition, that will be marketed, because that pays. One such tradition is the manager's uniform, unflattering as it is; symbolically the manager is one of the boys, who defends his team as he waddles from the dugout to argue with the umpires. His clothes mark him as an employee, not an executive. Yet, while the manager argues, preoccupation with rules is carried to the point of absurdity; a game is stopped because of the length of pine tar on a bat. Even indoors, on artificial turf, baseball continues in its ritual fashion; a runner must still touch all bases as he trots around; no one times the pitcher as he prepares to deliver the ball.

For even if all major-league baseball were ultimately to be played indoors before an invited audience, it would not by definition cease to be America's national game. Indeed, by then it might more truly than ever deserve that title, because it would reflect Americans' fascination with efficiency, comfort, and applications of technology, values that Americans have prized at least since the middle of the nineteenth century.

Television, then, has not fundamentally altered baseball. It has tampered with the style, rules, and conduct of the game much less than the game was altered prior to the 1950s. It has faithfully followed the tradition of spectacle nurtured from the 1880s. TV producers have made every effort to sustain the sports mystique, and to preserve the essence of the game.

Let us imagine Babe Ruth on television. We would have seen the crudity, the belches, the hangovers that the sportswriters omitted to mention. But we would also have seen the awesome power, the immense talent, and the sheer charisma of the man. He might not have been America's hero, but he would have been as superb a ball player on TV as he ever was in the flesh. If we cannot love baseball unless we are blinded by mythology, the fault lies not in television but in ourselves.

3

FOOTBALL

"Football will never be commercialized," wrote Bill Edwards in the December 4, 1920, edition of the *Philadelphia North American.* "The essential features of the game, the demands it makes on the players spiritually, the innate sportsmanship it requires of its adherents make the possibility remote of it ever being exploited professionally with any degree of success." A few years later Bill Edwards was president of a fledgling professional football league.[1] But in the 1920s and 1930s, big-time football was still college football; unlike baseball, the professional game of football had its roots in a college sport. But what college coaches refused to acknowledge was that football had been thoroughly commercialized before it was ever played regularly by professionals in name. Professional promoters simply cashed in on the market created by colleges and heightened the elements of spectacle intrinsic to the college game. It was not television that created football as we know it, but the desire of college administrators to market their institutions. The television and professional football industries have only refined and popularized an already tested product.

In 1928, Princeton's coach, William Roper, wrote, "There is money in professional football but not enough to have the sport continue in an exploited, circus-like manner employed by the promoters, who, after all, handled it like a boxing bout, a show and a band concert." Roper concluded that the professional game "will be first, last and always, of minor importance to the intercollegiate game of football."[2] He did not recognize that the colleges had already created conditions that would make the college game an adjunct to that of the professionals. In 1936, the first college draft was held, and although the first pick, Jay Berwanger, could not be persuaded to play professionally, the subordination of the college to the professional game was thus symbolically established.

The first college games of significance to the development of football were played in 1874, between Harvard and McGill.[3] In 1869, when Princeton and Rutgers had played the first intercollegiate football game, the game resembled soccer; and when Yale, Princeton, Columbia, and Rutgers in October 1873 drafted the rules for the game to be played by the Intercollegiate Football Association, the rules were based on those applying to soccer. Harvard was then playing what it called the "Boston Game," which was much more akin to rugby, the game McGill played. When these two teams met in 1874, the first game was played under Harvard rules, the second under rugby rules.[4] So much did the Harvard players enjoy the second game, they adopted the McGill rules.

Rugby, once described by Heywood Hale Broun as "football in underwear," was the winter game of English private boarding schools (called in England "public schools"). Fifteen men played on each team, and the oval ball could be kicked forward, carried by a player who ran with it, or passed sideways and backwards; no forward passing was allowed. A player carrying the ball could be brought down by the opposing team; as soon as the ball reached the ground the player had to release it. The ball could then be put in play only with the feet. When certain rules had been broken, a "scrum" was formed involving three lines of players on each side. $\circ^{\circ}_{\circ}{}^{\circ}_{\circ}$ The front row lined up with their arms around each other, leaning forward from the waist. Two players from the second row put their heads in the gaps between the front row bodies and shoved against the front line. The third line player did likewise in the gap between the other two. Two more players on the second row, one at each end, put an arm around one player and shoved against the front row. The ball was then placed between the opposing team lines and had to be hooked back out of the scrum by a player's foot; the ball could not be picked up by the players actually lined up around it, but only by those waiting outside.

In 1875, Harvard challenged Yale to a football game under what were called "Concessionary Rules" agreed between the two colleges. Over a thousand paying spectators attended,[5] including two Princetonians who persuaded Princeton to adopt the game. In 1876, a new Intercollegiate Football Association was formed by Yale, Harvard, Rutgers, Columbia, and Princeton to play a game that was very close to rugby. Yale finally refused to join the association (while agreeing to play football games with the other members) because Yale's captain wanted eleven men rather than fifteen on a team, and only goals, not touchdowns, to count toward the score.[6]

Excitement about intercollegiate football grew. In 1873, Michigan had invited Cornell to play at Buffalo. President Andrew White had replied, "I will not permit thirty men to travel four hundred miles merely to agitate a bag of wind." Yet in 1878 Yale faculty members for the first time allowed students to miss class for the football game with Harvard;[7] it was the thin end of the athletic wedge. But the play was still not wholly satisfactory for spectators. When the ball was passed, the game was open and interesting; but when the ball was dead, the scrum was incredibly boring to watch. Usually eight men lined up behind the ball in three lines. The front men kicked the ball forward while the rest pushed; the other men on the team stood about. Further, scrums occurred more often in the American game, because in Britain a player could be stopped without necessarily being knocked down. As Alexander Weyand noted, "In the American game, the aim was to knock the runner down. It was believed that, if he were hit hard enough, he would have no opportunity to pass to a teammate." In 1879, the Yale-Princeton game provoked the spectators to hiss; as The *New York Times* put it, "For nearly ten minutes the men struggled without gaining ten feet either way, the 'backs' of each side being nothing but interested onlookers."[8]

Walter Camp, Yale's captain, accordingly proposed some rule changes, which were accepted at the 1880 IFA convention. Instead of the ball being fought over by both teams, one side would be given possession of it. This team would then be able to plan an attack and use plays they had previously practiced. Camp also proposed that the number of players on each team be reduced to eleven, a point Yale had been fighting for since 1876.

American football was not, however, out of the woods. Camp had not anticipated that under his new rules one team could hold on to the ball; in the 1881 Thanksgiving game between Princeton and Yale, Princeton kept the ball for all but four and a half minutes in the first half, while Yale had it for the whole of the second. The spectators again made their feelings clear; so Camp proposed a further rule change. If in three plays a team could not move the ball forward five yards, or had not been moved back ten yards, then the ball had to be given to the other side.

From 1882, then, American colleges began to play a distinctively American game. Even earlier, however, a specifically American idea had been put in place; in 1876 it had been agreed that league games were to culminate in the declaration of a champion team each year.[9] Emphasis in the college games was thus placed on winning; whatever the process, the result was to count.

The championship game quickly began to draw large numbers of spectators. Played in New York on Thanksgiving Day in 1881 to increase the gate, the game drew 10,000 spectators; in 1884, there were 15,000.[10] Newspapers publicized it as a fashionable event; New York's social set attended. As Guy Lewis puts it, "College prestige gave football a level of respectability. It enjoyed a social standing not accorded to such professional contests as baseball. Because it made the calendar of the fashionable set, the football contest was an attractive event." As such, the game itself to many spectators was secondary. By 1887, the championship game attracted 23,000 spectators. Newspapers fed on their own publicity; as week-long advertisements in The *New York Herald* proclaimed in November 1889, "You'll know more about the Princeton-Yale football game than if you were present if you read Walter Camp's description."[11]

Fueled by such flames, the popularity of college football in the East continued to grow, aided and abetted by the colleges themselves. In 1883 the Harvard committee on athletics wanted to disband the team because they considered "a manly spirit of play" to have been overcome by "a spirit of sharpers and of roughs."[12] But the Harvard Athletic Association had embarked on an expensive program of remodeling Jarvis Field. Far from the team's being disbanded, the Yale-Harvard game was moved to New York to increase the gate. As Weyand remarks, "Ten years after Harvard apologized for charging admission to the game with McGill, football had become important enough to dictate university policies."[13]

Spectators loved the game and the trappings surrounding it. As Alexander Johnston wrote in 1887, "The enormous crowd, the coaches filled with men and horns, the masses and shades of color among the spectators, the perpetual roar of cheers, including the peculiar slogans of almost all the Eastern colleges, combine to make up a spectacle such as no other intercollegiate game can offer."[14] Yet with hindsight, the game itself was very dull. The ball still could not be passed forward; as Roper remarked, the result was "a cross between a battle-royal and a cattle stampede." Spectators often sat through periods "when they never saw the ball at all, but just a drab mass of twenty-two players eternally pushing and shoving each other up and down the field."[15]

The game also became exceedingly dangerous; in 1892, Harvard first demonstrated the "flying wedge." Players grouped themselves in a *V,* and began to run before the ball was played; at "the last moment . . . it was legally put into play and passed to a player within the walls of the V."[16] The runners crashed into the opposing line, carrying the ball forward, but also threatening serious injury to themselves and their stationary opponents. By 1896, this and other "mass-momentum" plays were abolished, but mass plays of one sort and another continued to the point that in the 1905 season, eleven high school and three college players were among the eighteen players killed playing football, while 149 other players were seriously injured.[17] Just after Thanksgiving, Columbia's president abolished football on his own authority; neither students nor alumni were consulted. After the season, Northwestern suspended football, the University of California and Stanford both returned to rugby, and the president of Harvard recommended that football be abolished.[18]

Spurred by President Theodore Roosevelt's interest, sweeping rule changes were announced in 1906, the most fundamental of which was the legalization of the forward pass. It was very restricted in that it had to cross the line of scrimmage "five yards from the center," and had to be passed from at least five yards behind the line of scrimmage. However, the possibility of passing forward not only opened up the game, but enabled smaller, lighter men to play than the old bruising style had allowed. This in turn gave colleges with few students a chance to compete at the intercollegiate level.[19]

To assist officials, lines were painted parallel to the sidelines at five-yard intervals. As lines were already painted across the field, the "gridiron" was born. But coaches did not know how to use the forward pass, and were worried about the risk of interceptions; much heavyweight play continued. In 1909, thirty-three players were killed and 246 injured, seventy-three seriously.[20] More rule changes were made, including the outlawing of flying tackles. In 1912, the rules governing the forward pass were further liberalized, although it still had to be delivered from at least five yards behind the line of scrimmage. In 1913, Notre Dame's dazzling use of the forward pass under Jesse Harper showed other coaches how the game could be opened up and yet won.[21]

By this time, college football had long ceased to be a pleasant winter pastime for interested students. The game had spread; on May 30, 1879, the first intercollegiate game was played in the Midwest; in 1885, Colorado College played Denver in the first Western intercollegiate football contest; in 1889, the intercollegiate game between the University of California and St. Vincent's College was the first west of the Rockies.[22] Not only was the game popular; it made money. The Chicago-Michigan game played in the Chicago Colosseum in 1896 brought in $10,812. This was held to be the largest sum made at a single football game in the Midwest up to this time,[23] but it is nevertheless a huge total. And not only did football games bring money; they brought prestige.

In 1888, Trinity (later Duke) beat North Carolina. Charles Crowell, Trinity's president, later wrote, "That long-talked-of-victory added not only to the athletic reputation of Trinity throughout the State but it gave to the College an indefinable prestige of a general but most effective kind."[24] So important was football believed to be by President Charles Adams of Wisconsin that he exerted his influence to allow an academically limited player to continue in college, although the faculty wanted him dropped.[25] In June 1893, the financial problems caused by Leland Stanford's death combined with a nationwide economic crisis left Stanford University unable to pay its professors. Yet agreement was reached on June 12 to pay a coach $1,000 and expenses to train the football team. In December the year before, the *San Francisco Examiner* had made matters clear: winning "is looked upon as the greatest possible advertisement, and advertising is now believed to be of the very life of the rival educational institutions of California."[26]

Alumni were as clearheaded as presidents. In 1895, authors of a letter from the Lafayette alumni advisory committee to the alumni sought subscriptions to support the football team, because, "rightly or wrongly, college athletics attracts the public attention, and a college which is an athletic failure ceases to be attractive to a large and important clan of students."[27] In 1903, even professors took part in pep rallies at the University of Utah, which was scarcely surprising since President Joseph Kingsbury told the regents that "they [athletics] are also considered to be one of the very best means of advertising a college or university."[28]

By the early 1900s control of college athletics had passed from students; professional coaches were the order of the day. Their tactics were often dubious. In 1899, Columbia hired George Sanford to coach, who in his first season arranged the hiring of outsiders to play on the Columbia team, which beat Yale. What he had done was discovered; but his services were retained the following year.[29] In 1908, Percy Haughton was hired as the first professional coach for Harvard, because Harvard had won only five of twenty-seven games against Yale; the members of the selection committee who noted their dislike of Haughton's conduct as a player while at Harvard and the fact that he had coached professionally at Cornell were ignored.[30] As Lorin Deland wrote in 1910, winning is all. A *Boston Daily Advertiser* editorial had stressed the overriding importance in college athletics of players' physical well-being and general student interest, both of which, the author considered, were more important than winning. Deland belittled the editorial, insisting that "victory by honest, clean methods is, or ought to be, the object which Harvard men are trying to attain." Deland pointed out that Yale succeeded where Harvard failed because Walter Camp "coached the coaches."[31] In hiring Haughton, Harvard tacitly acknowledged that nineteenth-century values were being abandoned; Harvard was now going to do whatever was necessary to win.[32] Whatever the rhetoric, the point of a college football game was not to play; it was to demonstrate superiority.

A few college administrators were far from happy about the commercialization of college football. One of them was President John Abercrombie of Alabama, who resigned in 1911 after three years of battling the alumni over football. He wrote, "I have no ambition whatever to preside over a corruptly conducted athletic club though it be called by the dignified name of the University of Alabama."[33] And while most journalists were happy to abet the college administrators who were marketing football, because football news sold papers,[34] a few writers sounded the alarm. As early as 1892, Edwin Godkin used his publications the *Nation* and the *New York Evening Post* to decry the importance attached to college athletics. Casper Whitney, the sporting editor of *Harper's Weekly* from 1888 to 1890, seriously questioned the commercialization of college sport in 1898. By 1905, *McClure's* and *Colliers* were engaged in muckraking college athletics.[35]

Sufficient questions were publicly raised to persuade the Carnegie Foundation to report on college athletics in 1925, 1927, and 1929. The last report, the most thorough ever prepared on college athletics to that date, was a blistering condemnation of the status quo, particularly with reference to football, which had "been transformed from a game played by boys into a profitable professional enterprise." The authors were quite clear about what ought to be done: "The paid coach, the gate receipts, the special training tables, the costly sweaters and extensive journeys in special Pullman cars, the recruiting from the high school, the demoralizing publicity showered on the players, the devotion of an undue proportion of time to training, the devices for putting a desirable athlete, but a weak scholar, across the hurdles of the examinations – these ought to stop and the intercollege and intramural sports be brought back to a stage in which they can be enjoyed by large numbers of students and where they do not involve an expenditure of time and money wholly at variance with any ideal of honest study."[36]

What then was Yale to do with its Bowl, which had cost $400,000 in 1914 and seated 61,000, or Princeton with its Palmer Bowl, opened in the same year at a cost of $300,000? After Bob Zuppke had come to coach at Illinois in 1913 and his team had begun to win, the stadium's capacity had been increased from 4,500 to 70,000.[37] Were colleges across the nation going to abandon their investment and their most reliable source of instant fame? Naturally not.

For colleges had marketed their football teams with great success. While removing the game from student control and making it an arm of public relations, most administrators maintained the fiction that football players were first and foremost college students. Yet no stone was left unturned, first to win, and then to ensure that the crowd was entertained during the game. In 1890, Yale bought an English bulldog for a mascot. The halftime drill show put on at Vanderbilt in 1892 was one of many, and when area residents complained about dull play in the same year, Nebraska officials promised "more running and kicking and grandstand plays."[38] For Stanford's first game in 1892, the *San Francisco Examiner* reported that "students draped the ball park with colored cloth and paper, San Francisco merchants decorated their windows. . . . A chartered train, draped in red bunting, transported Stanford's students and faculty to the game site." In 1896, Wisconsin elected its first cheerleader, copying easterners. In 1897, California and Stanford both had bands; colored balloons were floated up from the field, and Stanford students in the stands had been organized to use cards to show an *S* on a dark background.[39] Much of the pressure that led to the changed rules in 1906 had been building up over the years among midwesterners, who were anxious to provide a more interesting game for spectators. Camp and his supporters, whose ideas had dominated the game since its inception, found themselves outvoted.

The rule changes of 1906 and 1912, in spite of renewed public concern about the physical dangers of football, led to greater spectator interest. In 1914, about "450 colleges, 6000 secondary schools, and some 15,000 other teams [were] playing football, with an overall total of 152,000 active players."[40] By the 1920s, high schools were outdoing the colleges. "During the years of boom and depression the game most highly publicized in the newspapers of all but the largest communities, was interscholastic football . . . and high schools surpassed the universities in the enthusiasm with which they organized pep rallies, athletic clubs, cheerleading, and victory celebrations."[41]

Here was a genuine American game, unlike any played elsewhere in the world, since it had moved so far from its rugby roots. It was played across the nation, but no one thought of calling it America's "national" game because baseball had preempted that title. And unlike baseball, the game was dominated by teams that called themselves amateur because the players were not paid, although admission was charged and the games were thoroughly commercialized.

In these circumstances, honestly professional football at first struggled to secure a share of the entertainment dollar. What could it offer that the commercialized amateur game did not? The college game had been marketed as one in which "we find most of the red-blooded ideals which we are proud to believe are particularly American."[42] When buying tickets to college football games, spectators were not merely affirming their allegiance to their teams, but could understand that they were supporting other sports that administrators believed could not exist without the subsidies they received from football. Moreover, no college athlete had been forced to play; rather each player was disinterestedly giving of his best for the good of the team. Further, the spectator was entering a world of infinite possibility. As sportswriter Heywood Broun put it in 1922, "It is not his [the sportswriter's] fault that the general public is romantic and demands its heroes. The tradition which gave the whole credit of victory to the king or emperor, or at any rate some plumed knight, has descended into our own day and now works to the advantage of the backfield men. If every opposing tackler should suddenly be struck dead by lightning the newspaper story would still speak of the brilliant run of the half-back who walked down the field stepping over the prostrate foe until he had crossed the goal line."[43]

One source of support for the professional game was those Americans who had no thought of going to college. Even by the 1890s, numbers of high schools were playing football; the toughness of the game appealed to the men of the Pennsylvania coal belt and the factory hands of New York, Ohio, and Rhode Island. Intercity rivalries were satisfied by semipro leagues; but there were no wealthy entrepreneurs ready to risk their money on trying to rival the established college games. In 1920, the American Professional Football Association was formed with twelve teams; it died in a year.[44] In 1921 another association was formed, and in 1922 called itself the National Football League. Lacking capital and an emotional base for fans, it struggled; the Chicago Bears finished the 1923 season with a loss of $366.72.[45] In 1925, George Halas persuaded Red Grange, the "Galloping Ghost" from Illinois, who had had a spectacular college career, to sign with the Chicago Bears and to play exhibition games on the road, including eight games within twelve days. Spectators poured in to see their idol; 35,000 in Philadelphia; 73,000 in New York, and even 5,000 in Coral Gables, Florida.[46] But spectators failed to turn up for subsequent professional games. The depression made the professional game even more vulnerable. As Halas put it, "Of the twenty-two clubs in the League in 1926 and the eleven which had formed subsequently, only ten were operating in 1931, and four of these disappeared during or after that season."[47]

To survive, the professional game had to offer something different from the college game, something more exciting to spectators. As chairman of the league rules committee, Halas realized that the NFL had "to make radical changes to open up the game: permitting passing anywhere behind the line of scrimmage, bringing in out-of-bound balls and restoring the goal posts to the goal line." These changes reduced the number of games that were tied and increased scoring, both crowd-pleasing moves.[48] As Will Rogers wrote after watching an exhibition game in 1934, this was a game, "where you can pass from everywhere, anytime.

"Now, as football is not only the backbone but the gravy of college existence, you fellows better open up your game, for this pro-game was made for an audience. No penalty every minute to make an audience sore, nobody getting hurt every play, referees not in the way of players."[49]

Thus by 1934, American football had become the game we now know. Walter Camp, the man whose energy, drive, and single-mindedness had been chiefly responsible for making American football the nation's premier college sport, had lived to witness its transformation from a slow, grinding battle of weight to a swift, open, complex sport. Camp tried to retain control of the game's development long after it had outgrown one man's influence; but he and his contemporaries had seen the metamorphosis of the sport. The rule changes all had been made to attract and keep spectators.[50] The football that spectators saw in 1984 was fundamentally similar to the game their predecessors saw in 1934; it bore little resemblance to that played in 1914, and virtually none to that of 1879.

To increase spectator interest, the professional teams divided themselves in 1933 into two divisions, East and West, the winner of each to meet in an end-of-season championship game. So the professional game had not merely become more complex and visually varied, but even during the depression settled into a rhythmic and comprehensible competitive structure with a clear season-by-season result.

The league also took steps to equalize the teams. By the mid-thirties, the Bears, Giants, and Green Bay were stronger than other teams; but spectators would not come to, or stay at, a walkover game. Bert Bell,[51] owner of the Philadelphia Eagles, proposed a college draft system, simply to make teams more competitive; the draft was in place for the 1936 season. To survive, franchises were moved. George Marshall took the Redskins out of Boston after the club won its division in 1936 and the Boston press failed to notice it. Marshall went to Washington, where he did not have to compete with Harvard. In Washington he produced marching bands and halftime shows for the spectators, reproducing the carnival atmosphere of college games.[52]

Thus, constrained by the college game, and well before the advent of television, the NFL learned how to craft the game to meet spectators' demands. Owners concentrated on making each game's outcome unpredictable, its progress marked by speedy, visually interesting play.[53] Rules were altered to achieve just those ends, and franchises were placed where dollars were to be made.

Meanwhile, the college game continued to flourish. The 1929 Carnegie report was widely read, discussed, and ignored by the very intercollegiate powerhouses at whom it was directed. Although the depression cut into gate receipts and college athletic programs were curtailed nationwide,[54] many colleges, among them the most prestigious, continued business as usual. In a sense, they had no choice. President Charles Eliot of Harvard had realized in the first decade of the twentieth century that football could be neither abolished nor reformed. It had become an integral part of college life; and given the competitive values of American society, it was unthinkable not to do everything possible to enable one's college team to win. If that meant turning the game into a spectacle that was professional in all but name, so be it. And until after World War II the colleges could persuade themselves that they were not simply processing "meat on the hoof."[55] College players knew that there was no future in the game for them after college was over. If a few ringers were brought in and some incompetent students retained as athletes, no young man could regard his college career as a mere stepping-stone to a life of riches in the professional game. If colleges were cynically debasing themselves for prestige, they probably corrupted and shortchanged directly few of their student athletes, most of whom were swept up in the glory and fun of a prestigious sport.

Prestigious it was: 110,000 spectators watched the 1926 Army-Navy game in Soldier Field; 112,912 saw Notre Dame beat Southern California in 1929; 93,508 watched Michigan beat Ohio State in 1933,[56] and 81,000 came to the 1935 Notre Dame versus Ohio game.[57] Not content to rest on their laurels, colleges agreed in 1934 to reduce the size of the ball to make throwing easier;[58] officials knew that spectators like to watch the game in the air more than the game on the ground.

Colleges had the stadiums and the support of the elite; alumni were watching the future leaders of America honing their competitive skills and demonstrating their courage in a situation that symbolized both college unity and college competence. If a college could not win on the football field, how competitive were its other activities?

After World War II, however, prospects brightened for the professionals. The workers of America now had far more disposable income and were ready for diversion. The professional game had developed a degree of specialization that enabled players to enjoy longer careers and hence to secure fan recognition. The possibilities inherent in the forward pass had been exploited, and the professional game was both exciting and well executed. The quality of the game was well worth watching. The market seemed ripe for development. However, the NFL owners wanted to limit franchises; they liked the cozy club atmosphere of their ten teams, and wanted to ensure control of their product.

Denied an NFL franchise, Arch Ward in 1944 set up a rival league called the United States Professional League, which was reorganized as the All-American Football Conference in 1945. After bitter and costly competition, three AFC teams, the Cleveland Browns, the San Francisco '49ers, and the Baltimore Colts, joined the NFL in 1950.[59] Now the league had teams coast to coast, but none in the South; even so, football had a better geographical claim than baseball to being the national game.

The NFL built on and added to the spectacular elements college football had thrived on. By 1950 the NFL could count an audience not only of workers, but of those who had experienced football at college, but who were no longer so emotionally involved with their colleges as their predecessors had been. In 1929, the authors of the Carnegie report had noted the fact that American universities had already become what Clark Kerr was later to call "multiversities."[60] The authors wrote, "The question is whether an institution in the social order whose primary purpose is the development of the intellectual life can at the same time serve as an agency to promote business, industry, journalism, salesmanship and organized athletics on an extensive commercial basis."[61] The organization of graduate schools had shifted attention from teaching to research, and consequently many undergraduates were getting short shrift from their instructors. The authors of the 1929 report did well to be uneasy; but their analysis did nothing to alter the direction of educational policy. By 1950, there were numbers of graduates whose experience of college intellectually and socially bore no resemblance to Ivy League expectations; these graduates were not therefore tied to the college game in the same way. They did, however, understand football; and professional teams could provide an outstanding game for their inspection. The NFL began solidly to prosper.

The owners kept their goal of increasing spectator interest carefully in mind. Free substitution was experimented with during World War II, and established permanently after the 1950 season;[62] the first sudden-death game was played in 1955. Meanwhile, from about 1950, the NFL teams began experimenting with television.

It quickly became clear that football suited television very well; the ball was large enough to see and the action sufficiently predictable to allow close-ups without distorting the experiential basis of the game. Even in black and white, a football game could hold a fan's attention. But televised games in the Los Angeles area drastically reduced ticket sales, and no owner wanted that. So each owner experimented by broadcasting his team's games outside the area ticket holders came from, and often found himself competing for viewers with another team. George Marshall, for instance, beamed his Washington Redskins into Georgia, but couldn't go further south because George Halas and the Chicago Bears already controlled the television cables through Louisville, Kentucky and Jackson, Mississippi.[63]

During the next ten years, owners realized that they needed to act together to reap the maximum benefit from TV revenues. The NFL first agreed to black out on TV all home games within a seventy-five-mile radius of town.[64] George Halas, Daniel Reeves, Tim Mara, and Bert Bell then proposed in 1960 that all clubs should assign their TV rights to the league as a whole, which would negotiate with the TV companies on behalf of all the NFL teams; all revenues, regardless of which club games were actually televised, would be shared equally among the clubs.[65] But Bell, by this time NFL commissioner, died before these TV contracts were actually made. His successor, Pete Rozelle, not only brought the idea to fruition, but arranged in 1961 for special legislation to exempt such pooled contractual agreements from antitrust laws. The fact that the legislation passed so quickly and easily through Congress is an indication of the widespread support professional football now enjoyed in high places. The game that had been so carefully nurtured with spectators' interests in mind had proved to be one that might have been made for translation to a screen.

Rozelle now proceeded to use a national medium to market what he conceived to be a national product. While baseball owners continued on their chaotic way, NFL clubs were welded more and more closely together, the fate of each inextricably woven into the fabric of the whole. By 1977, ten years after the incorporation of the rival American Football League, Rozelle was presiding over a "league of 28 teams, each collecting more than 2 million dollars yearly from the networks," and attendance at stadiums had tripled, to 11 million.[66] By 1979, NFL football games were regularly shown in Mexico, and millions of Mexicans who had never been to the United States were Dallas Cowboys fans.[67] By 1980, weekly tabloids were published on several NFL teams, which had a circulation far beyond their local area; the *Dallas Cowboys Official Weekly,* the most successful, got more than two-thirds of its circulation outside Dallas and its environs.[68] TV was enabling mobile fans to keep up with their "home" teams, or to adopt teams if they were too far from an NFL club to see a team in person.

This success story would seem to indicate that professional football owes its present popularity entirely to TV. It all seems to fit; the World Football League (1973-75) had no TV contracts with any of the three major networks and failed. The American Football League (1959-69) had such a contract and therefore survived long enough to force an NFL merger. Unfortunately for this thesis, the United States Football League, which played its first game in 1983 fully equipped with ABC and cable contracts, only a year later was in deep trouble.

The first overnight USFL rating in a six-market average was 16.1; in 1984, the USFL's debut game had a 9.0 rating in a six-market average.[69] Spokesmen for ABC and the ESPN cable network both declared themselves satisfied with the 1983 season; but after an almost steady ratings decline, the prime-time game on June 17, 1983, got only a 4.8 rating, which was not only the lowest of the week, but the second lowest in TV history for a prime-time sports event. The average rating for the whole 1984 season was 5.5.[70]

What went wrong here is easy to discern. Not only were the USFL games being shown at a time when football is not supposed to be played, thus offending traditionalists, but they were of relatively poor quality. Nor did they have meaning. Football fans know what they want, and will not accept substitutes. As a spokesman for ABC remarked ruefully about the 1982 strike, the absence of Sunday football "did absolutely nothing for college games on Saturdays."[71]

In giving credit to TV for a league's survival, we forget how under-capitalized the WFL actually was; USFL teams reportedly lost $80 million in the 1984 season.[72] We also underestimate Lamar Hunt's acumen. Denied an NFL franchise, he and another Texan, Bud Adams, formed their own league, the American Football League, in 1960. The NFL put a competing franchise in Dallas; so just as Marshall had done in the 1930s, Hunt moved his franchise to Kansas City, where he had no competition. The AFL certainly sold its games to ABC; but had Hunt not drawn into his league owners with financial resources to match his own, the AFL could never have survived long enough to force compromise upon the NFL. Hunt used TV as a marketing tool, but when the opportunity presented itself he played a leading part in the negotiations that brought the AFL under the NFL's umbrella.[73]

In assuming that TV created professional football, we also underesti-mate both the skill with which Rozelle used it as his primary marketing instrument, and the elements of the game and league structure that had already been put in place to keep and enlarge spectator enthusiasm. Well before the advent of TV, the game had been opened up and speeded up, and attempts had been made to equalize team strength. It had been marketed as representing honest, manly virtues. When TV promised greater revenues than they had hitherto experienced, NFL owners eagerly experimented with it and had worked out an excellent marketing con-cept before Rozelle took office. What Rozelle did was to capitalize on past experience in changing rules, raising scores, providing spectacular play, and ensuring unpredictability.

Substantive rule changes had been made in the 1930s to make the professional game more attractive; in 1970, Rozelle selected a rules committee and gave its members a series of comments clipped from eighty-five papers nationwide that claimed that football was becoming dull.[74] Rules were accordingly changed to increase unpredictability and tension. When, for instance, too many games were being settled by field goals, which lack the excitement of touchdowns, the goalposts were moved back ten yards, and unsuccessful attempts from outside the twenty-yard line were penalized.[75] The 1974 season thus offered more tension and forced coaches into making more decisions, because it was no longer axiomatic to try for a field goal every time the team moved within thirty-five or forty yards of the goal line. In 1977, head slapping was outlawed; this again helped the offense, besides cutting out one obviously violent play. The bump rule of 1978, which allowed more freedom to pass receivers, made the long pass safer for the offense; it is a play crowds love to watch.

Rozelle knew, like Halas and others before him, that American audiences like high-scoring games because they are an indication of action and result. By 1980 rule changes had ensured that an average of forty-one points was scored each game, six points more than the 1974 average.[76] And this was in spite of the increased number of time-outs for commercials. But since the 1920s, at least, football has been a game of short bursts of action. Insertion of more commercials can hardly be held to disrupt the rhythm of a game that is so dependent on a coach's choice of plays as to have no predictable ebb and flow. And should spectators become intolerant of frequent commercials, NFL officials and TV executives will be the first to pay attention, for both are dedicated to keeping viewers in their seats, at the stadium and at home.

Since the early thirties, the NFL had tried to ensure competitive balance. Knowing that no TV audience would long remain with a runaway game, Rozelle has been careful to maintain strict draft and eligibility requirements and limited rosters, while setting his face firmly against free agency. Rozelle does not want to unbalance the league by allowing richer teams to have the benefit of better players.[77]

In 1978, the National Football League Players Association went to court because their executive director, Ed Garvey, claimed that the owners were not bidding for free agents as they should have done under the March 1977 agreement. Garvey maintained that only six of ninety-three free agents received offers, which indicated bad faith on the part of management. NFLPA lost its case, and Rozelle's efforts to ensure balance were not undermined.

Rozelle also continued the ongoing crusade for football's purity. From its earliest days, college football was marketed as not only a manly, but a gentlemanly, game, free from the taint of gambling and corruption professional sport was often associated with. According to Halas, Joe Carr, the first president of the NFL, "let all managers know that if he caught any owner or manager betting on the result of a League game, he would ban the individual from the League forever."[78] Yet Bob Curran alleges that in 1946, when Bert Bell, the owner of the Philadelphia Eagles, became NFL commissioner, "professional football was so suspect that the games were not carried on the board by the major odds-makers."[79] Bell worked to change that perception, and Rozelle inherited an organization that had marketed itself as representing honesty. In 1963, Rozelle suspended Paul Hornung and Alex Karras for placing bets on their own and other teams. When Joe Namath, in a glare of publicity, was forced to choose between playing football and remaining part owner of a club frequented by gamblers, the public image of football was being carefully preserved. It was particularly important to show that players were being thus controlled, because no one knew exactly what owners were doing, although rumors were widespread. Heavy, as well as illegal, betting is part of every NFL game, as the well-publicized points spread attests;[80] but Rozelle knew well that no large TV audience will long remain faithful to a sport its members believe to be fixed.

But in spite of Rozelle's efforts to build on a traditional base, all is not well with the NFL. It is the cracks in the NFL marketing facade that indicate most clearly that TV promotion alone is not sufficient to make or break any particular sport, even in the United States. In the 1980s, the NFL has experienced problems with competitive balance and revulsion against the game's violence and drug abuse by players. Its sexism may yet be its undoing. And Al Davis has undermined the owners' unity, carefully cultivated since the 1930s.

NFL expansion, for instance, led to problems of competitive balance. As an *Inside Football Report* noted in 1978, twelve of the NFL's twenty-eight teams had garnered something like 90 percent of the play-off spots since 1970. By 1978, Rozelle had already inaugurated "position scheduling," which rearranged schedules so that weak teams played each other, with the intention of spreading play-off games around and of making all games (except the play-offs) closer. Critics argued that this was not merely unfair, but a high road to mediocrity. Rozelle's reasoning, however, was clear; crowds want to watch a close game, not a well-executed bloodbath. Rozelle is forced into such moves, because he cannot compel owners to think before they act; nor can he distribute among them his own skill and wisdom. Rozelle could not, for instance, stop Robert Irsay calling the plays for his Colts,[81] whatever the effect on a 1981 game, nor could Rozelle prevent the firing of Bum Phillips, even after the Houston Oilers had become a new and enormously attractive NFL force. Rozelle cannot force owners to recruit wisely. Within the limits of his powers he tries to ensure that the NFL markets a standardized product, so that viewers can be sure that what they watch will live up to their expectations. In so doing, he is merely following the lead Bell set in the 1930s.

The eye of the camera, however, has revealed to viewers more than the early promoters of football wanted spectators to see. Almost from its inception, football has had problems with its image as a violent game. John Underwood's *The Death of an American Game: The Crisis in Football*[82] is just the latest outcry against a sport in which injury has been commonplace and death a real possibility. Coaches have been paid since the early twentieth century to win at all costs; what TV has revealed is the truly brutal nature of football played according to the rules. In the stadium, many spectators are too far away from the players to appreciate properly the damage players inflict on each other; TV close-ups demonstrate not only the bone-crunching nature of the collision, but show us the contorted face and twitching body of the injured player, on the field and on the bench. Viewers cannot overlook the implications of football's "controlled violence." Yet at the same time TV producers are careful not to dwell on injuries. If a player is down for long, a commercial is swiftly slotted into place; commentators condemn late hits and illegal play, while briskly pointing out that football is a "physical" game. In the journalistic hullabaloo that greeted Jack Tatum's *They Call Me Assassin,* there was very little comment on Tatum's sensible suggestions about the ways in which the rules could be altered to make the game safer;[83] rather, attention was concentrated on Tatum's frank admission that he was paid to inflict as much lasting damage on his opponents as possible. That, as college players knew in 1879, is the way to win.

In marketing football, there is a fine line between showing viewers a competitive, courageous, physically demanding game, and a lethal battle. TV broadcasts do not linger on the gory details; it is the print media that discuss sports medicine, cite improper treatment of professional athletes' injuries, and bring home to the public the lasting physical cost of playing professional football. What TV has inadvertently done is to make clear to every viewer that, played legally, football is deadly. It always has been; now we see the damage in close-up.

If violence is an old problem, drugs are a new and potentially very damaging one. For years, NFL teams could not publicly admit that their players might have drug problems. To do so would, first, cast doubt on the validity of the carefully constructed competitive structure of the league, for who knows what a hopped-up player could do to his team? Second, a sport cannot be marketed as a repository of manly American values if it is played professionally by a bunch of junkies. Accordingly, when in 1972 psychiatrist Arnold Mandell discovered and then made public the drug problems of the San Diego Chargers, the full resources of the NFL were engaged to silence him.[84] Ten years later, Rozelle was doing his best to salvage the NFL's credibility by publicizing both the efforts to rehabilitate players who had drug problems and the sentences imposed on offenders who had been caught. To remain popular, football must at least appear to be played without stimulants.

Television, as a medium, was not responsible for the NFL's drug problem. Drugs became commonplace on campuses during the 1970s, and players simply took the habit with them into the professional game. Their higher salaries there helped them procure more exotic chemicals. It was the print media that exposed NFL drug problems; TV producers were still, long after the horse was out of the barn and galloping about the pasture, trying to close the barn door and maintain the football mystique.

Forced to deal with violence and drugs, the NFL has not yet dealt with its sexism, which telecasts have underscored. Football is a male game, and its physical demands will ensure that it remains so, even if some women choose to play a version of it. When cheerleaders appeared as part of football's spectacle even in the 1890s, their activities could be regarded as simply part of the brouhaha that surrounded any game. On television, their sexual connotation was not merely emphasized and heightened, but became their raison d'être, whatever their own protestations. Their costumes and routines are obviously designed to titillate; camera shots and angles do not reveal the group choreography, which cheerleaders persuade themselves they are there to demonstrate.[85] Cheerleaders have nothing whatever to do with the game's progress or outcome; their presence simply serves to remind viewers that football is a male-bonded activity, to which women can contribute only encouragement, and, by implication, become available as spoils after victory is gained. Because Americans who can afford to buy stadium tickets belong to social classes whose members are increasingly affronted by overt treatment of women as sex objects, cheerleaders may soon come to be regarded as old-fashioned. If they do, it will be at least in part because television has punctured the illusions that cheerleaders are one of the techniques of crowd control or help generate vocal support for the home team. TV has revealed more than we expected to perceive.

Rozelle inherited, and continued to nurture, an organization in which owners cooperated with one another. Ed Garvey constantly protested during 1981 that NFL owners did not even care about their teams winning, because they got the same TV revenue whatever the results. But this cozy owner relationship was rudely disturbed by Al Davis, when he sued the NFL because it refused to let him move his Raiders from Oakland to Los Angeles. TV and radio rights in 1982 represented only just over half an NFL team's revenue;[86] Davis made the point that he wanted a more profitable stadium for his team, although he was of course considering the Los Angeles cable market. He did not conduct his suit quietly; no American can now be unaware that NFL owners are competitors for the entertainment dollar, not partners in a philanthropic enterprise run for the benefit of the American public.

If owners see football as a business, so do the players. The money that television made available, as in baseball, allowed football players as a group to secure agents and pay for the services of high-priced union officials. Yet Ed Garvey's success did not match that of Marvin Miller. Football players are still drafted and either play for whichever NFL team secures their services or have to leave the league; if they play out their option, they still find it extremely difficult to market themselves to another NFL team. By no means have all football players benefited much from TV endorsements; particularly if they are buried on the line, their market value does not amount to much. Contract terms are financially extremely important to a player; TV money does not guarantee that those terms will always work to a player's benefit. But no fan can now be deluded into believing that players are embarking on their NFL careers for love of the game alone; and when Herschel Walker signed his USFL contract, he publicly gave notice that many college players consider themselves professionals too.

Walker, in fact, was simply following the example of his mentors. In 1975 a group of colleges playing big-time football in the National Collegiate Athletic Association's top division formed an association that in 1977 called itself the College Football Association. Its members wanted greater autonomy within the NCAA, and when they failed to get it went to court. The universities of Georgia and Oklahoma filed suit on behalf of the CFA against the NCAA over television revenues, claiming that institutions should be able to make whatever contracts they liked, regardless of NCAA rules. By 1983, when the Supreme Court decided to review the case after two federal courts had ruled against the NCAA, the CFA (by then a group of sixty colleges) had officially withdrawn from the suit. Nevertheless CFA members were all ready to negotiate TV rights individually, outside the NCAA's purview, should they be given the chance.[87]

By challenging the NCAA in court, the College Football Association demonstrated that their allegedly amateur teams are actually businesses. The NCAA was not, to their minds, maximizing the TV profits they could make. Already commercial enterprises in 1929, big-time college football teams in the 1980s wanted to exercise direct control over a source of revenue that had hitherto escaped them. In so doing, they seemed unconcerned with the fact that they were running the farm system for the professionals at no charge and employing players whom they call students so as to avoid paying them anything close to what they are worth.[88] Television, however, has not caused such activity; it has simply been used to perpetuate it. Just as colleges used the print media in the 1890s to publicize themselves and generate revenue to run a "competitive" program, so they now wish to use TV. The game has not changed; the stakes are simply bigger.

It is the more tempting for the football industry at all levels to try to derive every last dollar from televised football, because it is a game that translates superbly to a screen. Professional football may be played in a gleaming new municipal stadium, but it descends from the games watched by thousands in the elite Ivy League structures, and those remembered by hundreds of thousands who gave allegiance to players regarded not as "Saturday's children" but Saturday's heroes. This link with the college game is symbolically preserved in the material provided on each player; when his photograph is shown on the screen his college is cited, and commentators frequently mention a player's college long after he ceases to be a rookie.

Before the game begins, the "sacred space" is honored. Players line up, helmets under their arms, during the singing of the national anthem. The teams are on opposite sides of the field, for the "sacred space" is to be contested; football is a game of territory. Yet all are bound together as Americans, and as such they stand. The camera pans the players warily, and if anyone is chewing gum, looks bored, or is otherwise not presenting a symbolically patriotic front, he is quickly passed over. As in baseball, the national symbols of flag and anthem are honored, to set the game in the context that transcends it.

Never is a football game ended until the final whistle is blown. Real time becomes not only "sacred time," but is transformed during a football game, for it can be deliberately extended or conserved. In the last desperate quarter, plays may be used solely to stop the clock; two plays may be called in the same huddle to give the team holding the ball game time it would not otherwise have. Similarly, time may be "eaten up" by a team that does not want to risk losing its lead. But this kind of play is dull for the spectators, so the NFL has made sure that it is risky. For not only must the measurable gain be made; but each team has theoretically been drafted by NFL rules to be equal to the one opposing it. A defense, supposedly as skilled as the offense, will extend itself beyond its limits to try to jar the ball loose, while praying that a moment's inattention on the part of one of the offensive players, nowhere near the ball, will involve a life-giving penalty. The use of time-outs has become a fine art.

A football team palpably represents the "bond of brothers," for no one member can make or break a game. Indeed, one man's superlative skill may even be blunted by the inadequacies of his teammates. No one who watched Jim Plunkett's torments with the New England Patriots could be unaware of a quarterback's need of protection; and what might O. J. Simpson have achieved had he not had to spend his best years with the Buffalo Bills? It is not every coach who takes Tom Landry's position that individual team members may not entertain the crowd when they have a moment of triumph, but television cameras always focus on the butt-slapping, shoulder-patting, and other manifestations of rejoicing when success is achieved. Similarly, when the field goal is missed, the pass is dropped, not only is the anguish and chagrin focused upon, but also the gesture of commiseration often extended to the man who has missed his assignment.

The cameras also reveal "spirit." Viewers are shown the heaving, panting player as he slumps onto the bench, his face buried in an oxygen mask; they watch Danny White crying on the sidelines. There are close-ups of a triumphant team on its feet, when the momentum of the game has swung, and shots of the hanging heads, the glumness, of their opponents. Viewers are made aware that the players are trying, that they care. Whatever they may read in the press about owners not worrying whether they win or lose, viewers can scarcely fail to be convinced by what they see on the screen that the players are consistently giving their all.

Just as in baseball, TV viewers are encouraged to "root." Similarly, replays and commentary encourage them to marvel at a player's growing skills and the extension of his native talent, while the matching of teams encourages every viewer to believe that both teams are pushing each other to the limits.

All viewers also know that what they are watching is a kind of chess game. They are aware that every move made by both teams has been plotted theoretically before they ever step on the field. The NFL has done what it could to ensure that the teams who meet will be equal; each head coach has then worked with the material he has to make sure that his team's play epitomizes his own philosophy of football, whether it be Vince Lombardi's running for daylight or Tom Landry's running of precise and complex patterns.

The coach's position in relation to the team is underlined by his dress and actions, clearly shown by the sideline shots. He does not wear the team's uniform; he is not "one of the boys," who happens to be directing operations. He is in charge of affairs, and although he will not set foot on the field, his influence will be felt throughout the game. He does not always wear a headset because one of the players or other coaches gives him information or runs errands; he is the executive, in charge of the operation. Yet he has to win; he does not own the team, and like any of the players, he is an employee. He does not receive the trophy at the end of the successful season; the owner does that. All of this hierarchical organization is shown to the viewers; if they overlook it, they have only themselves to blame.

Every viewer knows that each team has studied films of the other and has developed a game plan that it believes will use its own strengths and capitalize on its opponent's weaknesses. The outcome of the game will not therefore depend on continuous improvisation by brilliant players, but on practiced skill in execution and readiness to make use of any and all the mistakes one side can fluster the other into making.

Viewers also know that what they are watching is important. Each televised professional game represents one sixteenth of the full season; each postseason game en route to the Super Bowl represents victory or elimination. No one knows which of the World Series games will be the crucial one, so excitement cannot be generated to match that which surrounds the Super Bowl. The NFL carefully restricts its product, not simply because each game requires preparation and too long a season involves too many injuries, but because too many games reduce the inherent importance of each one. It matters less how often NFL football per se is televised, than that each game shown shall possess a value in itself; viewers can then decide whether they will watch every game that is televised or restrict themselves to watching teams they care about.[89]

Football is a game of continual crisis; it was structured to be so well before the advent of TV. Because play stops every time the ball is dead, fans and spectators have time to savor the crisis and plan how to deal with it. On every play, the coach makes deliberate choices, but on some he is obviously battling the fates. Should he settle for a field goal or go for the extra yardage; should he risk the interception or settle for less territory? The precise patterns that everyone has spent so long perfecting are disrupted by defensive players who anticipate and react fractionally quicker than expected, and by offensive players who move with fractionally more agility and speed than anyone knew they possessed. A momentary lapse of concentration on either side may bring disaster. What seems to be a crisis may be averted because the team has prepared for it; one well-executed play may allow a team to escape its apparent fate. Games may even be won and lost on a "Hail Mary" pass. Football's bread and butter is consistent execution, but there is always the jam of the unanticipated. The game therefore possesses intelligible order, but unless the teams are hopelessly ill matched, it can rarely be monotonous.

For even football's bread and butter provides visual variety that translates well two-dimensionally. Players shuttle in and out; long passes alternate with short, and with ground plays. As each play starts from the same place, the camera crew knows where to go; if the ball is momentarily lost because it is faked, the viewer applauds a successful conjuring trick. And even when the development of the play appears to be obvious, the result may be surprising; Robert Newhouse or Earl Campbell crash into apparently solid lines and yet make yardage, while lesser players are buried almost before they reach the ball. What star players perceive and capitalize upon are chances that are invisible to those of lesser caliber; their timing appears little short of miraculous. The game is full of subplots, for teams can be compared with regard to time of possession, yards gained, third downs converted; individuals' statistics provide similar food for thought. Team and individual statistics can be compared across a season or over the year; the subplots help to build a heritage.

In translating football for viewers, TV executives have determined to make it intelligible and attractive. To watch a football game is therefore to be deluged with information.

First, the players are personalized. Because they are hidden by their helmets and paddings, since 1970 they have worn not only numbers but names on their jerseys. The starting teams are introduced individually and shown to viewers as they lumber through the gamut of cheerleaders. The photos of players who perform well or ill are shown on the screen between plays, with added details about their career length and the college they attended. As players run in and out of the huddle they are named; when a play is over, individuals are followed back to the huddle or sidelines, while a commentator names and discusses them. Every effort is made to show football players as people, not simply as team units; players are often shown on the bench, with their helmets off, where they can be recognized. A player such as Rocky Blier who has a genuinely moving background is a commentator's godsend. In spite of the commentator's effort, some players go virtually unnoticed because of the positions in which they play. But if television has made the faces of some players better known than they were in the days of print, it has not deliberately consigned others to oblivion; players in some unsung positions have always labored in obscurity.

Second, spectators are informed about the game in progress. They are constantly reminded of the state of play by the commentators; insets on the screen give the score, shots of the scoreboard show the time, and statistics such as rushing yards gained serve to recapitulate the game as well as to explain its progress.[90]

Third, commentators try to teach spectators to understand football. Replays, with or without a chalkboard, are used to show precisely why and how plays succeeded or failed. In a game between the Detroit Lions and the New York Giants, there were fifteen replays in the first half and twenty-five in the second. After a play is over, commentators may discuss the performance of particular players and then suggest what plays might be sent in, given the particular situation the team faces. In teaching viewers to understand the game, commentators are following an honorable tradition, well established in print. As early as 1913, Herbert Reed, for instance, wrote a book called *Football for Public and Players* because "it is the spectator who needs the coaching nowadays, and it is in the hope of clearing away for his benefit . . . much of the mystery that has been deftly thrown around the game . . . that this book is offered to a sometimes puzzled football public."[91] Commentators do not always do their job well; the best, however, provide footnotes to the game that can help viewers understand the text.

Fourth, spectators are expected to become enthusiastic about football. Plays are shown in slow motion, not simply so that what is happening can be comprehended, but so that the artistry will be apprehended. Spectacular plays are shown over and over again, so that we can appreciate just how difficult the game is to play, just how athletic a man has to be, just how determined and tough he must be to endure. Preston Pearson's beautiful leaping catch in a December 1980 game against the Rams became more exciting, not less, as it was repeated, for there is a level of artistry that ordinary mortals need time to encompass. Viewers are also incited to enthusiasm by seeing shots of the stadium crowd when its members are excited; in the Lions versus Giants game, stadium supporters were seen four times in the first half and five times in the second, always when a score or spectacular play had aroused their visible admiration.

As viewers we do not, of course, have to pay attention to any of this. Many people do not. But if we care to take advantage of it, we can move into the company of those who enjoy *A Thinking Man's Guide to Pro Football*.[92] For football can be enjoyed on many levels. TV producers, in providing shots of cheerleaders, as well as replays and explanations of the most complex facets of the game, are trying to appeal to everyone who might be watching.

In translating the game, however, TV executives do no violence to the essence of the game, in Novak's terms, nor do they violate the stadium experience. A typical sequence of shots is to be seen in the "Monday Night Football" game between the Rams and Cowboys on December 15, 1980. A shot of the line of scrimmage is shown from above, sideways to the line, so that the positions of all the players on the line and several beyond it can be seen. The handoff to Dorsett is shown more closely and the play is followed until Dorsett is picked off by Butch Johnson. Johnson is followed in close-up back to the huddle. A long shot of the field acts as the background to next Monday's schedule; then the scrimmage line is shown from the same angle as before. The pass is followed to Preston Pearson, and a close-up is then shown of the catch, followed by a replay from another angle. Again, the viewer is placed above and to the side of the line of scrimmage; the pass is followed to the interception by Rod Percy, and the camera zooms in on him as he runs. After a close-up of the triumphant Percy, a replay is shown from two different angles. The viewer follows this action just as he would at the stadium. What he sees has been framed for him and interpreted by commentators; but all of these interpreters are trying to remain true to their text. Americans understand football.

TV, then, has not altered American football, but has brought it to a wider audience than Camp could ever have dreamed of. TV could not, however, have been used as football's primary marketing tool after 1960, had not the fundamental rule changes required to make it a mass spectator sport been accomplished before that. By the time TV became available, football's structure and its relation to the needs of American spectators were well understood. Americans wanted competitive balance, high scoring, a variety of plays well spiced with the ball flying through the air, and a result. All of this had been accomplished before World War II; even without TV, professional football would have become America's winter game in the affluent postwar days.

For TV simply took the traditional elements of the game and heightened them. Radio announcers had broadcast college games;[93] the televised game carefully nurtures the college link. The officials' signals were originally designed so as to let everyone in the stadium know what was going on; now the referee is equipped with a microphone as well. American audiences are dedicated to following the ball; the TV cameras rarely lose sight of it, providing just sufficient glimpses of the pattern of the players to allow intellectual viewers to put the game together in their heads. The spectacle of the college game is retained; close-ups are shown of the homemade banners and specially dressed spectators. The cheerleaders are focused on, the colorful uniforms of the teams and their jazzy helmets are displayed. TV has, however, dropped the halftime shows, designed as they were for viewing from a distance, and not being sufficiently predictable to translate to a small, two-dimensional screen.

The NFL's present problems are not specifically to do with TV or even with the USFL. Rather, its malaise is much more deep-seated, to the point where we may in 1994 see a book entitled *The Rise and Fall of Football as America's National Sport.*

TV was not responsible for the availability and use of drugs in society at large that spilled over into the NFL. (Indeed, if football is so painful a game that it is not possible to play it as a professional without drugs, the sooner it disappears from American life the better.) More fundamental is the change in American views of what constitutes masculinity. Thirty years ago, "real" American men not only did not eat quiche, but did not change their babies' diapers, seek child custody, voluntarily attend the ballet, or publicly show grief or tenderness. In 1986, American men do not have to prove themselves by being physically tough or by inflicting and accepting pain as a necessary part of athletic activity. Tennis is no longer for Americans a "sissy" sport.

During the 1960s, some professional players began to wonder what their sport really consisted of.[94] After Lance Rentzel published *When All the Laughter Died in Sorrow* in 1972, it was no longer possible to believe that football, by definition, "built character." How, asked members of the "me" generation, could self-discipline be learned when one was required from junior high school onward to obey a coach's whims without question? And if this "self-discipline" had really been acquired, why were grown men subject to bed checks? Players who had loved their professional football careers continued to publish books;[95] but serious questions were being raised about the physical and mental costs of playing football.[96]

As TV has nothing to do with all this, so it had nothing to do with the burgeoning popularity of soccer. Suddenly American youngsters found they could play a game in which they could do what they wanted, not just what the coach told them to do, from which they did not emerge black and blue. They did not sit about on the bench, and they could be male or female and of any size and shape. They could practice on their own. Their parents discovered the game was considerably cheaper than football and caused far fewer injuries. Soccer was not wholly controlled by the schools; clubs made interesting trips, even abroad, and nobody fussed about the players' grade point averages or whether they could or could not attend a soccer camp.

Some American fathers were alarmed; they themselves did not understand soccer, and they felt their sons were giving up an all-American game for a European import. But even the schools could not resist the tide; soccer posts have gone up on athletic fields all over the United States. It began to dawn on Americans that soccer's World Cup is international.

What is being created in the United States is a generation whose experience of and interest in football is limited. At the same time, the overt professionalism of the college game may well have alienated the future alumni on whom the support of college ball has always depended. When football scholarships are awarded openly to students who have no hope at all of surviving in a college classroom, and particularly when they are awarded to blacks who are cynically brought to predominantly white colleges, it becomes obvious to the most naive of freshmen that the college is running a business. Why, in later years, should that business require or receive the support of their time or pocketbooks? It will be some years before the effects of such value changes are manifest; but unless colleges start work on the image they are now portraying, alumni support for athletics will inevitably crumble.

NFL and USFL owners looked carefully at TV markets. They might do well to start planning their own farm teams, for the professional game now rests wholly on the nation's formal educational system. If that plank rots (and the termites are already nibbling) the NFL will have no product to offer the TV industry.

Football's problems were not caused by TV. However much it enlarged the sport's audience, TV did not create American football, nor will it break it. This marvelous, complex sport, so satisfying to watch, will only die if those who play and organize it allow it to be turned simply into a means to a profitable end.

4

NATIONAL
DIFFERENCES

In translating baseball and football for the viewer, U.S. television producers have worked within the conventions already established by the stadium game. Both baseball and football were organized from their early days to attract spectators. The so-called amateur game of college football was altered precisely so as to fill stadiums, long before the professional game became a threat. In both baseball and college football, winning was of paramount importance, whether the players were professional ball players held to their original clubs by the reserve clause, or lads who thought of themselves as giving their best for their alma mater even if they literally killed themselves doing it. Both games were spectacles; "Take me out to the ball game," meant "Entertain me."

Television simply developed what had already been established. And that symbolized far more than the conduct of games; its content was imbued with deep-seated cultural values. "Values" have been much debated; by a value I mean what Clyde Kluckhohn called, "a conception, explicit or implicit, of the desirable . . . which influences the selection from available modes, means and ends of action."[1] Values can and do change; nevertheless, TV producers on each side of the Atlantic face audiences who have different notions about what is desirable. These notions affect the TV industry itself; its powers, prerogatives, and uses have been constrained in Britain and the United States by different conceptions of the desirable in public life.

It is extremely difficult properly to describe, much less analyze, the cultural differences between nations.[2] However, certain gross distinctions can be made between American and British conceptions of the desirable. Many of these distinctions affect the ways in which Americans and the British play and watch their national games, and therefore, the way in which these sports are handled on television. Television producers fit their product to what audiences will accept. What Americans and the British want from TV sports are not necessarily the same; the Atlantic is a much wider ocean than has usually been supposed.

For it is only since World War II that British conceptions of professional sport have approached what American organizers of commercialized sport took for granted in the nineteenth century. Until after World War II, the British establishment's ideals of amateurism permeated cricket, and to some extent soccer, even though professional soccer was run by the middle class for working-class players and spectators.[3] For amateurs, the prime object is to play with all one's might whatever the result. To win is a bonus, not the sole aim. This gentleman's code, promoted zealously during the period when cricket and soccer were commercialized for the masses, held little appeal for the working class. Tony Mason points out that working-class soccer supporters in the late nineteenth and early twentieth centuries were much less interested in good play than in seeing their side win. Moreover, the professional players they were watching often failed to demonstrate the ethic of sportsmanship playing hearty games was intrinsically supposed to develop.[4] But until World War II swept away in Britain the deference traditionally given to birth and inherited wealth, it was the amateur ideal that was espoused by those who controlled British sporting life. People high in social status took their creed for granted; those lower down the social scale with any aspirations toward gentility paid at least lip service to it. Britain is still a class-conscious society, but amateur ideals in sport have withered as the power of the class that imposed them has been attentuated.

The postwar influx of Pakistanis and Jamaicans turned Britain into a multicultural society. Devoted to cricket, the West Indians brought their own traditions of spectatorship to cricket grounds, and refused to modify them in accordance with established British custom. They acted as if they expected cricket to be exciting, and cheered on their own side exactly as they would have done a soccer team. Yet they also understood the game's subtleties, so their exuberance may actually have affected the game less than the turbulent atmosphere suggested. But it is obviously more tempting for players to abuse each other verbally when the ground is noisy than in the sepulchral silence that used to characterize cricket matches. It is too soon to tell whether the change in spectators' behavior really affects what professional cricketers do.

The demise of the cult of amateurism and the advent of multiculturalism (with the overt racism it has spawned) are but two of the fundamental social and economic postwar changes that have affected British conceptions of what constitutes a sporting event. British sports telecasting now reflects the ambivalence between continuity and change that has marked professional cricket and soccer at the grounds themselves. The obvious commercial purposes of baseball and football are still not as clearly served by cricket and soccer, and so confusion now exists between community tradition and the need to balance the books.

Much of the substance of a BBC sports telecast therefore transmits conventions of sport established in the nineteenth century. Yet the very existence of limited-over cricket, which is televised just like the test (international) matches, points to a change in what the British regard as desirable in their national summer sport.

Yet while changes in British conceptions of sport have undoubtedly occurred, it is true that Americans and the British still have fundamentally different ideas about the nature and purpose of competition, which in turn constrain and are constrained by their educational systems, attitudes to community, the social status of entrepreneurs, class-consciousness, and the relationship between the spirit and letter of the law. Members of these two societies also differ in their view of sport as entertainment, and the arts of listening and acquiring information. The history of the two broadcasting industries is fundamentally different, as is the structure of the sports industries themselves. On either side of the Atlantic a sports telecast is imbedded in a complex cultural context.

Profoundly different conceptions of competition suffuse American and British life, and go far beyond what happens on a playing field. There are other fundamental differences between the United States and Britain about what constitutes the desirable, but as competition lies at the heart of a professional sporting event, it must be tackled first. American and British attitudes to competition are most clearly demonstrated by their respective educational systems.

However it operates in practice, the American educational system is ostensibly designed to allow anyone who perseveres to compete; in Britain, it operates overtly as a sorting machine. Writing in 1960, Ralph Turner distinguished between the American and English educational systems by asserting that "elite status" is achieved in the United States by what he called "contest mobility" and in England by "sponsored mobility."[5] Turner suggested that in both countries most people take for granted a specific view of the way in which social advancement is and ought to be acquired. This "organizing folk norm," as he called it, is by no means all-embracing; in the United States the Roosevelt and Kennedy families have certain doors opened for them that remain shut to other Americans, and in Britain, comprehensive schools are run on the premise of giving all children "equality of opportunity."[6] But the fact remains that Americans believe that everyone who wants it should be allowed to "get an education," whereas the educational system in Britain is intentionally selective. Children are sorted out in their early teens; they do not graduate from high school with indistinguishable diplomas, but leave school at sixteen or eighteen with nationwide differentiated and graded certificates, the most respected of which are gained through passing external, largely essay examinations. Americans believe everyone deserves access to every kind of national resource; the British still tend to think that "where everyone is somebody/Then no one's anybody."

Turner's distinction is important. While in America an educational pecking order certainly exists, this order does not produce anything like the equivalent of the British establishment. In 1959, Oxford and Cambridge graduates numbered over a third of the members of the House of Commons, by no means all of them Conservatives. The upper echelons of the civil service, the church, and the law were similarly staffed.[7] The route to Oxford and Cambridge is often via Britain's public (i.e. private) schools. By 1982, Anthony Sampson believed that "school and university backgrounds have lost some of their significance in Parliament." But he also remarks that "there still remains a remarkable educational elite which has maintained its continuity and influence through all the political upheavals. Few people in the early Wilson years would have predicted that in 1982 the chairman of the BBC, the editor of *The Times,* the Foreign Secretary, the Heads of both foreign and civil services and half the chairmen of the big four banks would all be old Etonians, while the Home Secretary, the Chancellor, the director-general of the BBC, a bevy of judges and the other two bank chairmen would come from the rival foundation, Winchester. Such a lasting duopoly must surely have some significance in Britain's anatomy."[8]

In the United States there is nothing comparable; instead, many alternative avenues to political and educational advancement are open. Educationally, people can "start over" at any age; they can begin work in many disciplines at college without any prior training, even when these disciplines are regularly taught in high school. In Britain, in spite of the creation of the Open University and the existence of an array of colleges for further education, it is virtually impossible to seek credentials by "starting over." As most privileged and/or clever British children try to get into Oxford and Cambridge and without automatically doing graduate work take up careers in politics, law, medicine, and multinational corporations, an establishment exists that has no counterpart in America.

In a society where mobility is usually achieved by sponsorship, the importance of competition is played down. In Britain one "stands" for elected office; in the United States one has to "run" for it. Sponsors, not contestants, set the competitive pace. Those sponsored must live up to their mentors' expectations, but they do not have to concentrate on defending themselves against their rivals, and both parties assume that the expectations can and will be met.[9] A contest, however, is never finished; in American public life one must be, and be seen to be, keeping up, for to fall behind is by definition a demonstration of personal weakness.

TV producers working in America and Britain thus have to deal with quite different public attitudes toward the value of competition. I am not suggesting that the British do not want to win elections, awards, contracts, or sports contests; they do. But there is still in Britain a tendency to believe that success hinges as much on innate qualities that need nurture as on acquisition of attributes that can be learned. A sponsor can perceive those innate qualities and provide the conditions under which they will develop: as the coach remarked in *Chariots of Fire,* he couldn't put in what God had left out. In contrast, a properly organized contest sorts out those who will strain and labor from those who will not bother to make the effort. To fail to win a contest is to have failed to have tried sufficiently hard. In her autobiography, Christine Evert Lloyd mentioned the difference between her husband's training in competitiveness and her own. "In England, losing wasn't the end of the world, he has told me; if you lost well, that was okay as long as you tried. In the United States, young Americans have been taught that [being] number one is the only thing that matters: It doesn't matter how you do it as long as you do it."[10]

This concern with process rather than result goes beyond interest in any specific contest. In 1969 it was suggested that league cricket should be introduced to villages in Sussex, a county in England that had always been quite content with friendly matches. All players in these matches paid a membership fee to a club; they were true amateurs in that they paid to play. One club was so averse to the idea of substituting league for friendly matches that it wrote to other clubs, pointing out that "playing for points" would lead to the end of friendliness, and that the league would dictate the fixture list (the team schedule). Worse still, a "weaker player" selected because "he is a good type, does a lot of hard work for the club, enjoys the beer and social atmosphere" would be left out of the league team; umpires would be held accountable for bad decisions instead of their being "forgotten over a glass of beer." As "friendly competitive cricket" had been "played on Sussex village greens for more than two hundred years," why change it now?[11] A clearer statement of concern with process rather than result could hardly be made.

But attitudes change. By 1979, famous Sussex village teams were playing in leagues. And as John Bale points out, league cricket had always been characteristic of the north of England, where the mores of the working class exerted a more powerful influence than in the south.[12] For the cavalier attitude to winning of the British upper class could be sustained only by men who understood themselves to be superior to the rest of the world in everything that mattered. As the British Empire crumbled, and with it the effortless arrogance of the British ruling class, so did British attachment to amateurism.

A careless attitude to winning may derive not only from a greater concern with sportsmanship, but also from the inner certainty that one could always win if one took the trouble to try. Results become important precisely when teams are not sure they are "winners," just as one says, "I'm as good as you are" only when one fears one is not. Before World War II, Britain's world leadership was a fact of life; by the 1960s, the United States and the USSR had taken her place. The results of postwar international soccer matches, games that multiplied as travel became easier and money more plentiful, gave the Football Association an equally rude shock. British teams no longer automatically beat any foreign side who had the temerity to play them. The hysterical rejoicing when Britain won the World Cup in 1966 is to be explained by the assurance it gave that while the heavens had been shaken, some stars remained in place.

Yet if winning became more important after the war than before it, to win was by no means the only reason for playing; in both cricket and soccer it has always been honorable to draw (in the United States, to tie). Indeed to gamble on winning rather than to play for a draw may be regarded as rash and simpleminded. Mass legal gambling on British soccer, "the pools," depends on draws. In contrast, U.S. soccer sponsors invented the "shoot-out," because U.S. spectators require a result. Few soccer matches, other than Cup Finals and World Cup or other ethnocentric games, are televised live in Britain. Instead, British viewers watch on Saturday evenings an edited "Match of the Day" the result of which they already know. To treat U.S. football games similarly would spell network disaster, because Americans want to know what is happening while it happens, not after the event.

Who cares about watching a sports event in the United States after it is over? Virtually every other popular TV show appears in a rerun; past Super Bowls and World Series games lie quietly in their film racks. When baseball players were on strike in 1981, Americans declared themselves to be suffering from withdrawal symptoms; but the networks did not attempt to show past games. Only connoisseurs care about the process by which a competitive result has been achieved; the network executives, probably rightly, decided that baseball connoisseurs were not great in number.[13] When the Super Bowl was shown during the 1982 NFL strike, it achieved the princely rating of 5.6.[14]

Sponsored mobility can occur only in a society that contains a stable elite, confident of its own position and values. It presupposes concern with tradition. Contest mobility looks to the future. The millions of immigrants who poured into the United States during the nineteenth century wanted a better life not only for themselves but for their children. They stuck it out, even when those very children began to despise them for their odd and old-fashioned ways, determined to make their vision a reality.[15] Similarly, the founders of the new towns mushrooming in the plains and mountains were dazzled not by what was, but by what could be.[16] Isabella Bird, an Englishwoman traveling through the Rockies in 1873, misinterpreted much of what she saw because she interpreted her experience in British terms and lacked American vision.[17] As Vergil Gunch put it to Babbitt, "You don't want to just look at what these small towns are, you want to look at what they're aiming to become."[18] By the same token, chambers of commerce in the new towns could brook no discussion of possible flaws in their cities; to fail to boost or be optimistic, let alone to cavil, were marks of the wrongheaded, the drones of the community. Boosting was not confined to small towns, and a winning baseball team could be used as a means of enhancing even a big city's reputation. When the Red Stockings, baseball's first professional team, returned to Cincinnati after their triumphant 1869 tour, a leading merchant said, "Glory, they've advertised the city, sir, advertised us, sir, and help[ed] our business, sir."[19]

A small town's future was also bound up with the aspirations and achievements of its children. The most tangible of those achievements, which could be revived every year, was the performance of children's sports teams. The capture of a district or perhaps even a state title demonstrated that the town was worth something, whatever its size and appearance, because it produced winners. In Texas at least this is still true. As Al Reinert writes, "High school football is the one thing that can both unify a Texas town and set it apart from the hundreds of other similarly rural and unremarkable Texas towns. . . . [Towns'] success at high school football is their one claim to recognition by the larger world, and thus it provides the clearest reflection of their own sense of worth."[20]

Nowhere in Britain can one see roadside signs cataloguing past glories of children's teams, usually named after a predator; the appointment of a games master (coach) is not noted in the local newspaper nor are his coaching skills publicly discussed, and school matches are not broadcast.[21] Children's school games are simply children's school games; civic pride, if it is manifested through sport at all, is related to adult sporting prowess. The destiny of small towns and villages in Britain has long since been determined; they have no position to jockey for. In any case, doing one's best for one's child does not in Britain include boosting the school teams.

For sport, like so much other British activity, is class-related. It was the playing fields of Eton, not those of Podunk Hollow Comprehensive, that were alleged to be the genesis of British military might; Eton, the symbol of the hierarchical, sex-segregated, expensive form of education to which children of the well-born and wealthy were subjected. Private schools in the United States have never been a model for public schools; from the end of the nineteenth century, schools designed for children of the British middle class were modeled as closely as possible on British public schools, and often staffed by their products. Until after World War II, the children of the masses, apart from those who demonstrated exceptional academic ability and who were sponsored by means of scholarships into the middle class, were given an education that was designed to fit them to be the hewers of wood and drawers of water in an industrial society. There was, therefore, no way in which any children's school team, even in a small village, could serve as a vehicle for that community's aspirations; the village's future did not rest on the desires of the hoi polloi. Further, as adults played soccer and cricket in their spare time, any rivalry between villages was settled by adults, not children. Such rivalries were often fierce; but they had to do with sports, not with the community's status in the eyes of the world at large, for that status was already established.

The sense of one's place in the world is missing from many American towns, large and small, because they have been founded so recently, their population is often relatively transient, and their opportunities seem boundless. With whatever frenzy towns and communities greet their championship teams in Britain, no one supposes the town's mental health depends on the state of a sports franchise. In July 1982, the California Supreme Court ruled that the City of Oakland could extend the power of eminent domain to the Raiders, whose owner sought to move the team to Los Angeles. The court noted that the team was responsible for an annual $30 million of economic activity; but was also swayed by the fact that the Raiders were alleged to have given Oakland " 'social, cultural and psychological' identity."[22] In this case, the law may indeed be an ass; but what is significant is that someone should seriously suppose that without a football team a flourishing urban area would somehow become faceless. American urban life is fortunately far more deep-rooted; but the perception of the need for competitive success, symbolically represented in a winning team, obscures the reality.

Similar concern for relative status has affected the development of college athletics. In the United States, colleges and universities proliferated during the late nineteenth and early twentieth centuries. Most of the newcomers were financed by state legislatures, and were, except in the eyes of their own alumni, more or less equally undistinguished. They therefore had to compete with one another to establish their status; the quickest and simplest way to draw national attention was to produce a series of winning teams. The Big Game[23] was the only established Ivy League tradition that was publicly understood and could be copied fast and easily. What the Big Game had done to football by 1929 I have already described; by the early 1950s, the rot had not only spread to other sports, but had led to bribery of college players. When some college basketball players who accepted money to organize the score for the convenience of gamblers were sent to jail in 1951, Red Smith wrote one of his most outspoken columns, remarking that these players could regrettably "not be accompanied [to jail] by their accomplices." Smith wrote, "There is no law that can reach the educators who shut their eyes to everything except the financial ledgers of the athletic department, the authorities who enroll unqualified students with faked credentials, the professors who foul their academic nests by easing athletes through their courses, the diploma-mill operators who set up classes for cretins in Rope-Skipping IV and History of Tatooing VII, the alumni who insist on winning teams and back their demands with cash, the coaches who'd put a uniform on Lucky Luciano if he could work the pivot play."[24]

College athletics were thus corrupt, and known to be corrupt, long before the advent of television. But corruption is a relative term. As long as colleges were required to look and be competitive to be regarded as successful, it is hard to see how athletic programs could have been conducted differently. By the 1950s, Ivy League colleges no longer needed to play this game;[25] their status was already assured. They could afford to refuse to give athletic scholarships and huge coaching salaries; their names and reputations were already made. Newer kids on the block had to attract attention.[26]

In Britain, universities cannot establish status through demonstrated athletic prowess, even if they would. British universities are financed mainly by the government;[27] each university argues its case with individuals who are appointed, not elected, and who probably were educated at Oxford or Cambridge themselves. To them, college sports are a hobby, and have nothing to do with the cerebral purposes of a university, so even to mention the successes of a specific university team would be a sign of unfitness to receive funding. Further, there is no real scrambling for status among British universities. This is not due simply to the preeminent position of Oxford and Cambridge, but derives from the fact that the rest of the universities in Britain have a specific intellectual mission, are very few in number, and are relatively so equal that they have very little to compete for. Many American public universities are obliged to admit every applicant who meets a minimum standard, and states often fund universities as they do elementary and secondary schools, on a per capita basis. Places at British universities are limited as they are at American law and medical schools; students are individually selected. All British universities thus occupy the privileged position of the Ivy League in the United States, and can afford to regard college athletic activities accordingly.

Of course, what Turner has to say about an "organizing folk norm" does not mean that what people believe and what actually happens are the same. Under American "contest" rules, football and baseball players ought to make their way by demonstrating that they play better than their peers; in fact, they must first compete for the coach's favor. Both football and baseball are, in reality, sponsored activities. From junior high school onward, aspiring football and baseball players learn to please their coaches; a player has no other means of putting himself in a position from which he is allowed to compete. The standards of excellence and methods of attaining them are set by people other than players, a characteristic of sponsored activity. So it continues into the professional game; however outstanding the player, if he becomes unacceptable, for reasons other than his athletic ability, to those who rule his sport, he will not be allowed to continue to compete.

Nevertheless, football appears to be a contest activity. Facilities and coaching are provided for the poorest student; college scholarships are dangled before ghetto youths as a means of escape. It is assumed that any talented individual can succeed, regardless of his background, and football therefore appears to promise equality of opportunity for all. Let a player, however, cross his coach, and his "opportunity" disappears. In baseball, a coach not only picks the team, but decides how long a pitcher shall pitch, how he shall pitch, how hitters shall hit, and even when they may run between bases. But baseball, even more than football, appears to be a "contest" activity, because a boy can hone his skills on his own, and may not need college before entering the pros.

On the other hand, tennis is still regarded as a "sponsored" activity, because young players need private coaching, use expensive equipment, and have to meet large travel expenses. But they gain entry to prestigious tournaments simply by winning lesser tournaments, which no one can bar them from entering. This is actually contest mobility, because no coach can relegate them to the bench; but they play for themselves, by themselves, in a sport that lacks traditional American roots, so they are regarded as being sponsored.

Paradoxically, therefore, sports that depend entirely upon a sponsor's approval and activity even during play itself, can be regarded in America as a channel of upward mobility for all who try hard enough to develop their talent. So powerful is the organizing folk norm that reality has been made to fit it; a youth is not regarded as a "born cricketer," but as an athletically talented individual who has earned the right to play football or baseball on his school team by "meeting the competition" on the way up.

Indeed, the organizing folk norm in America allows many people to believe that children who perform well on their school teams will succeed in the business world. In discussing the matter, "team spirit" is always stressed; but team spirit is needed every bit as much by a member of an orchestra or choir. The difference is that children playing a sport are learning to cooperate so that the group can compete; a member of an orchestra usually does not know what it is to be "a winner." Therefore it is assumed that music does not prepare American children for the real world, whereas team sports do.

The present differences between American and British views of the importance and function of industry and industrialists derive from the nineteenth century and epitomize a strikingly different view of competition. People who make money have won, by contest, a prize that can be shown off to and appreciated by anyone; as the most obvious and tangible rewards are to be found by the enterprising in industry, successful American entrepreneurs are highly valued. Herbert Spencer's application of the idea of the survival of the fittest to human social activities rather than to the development of species was readily accepted in the United States, although it had been rejected by most of his fellow countrymen.[28] In Victorian England, one knew one's place; without exceptional sponsorship, all the struggling and adaptation in the world could not ensure upward social mobility. Further, money alone could not buy respectability or prestige in Britain; and by the end of Victoria's reign, the British aristocracy had managed to imbue British industrialists with aristocratic values. As Martin Wiener points out, nineteenth-century British aristocrats were indeed capitalists, but their capitalism was "basically rentier, not entrepreneurial or productive." In seeking to become respectable (and therefore acceptable), even gifted industrialists grew inhibited; consequently, Weiner argues cogently, "lasting social and psychological limits were placed on the industrial revolution in Britain."[29]

In America, there was no aristocracy to coopt industrialists. By the mid-nineteenth century, whatever the accident of his birth, a man could begin again, even to the point of denying his past identity altogether. If he struck lucky in California, who cared where he came from? The gold rush was leavened with ruffians:

> Oh, what was your name in the States?
> Was it Thompson or Johnson or Bates?
> Did you murder your wife
> And flee for your life?
> Say, what was your name in the States?[30]

In nineteenth-century America there were no such people as "the rich man in his castle/The poor man at his gate," their stations in life ordained by the Almighty. Charles Sumner could tell his Yale undergraduate class to "root, hog, or die," as he expounded his own version of Social Darwinism, because it was supposed that there was still room in the America of the 1890s for an enterprising hog to root where none had rooted before. When Frederick Jackson Turner published in 1893 his explanation of what was American about Americans it was eagerly seized upon, because it articulated what Americans already "knew."[31] They had had the courage to break out of their European cultural mold and to take possession of their vast new territories in a way that allowed the best and smartest competitor, unfettered by birth and custom, to make his way in the world. As the pioneer had tamed the wilderness, so now the entrepreneur could exploit its riches. Later historians might call Rockefeller, Carnegie, and Morgan "robber barons"; such men could not exist at all in Britain, if only because there was nothing for them to rob.

A very clear example of this difference in attitude as it was epitomized in the 1930s occurs in Harold Nicolson's *Diaries and Letters*. Writing the biography of Dwight Morrow, Nicolson unwittingly offended J. P. Morgan. As Nicolson says, "I had written, in describing the immense expansion assumed by Morgan's bank at the outbreak of the war, 'It ceased to be a private firm and became almost a Department of Government.' I meant that as a compliment. Old J. P. appears to have regarded it as an insult . . . *I* feel it is the highest compliment to compare Morgan's to the Foreign Office. *They* regard it as an insult to suggest that they have any connection with the Government, or any Government. But, you see, the whole point of view is different. I regard bankers and banking as rather low-class fellows. They regard officials as stupid and corrupt."[32]

Of course, Nicolson was a civil servant by profession, but his attitude mirrored that of many of his contemporaries; British gentlemen served in public office and did not stoop to scrabbling in the marketplace for private gain. Even for Nicolson, bankers were preferable to tradesmen.

That British attitude has only just begun to change; "Dickens' disgust with the creed of economic success"[33] remains in the 1980s. As Sampson remarks, "The traditional British elite, fortified by their ancient schools and Oxbridge colleges, have maintained their edge over others – at some cost to the country. Their values are less closely related to technology and industry than to pre-industrial activities such as banking and the army."[34]

Yet a metamorphosis has begun. An MBA degree, unheard of in Britain twenty years ago, can now be earned,[35] and universities as institutions are trying hard to establish profitable links with industry, instead of twitching their skirts hastily away. As the dean of Londons' City University told the *New York Times,* "Business has not been recognized in Britain the way it has in America. Medicine, accounting, the law, the church have always had more status than business. But I think that's breaking down."[36] The breakdown however, is slow; a 1985 government policy document, *The Development of Higher Education into the 1990s,* stressed the need for linking university education much more closely to the requirements of business and industry. The report states, "The entrepreneurial spirit is essential for the maintenance and improvement of employment. Higher education should be alert to the hazard of blunting it and should seek opportunities to encourage it."[37] Mrs. Thatcher's government is putting heavy financial pressure on British universities to apply themselves to the marketplace. Nevertheless, in Britain almost everyone, however irreverent or cynical, still takes for granted the idea that some activities must not be commercialized. The Royal Wedding, the world's blockbuster, was transmitted free of charge.[38]

Tyrell argues very perceptively that baseball itself "was an active agent in the forging of the urban-industrial order." As the game was professionalized by 1871 and commercialized by 1876, it began to act as an agency of social control. "The emergence of professionalism involved a shift from concepts of moral uplift to those of order and organisation, from attempts to impose morality directly to attempts to inculcate ideas of team-work, discipline and competition. The role of money in baseball was thus not only to transform the game into a professional sport, but also to further the social disciplines of a market-oriented society."[39] Thus baseball did not, in Tyrell's view, simply reflect social values, but helped shape them. And America's national game was organized and advertised by American business.

Whatever muckraking was done, however much Populist legislation finally found its way into the statute books, the business of twentieth-century America has indeed been business. In the 1980s, while "old" money has its own mystique, "new" money wields enormous power and influence. As possession of advanced technology has frequently made the difference between living and dying in business, American money-makers have invented and saturated the market with the products of a continuing industrial revolution.[40] The world of planned obsolescence is the world of the competitor, not of the craftsman.

This concern with competition has other ramifications. As Ralph Turner points out, where advancement takes place through contest, "the most satisfactory outcome is not necessarily a victory of the most able, but of the most deserving."[41] The "most deserving" is the one who takes the time and trouble to understand the rules of the game thoroughly, and who perceives where and how they can be manipulated. The American film *Rookie of the Year* perfectly illustrates this point. A girl wants to play baseball; the coach of the team on which her younger brother plays gives her the chance to fill in for a boy who is hurt. The coaches of other teams are furious; their first thought is to find a league rule that will allow them to refuse to play the girl's team, without overtly stating that they do not want to accept the right of girls to play. In order to belittle the girl, in a crucial match the coach gives his pitcher instructions to walk her when she comes to bat. But the girl, too, knows how to use the rules. In the play-off game, her team is losing; she wins the game for them by pretending to be hurt and then haring off to the next base. For such deft trickery she is overwhelmed with praise by her teammates, coach, and parents; even the opposing team does not regard this play as unfair. They have been outsmarted, and they know it.[42]

The point here is that this trickery is not cheating, because it takes place within the rules. In a society that prizes contest mobility, cheating is a matter of breaking the rules, not manipulating them. As John Dizikes puts it, "The tendency to organize play was immensely strengthened in American culture because sport was a widely available means of controlling the looseness and limitlessness of life all about. The need for a native tradition, however, soon became the need to reject tradition. *Deception became a form of freedom from the past.* Once play became sport, Americans played a double game: the game within the rules and the game against the rules. One ordinary American gamesman put it simply. Having studied the rule book in spring training, Buck Ewing said to his players: 'Boys, you've heard the new rules read. Now the question is: what can we do to beat them?' "[43] (Italics added.)

In a society concerned with sponsorship, such an attitude is unthinkable. The game must be won according to the spirit of the law, not the letter. One may win fairly only by outplaying, rather than outsmarting, one's opponent. The spirit of the law, however, can be obeyed only by those who both know the law and understand its implications; consensus about how the game ought to be played must exist. In such a situation, the very rule book may be deliberately vague. As Kerr puts it, "It has always been the glory of Cricket that its Laws do not set out to cover every small point in a complicated game, but leave much unwritten for sensible interpretation by players inbued with its spirit."[44] This is the amateur spirit writ large or gone mad, according to one's point of view; but to fail to understand the spirit of the sport in which one has engaged under these conditions is to mark oneself as an outsider.

Until fairly recently, just such a high degree of consensus characterized British public life, however different in principle the activities of the major political parties appear to have been. This is partly because the top civil servants in Britain have great influence on the political process. The budget in the United States, for instance, is a public battleground, with the president, the Senate and the House preparing, submitting, and arguing about the figures. In Britain, Treasury officials privately advise members of the cabinet (all of whom are members of Parliament, and normally are elected members of the House of Commons). The cabinet, after private discussion, then presents the budget to the House, and it is very rarely changed, both because the House lacks the facilities to duplicate the work already done, and because votes on the budget are votes of confidence. In Britain, a government that cannot secure enough votes to secure passage of its legislation resigns, so while budgetary policies are debated, what the cabinet has proposed is usually what is passed. Permanent civil servants may have had much more influence on the budget, in fact, than elected representatives; the exact degree of their influence is extremely hard for an outsider to assess. The private nature of all this activity is accepted by the British public as a modus operandi because it is assumed both that some notion of fair play exists behind the scenes and that there is no effective way for anyone to challenge it.

In a country as heterogeneous as the United States, and one that lacks a nationally recognized establishment, not only are such private arrangements anathema, but every political question ultimately becomes a legal question. Conflict resolution in the United States depends heavily on the courts, even though it is abundantly clear that the legal system is not designed to handle complicated ethical and social problems. Crucial decisions affecting the development of the television industry have therefore been made by U.S. courts.[45] Similarly, American courts have been used to regulate the sports industry. The Federal League made its first challenge to the reserve clause in 1914,[46] and the Flood case in 1972 "represented the third time in fifty years that the [Supreme] Court had been asked to rule on the applicability of the antitrust laws to baseball's reserve system."[47] In any court, the letter of the law is of paramount importance. And in situations in which the letter counts rather than the spirit, rules must be devised to cover all foreseeable contingencies. To play to the rules of any particular sport is therefore in America by definition to play fairly, and creative manipulation of those rules must therefore be a sign not of unsporting behavior, but of intelligence.[48]

As conflict began to replace consensus in postwar Britain, and as the rights movement gathered strength, sports cases appeared in British courts. His Majesty's judges considered soccer for the first time in 1945;[49] almost twenty years later, soccer's maximum-wage law was struck down through court action. "Fair play" and "gentlemen's agreements" are redolent of amateurism; the more thoroughly commercial and professional cricket and soccer become, the more conflicts will be adjudicated in court instead of in the boardroom.

On both sides of the Atlantic, players whose livelihoods are at the mercy of the umpire will break the rules if they can get away with it. And while judgment calls are an inevitable component of every game, professionals want to hear as few of them as possible. Proper interpretation and enforcement of rules therefore becomes one of a professional's major concerns. Protests about calls by professionals are quite different from the umpire-baiting that baseball and soccer crowds have always indulged in, which are simply an aspect of ritual participation. A bad call costs a professional money. Concern for the spirit of the law is the sign of the amateur, one who cares more about game-as-process than game-as-result. Professionals obviously cannot afford to worry too much about process.

Willingness to accept the officials' interpretation of the rules also relates to ideas about what constitutes authority. In the United States, it is perfectly acceptable to question the decisions of the umpire; indeed coaches are expected to do it loudly, obviously, and energetically. Their songs and dances will not actually change the umpire's mind, and everyone knows it, but the ritual challenge to authority must be made. In the United States, everyone is equal, and if some are temporarily more equal than others it is as well that they should remember the fragility of their power. In Britain, soccer fans may shout what they like and may attack the referees if they can after the match; but no soccer coach, however irritated by the referee he might be, would consider it ritually incumbent upon him to challenge a referee's decision. Players' unwillingness to "play to the whistle" has been regarded in recent years as an indication of soccer's deterioration, and referees' powers to send off players have been strengthened.

Professionals play to make money, the more the better. In a country where commercialism is regarded as crass, no quarter can therefore be given to professional athletes. When soccer gave itself over to professional players, at the end of the nineteenth century, English gentlemen took to rugby.[50] Cricket remained a sport open to all classes, because the professionals were quarantined as a separate caste until after World War II; now that all sports are ruled by professionals, much less prestige is attached in British public schools to sporting prowess than it was even thirty years ago.[51]

In America, precisely the opposite trend has occurred. As the rewards to be obtained in professional sport have become more valuable, so have school athletic programs become increasingly more visible. School teams and their appurtenances are perhaps now among the few places where an American child is expected instantly to obey, to concentrate, and to exert himself or herself to the point of exhaustion, on pain of being excluded from the activity he or she wants to take part in. While the chorus of criticism about sports programs from journalists, sociologists, and educators has grown deafening in the last few years,[52] schools and colleges continue to model their programs after the professionals. They are hampered only by budgetary constraints; to overcome those, they must be "competitive."

While national views on what constitutes competition are fundamental to sports telecasting, there are other cultural constraints to which TV executives must pay attention. Ever since Von der Ahe combined professional baseball with beer, horseraces, and fireworks in the 1880s, Americans have regarded professional sport as a spectacle, not simply a game. This attitude rapidly filtered down to all levels of the game and in football especially has combined with isolated communities' need to provide something for everyone. Women have not until very recently played much sport at which spectators were expected; but they have been members of bands, drill teams, cheerleading teams and all the other appurtenances of a league game through school, college, and into the professionals.

Women were also expected to watch professional games; the White Stocking ballpark in 1871 even had special seating for ladies and city officials.[53] Watching football and baseball at the stadium and ballpark became by the mid-twentieth century a family affair, an outing. TV producers have seized on this element of spectacle and heightened it; the Dallas Cowboy cheerleaders owe their fame to the close-ups TV can provide. And in treating football as family entertainment, TV is building on an established U.S. tradition. Each game is presented as part of a total entertainment package, not simply as a contest of skill.

To the British, such attitudes border on desecration, for soccer and cricket are events in their own right. An American ballpark or stadium resembles a disturbed anthill, as spectators roam in search of refreshments or programs or just to move; the British tend to wait until halftime or other scheduled breaks before wandering about. There are no introductions, no cheerleaders, no halftime shows, no information from a referee and rarely any from an announcer, no bands or organs, no talking scoreboards, and in soccer grounds, very little seating. The BBC regularly broadcasts an edited version of a soccer match on Saturday evening, after which one or two stars of the match are interviewed, and some general soccer lore is discussed. The match shown is treated as an event, not as part of a total spectacle. Soccer matches have traditionally been watched by men, largely from the working class; TV producers have made little attempt to attract a wider segment of the viewing public.

Those who watch sports programs in America and Britain also differ in their attitudes toward information. In Britain, there is no equivalent of the eye-catching and constructive displays to be found at every visitors' center run by the National Park Service. Nor are public-service messages broadcast, much less the tasteless clichés about social problems prefacing a plug for plumbing fixtures or some other commercial enterprise "always concerned for the youth of our community." The British appear to assume that people visit museums because they are already interested, so to instruct them too clearly would be patronizing; and that people without common sense are not likely to acquire it through broadcast exhortations.

The American air is filled with information, from public-service advertisements about crisis phone lines to statistics on the local pollen count in the weather forecast. This information is often cast in terms that make a spurious claim to expertise; a "twenty percent chance of precipitation" simply means that it is unlikely to rain. To use numbers, however, suggests that someone understands what is happening and is in control of it; an expert is speaking. The British do not require such precision because they lack the ambivalent attitude of denigration and reverence toward "experts" that Americans often possess.[54]

This attitude to information affects attitudes toward sports commentary. When spectators believe they understand a game, they neither require nor welcome much from announcers. British TV viewers complained about the 1979 Wimbledon commentary (although by American standards it was both pertinent and pathetically sparse) on the grounds that the announcers talked too much. Alistair Cooke betrayed his British upbringing in a devastating commentary on TV golf announcers, citing Henry Longhurst's praise of "brilliant flashes of silence."[55] British commentators have few pauses to occupy in soccer, but they feel no compulsion to fill in the action gaps in cricket. A British academic, H. A. Harris, succinctly expressed British views when he wrote, "The best advice to a television commentator is, 'If in doubt, say nowt.'"[56] American TV executives are constrained to act as if their audiences may not understand what they see; British TV executives tend to assume that their audiences welcome the sort of conversation they would have at the event itself, and information on factors like wind and weather that their screen cannot give them.

The use of commentary, however, is related not simply to attitudes about information, but to habits of listening. Because American radio so soon became commercial, listeners rapidly learned when not to hear; the BBC, however, tried to train its listeners actively to listen. BBC radio still preserves much of the program content of pretelevision years, albeit on different channels. When U.S. network radio listening declined in the 1950s, and when money was required to fund the much more expensive TV shows, radio networks abandoned drama, including mystery plays, comedy and talk shows, children's and quiz programs.[57] As David MacFarland pointed out, by the early 1960s U.S. radio was broadcasting for those who wanted to devote the minimum of attention to listening:

"Stations programming music-and-news . . . provided a service that unlike TV, newspapers, magazines or even earlier radio programs, demanded little concentration by the audience."[58] In America, only public radio broadcasts programs that require close attention.

Musak and Walkmans are now as ubiquitous in Britain as in the United States, and British commercial radio is as mindless as American; but the old tradition of tuning in rather than tuning out still lingers. Many British schools do not have public-address systems; where such systems exist, they are not normally used to interrupt lessons, as often happens in American schools. When we are besieged by broadcast noise, we tend to ignore all of it. The establishment policy in Britain is still to anticipate an attentive audience, not one that has to be cajoled into awareness.

These fundamental differences in what is considered desirable in public life have affected and still affect the marketing of professional sport in Britain and the United States. American television producers have set out to market national sport in precisely those ways that fit the values Americans wanted to see reflected in sport before television was invented. Football, for instance, has been carefully tailored over eighty years to meet American requirements.

Viewers are provided with a staggering volume of information, not all of it by any means pertinent to the game in progress. They are also encouraged to prepare themselves for other sporting programs, and are reminded by players' appearances for charities such as the United Way that professional football players take their citizenship duties seriously.

Each professional player has survived long and rigorous competition to secure his place on the team; even Tom Landry announced that all starting jobs for the 1983 season were up for grabs at training camp. While sponsoring players through the draft, each team is on the lookout for players who want to try out as free agents; even though the final decision is made by the owner and/or coach, players appear to have been given every chance to compete with each other throughout their careers. They have apparently earned their way to the top, and ostensibly retain their places on the basis of merit alone.

Every game is played to win, and the varied scoring possibilities in football make a tie extremely unlikely even if the teams really are evenly matched. The uniform, the turf, the timekeeping, the headphones, and other gear surrounding the teams are miracles of modern technology. Football is a game of precision that may be won or lost by skillful manipulation of seconds. Professional football does not merely involve personal effort and talent, but the organization and technological expertise modern businesses the world over require. It represents the epitome of the efficiency Lorin Deland pleaded for in 1917.[59]

The game is conducted not according to the spirit but the letter of the law. Seven officials are required to keep the game going; each has a specialized function, and a rule infraction that has nothing to do with the movement of the ball may cancel the play. The Eagles will long remember Rodney Parker's touchdown catch that would have made the score 7-7 in Super Bowl XV, had officials not ruled that Harold Carmichael had turned upfield before the ball was snapped. Carmichael was nowhere near the ball; the infraction gave momentum back to the Raiders. Specific and detailed rules cover every foreseeable contingency, and so complicated are decisions that officials frequently have to confer before a final judgment can be made. A magnificent leaping catch may be nullified because someone else on the team, nowhere near the play, broke a rule; a touchdown may be called back for the same reason. Judgment calls still exist; but they have been made as few as possible, and commentators are quick to pounce on doubtful decisions. To express the spirit of the game is to play within the rules; when injury results from a legal hit, viewers are reassured by commentators. The player himself may be just as incapacitated from a legal as an illegal blow; but the first injury is sanctioned by the football and TV industries because it is rule-governed. Players continue to suffer each season; so long as they suffer lawfully, all is well.

TV, in short, has not changed the fundamental nature of the football product that has been marketed since the early 1900s. The use of the medium has simply made the game already shaped to suit an American audience accessible to a larger public.

Baseball has followed the same path. Rules, style of play, and ballpark accommodations were tailored from the early twentieth century to meet American expectations of excitement, spectacle, and family entertainment. While football overtly flaunted American fascination with technology, baseball concerned itself with the antithetical American ideal, pastoralism. American national sport has indeed epitomized "the machine in the garden",[60] television has done nothing to alter that dichotomy. British requirements for televised sport are rather different, and will be discussed in more detail in the chapters on cricket and soccer. What is clear is that while the British are definitely concerned about results, they are still primarily interested in process. Because professional sport has no ties with the formal educational system of the kind that exist in the United States, British television does not much concern itself with school or college sport. Because most viewers are assumed to be interested in and to understand the game they are watching, commentators are not required to entertain viewers. Nor are sportscasts vehicles for anything other than the event; they are ends in themselves.

Sports telecasting on both sides of the Atlantic, however, is influenced not only by national conceptions of what is desirable, but by the national histories of the television and sports industries. Before we turn to cricket and soccer, the history of those industries as it affects sports broadcasting must be discussed. This is the subject of the next chapter.

5

THE TV AND SPORTS INDUSTRIES

The conventions that govern the TV industry on both sides of the Atlantic did not arise from the industry itself, but came originally from radio. Significant differences still exist between the American and British television industries because their radio industries were set in entirely different societal contexts.

In the United States, Westinghouse began the first daily scheduled broadcast on radio in 1920; it fell into what TV producers later labeled "prime time."[1] By 1924, perhaps 2.5 million sets were in use,[2] and stations scrambled to meet programming demands. They used amateur and then professional performers, and whatever material they could lay hands on. In 1923, a court had supported the American Society of Composers, Authors and Publishers in its contention that WOR, Newark, was using copyright music for profit because listeners heard that the broadcast was coming "from L. Bamberger and Company, one of America's great stores."[3] Incensed, broadcasters paid for the use of material, even as they realized that what ASCAP had begun, other groups threatened to emulate. In that case, where was the money to finance broadcasting to come from?

Various ideas were put forward and experiments tried;[4] but while public debate was concerned with the financing of broadcasting another question was being asked in private. Who was going to make a profit from the use of radio sets and other broadcasting equipment? The Radio Corporation of America, founded in 1919, which included Westinghouse,

United Fruit, American Telegraph and Telephone, and subsidiary companies, had worked out patent and other marketing agreements, but by 1924, it seemed to the others that AT&T was trying to hog the market. None of the companies, however, wanted to discuss their differences in public because of the antitrust act. So RCA, GE Westinghouse, and AT&T decided to submit their claims to an arbitrator, in secret. But they had reckoned without the Federal Trade Commission, who chose this moment to charge these and other companies with conspiracy to monopolize broadcasting. Amid frantic and secret negotiations, the companies sorted out their empire; as a result, the National Broadcasting Company was formed.[5] In the advertisements announcing NBC in September 1926, Owen Young, the chairman of the RCA board, and James Harbord, its president, proclaimed that the new company's purpose was "to provide the best programs available for broadcasting in the United States," and that it was "not in any sense seeking a monopoly of the air." They also announced that one of the "major responsibilities" of NBC's new president "will be to see that the operations of the National Broadcasting Company reflect enlightened public opinion."[6]

Marketing arrangements having been settled, the public question remained. Where was the money to come from to produce "the best" (or indeed any) programs for broadcasting? By 1928, the question had been answered; advertisers supported the new broadcasting industry. In 1924, Herbert Hoover, then secretary of commerce, had declared, "I believe that the quickest way to kill broadcasting would be to use it for direct advertising ... if a speech by the President is to be used as the meat in a sandwich of two patent medicine advertisements there will be no radio left."[7] Yet having analyzed the radio fare offered by New York stations in February 1927, George Lundberg wrote, "The radio is at present used almost entirely as an entertainment device for the advertising of radio itself, and of the businesses which provide the programs."[8]

Further, when a network sold a time period, the sponsor decided what program should go into it; as Roy Durstine put it succinctly in 1930, "The public wants entertainment. The advertiser wants the public's attention and is willing to pay for it. Therefore, let the advertiser provide the entertainment."[9] NBC's "enlightened public opinion" therefore boiled down to the degree of enlightenment advertisers believed their audiences could stand.

Meanwhile, a U.S. District Court decided in 1926 that the secretary of commerce had no legal right to make detailed regulations about radio station licenses, as he had been doing since 1923 when the fantastic increase in broadcasting had begun to make the ether cacophonous. The court decision led to immediate chaos, as stations increased power, changed wavelengths, and extended their air time. Broadcasters turned to Congress to have order restored. In 1927, the Federal Radio Commission was established by the Radio Act; the granting of station licenses was to be in accordance with "public interest, convenience or necessity."[10] Further, these licenses were not permanent; in theory at least, a station that did not serve the "public interest" could find itself without a wavelength. Certainly, the FRC strictly enforced regulations that specified station location, frequency, and power; but while it concentrated on "public convenience" the FRC seemed much less sure what to do about "public interest," which the act had in no way defined.[11] When the BBC's Director General John Reith visited the FRC in 1931, he specifically discussed the public interest. As he wrote in his diary, the commissioners "were immensely tickled with the idea that they should exert their powers."[12]

Not surprisingly, as radio audiences grew bigger, advertising became more crass. Those who assume that television is responsible for the debasement of public taste cannot be aware of the complaints about radio in the 1930s. Not that the furor did much good; the Communications Act of 1934 that replaced the Federal Radio Commission with the Federal Communications Commission did not create the nonprofit channels that critics of radio had demanded.[13]

On April 30, 1939, RCA formally opened its TV broadcasting service. CBS, formed in 1927 and bought by William Paley in 1929, had also been experimenting with TV, as had other groups. By 1940, twenty-three stations were televising broadcasts. The FCC, however, had forbidden TV stations to sell time directly to advertisers. The FCC also ordered RCA to get rid of one of its two TV networks; in 1943, NBC-blue became the American Broadcasting Company. Wartime restrictions, however, stopped the growth of TV broadcasting.[14]

After World War II, television broadcasting was again licensed; by 1946, RCA had black and white sets for sale nationwide. It rapidly became clear that TV was very expensive; NBC decided that radio should finance it. The "public-service" programs, put on in response to the public debate about radio quality in 1936, quickly became casualties.

The FCC, however, was in no position to insist on a quality TV product. Tuchmann goes so far as to suggest that the FCC and the TV industry originally enjoyed a relationship like that of "a business and its house-union."[15] Whether or not that is now true, the radio industry had found little to fear from the FCC, so when the commission tried to insist on standards for television it found itself swimming completely against the tide. In 1946, the FCC forgot its customary role and issued a memorandum entitled "Public Service Responsibilities of Broadcast Licensees," which set out recommendations for programming in the public interest.[16] This "Blue Book," as it came to be called, listed specific instances of programming it deplored, and advocated balanced programming that would provide for minority interests and nonprofit organizations, as well as giving listeners a chance to hear programs that had no proven commercial track record. The public paid remarkably little attention to the FCC's concern for its welfare; broadcasters were outraged. Although the Blue Book may have prompted the National Association of Broadcasters to adopt a revised code for self-regulation in 1948, it affected the actual conduct of stations very little. Nor did the FCC really attempt to refuse licenses to offensive stations; by 1952, TV licenses had even been given to thirty of the eighty radio stations specifically cited for poor programming in the Blue Book, a number that amounted to about 28 percent of the total TV licenses granted.[17] "Free speech" on the air waves continued to be the most persuasive speech money could buy.[18]

For various reasons, the FCC refused to issue TV licenses between 1948 and 1952. But after 1952, when licensing was resumed, sales of TV sets rocketed; competition between networks for listeners meant that whatever was popular on one channel was quickly copied on the others.[19] The phenomenally successful "Milton Berle Show" ("Texaco Star Theater") of 1948 was overtaken by "Arthur Godfrey's Talent Scouts" in 1951. "I Love Lucy" was followed by a host of comedy series in the early 1950s; the success of "Gunsmoke" led to a spate of westerns in the late fifties, while quiz and giveaway shows proliferated, until Charles Van Doren was forced to admit in 1959 that he had been coached throughout his famous appearances on the "Twenty-One" quiz. The revelations that followed were a disaster; the networks were demonstrated to have wantonly manipulated the public for the sake of profit. In reaction, the networks turned to news and public-affairs shows; and as ratings increased, no one was prepared for the remarks of FCC Chairman Newton Minow at the National Association of Broadcasters convention in 1961. Calling network television a "vast wasteland," Minow cited the "procession of game shows, violence, audience participation shows, formula comedies about totally unbelievable families, blood and thunder, mayhem, violence, sadism, murder, Western badmen, Western goodmen, private eyes, gangsters, more violence, and cartoons, and, endlessly, commercials, many screaming, cajoling and offending, and, most of all, boredom."[20]

Scathing as Minow's denunciations were, they had little effect. For the next twenty years, critics continued to protest, and programming decisions continued to be made on the same grounds as they always had been.[21] Some excellent programs were produced, but the fundamental problems remained. Producers had to search for programs that would have the greatest appeal. Indeed, there was no possible way in which they could do anything different, unless they were to pull up their roots and start all over again.

For the truth is that American network television does very well what it was set up to do. It simply continued the tradition established by network radio, an industry that by 1928 existed for the purpose of profitably distributing advertising copy nationwide. Officially, broadcasting was supposed to have other purposes; but like so many other public institutions on both sides of the Atlantic, what the broadcasting industry actually did and what it was supposed to do were different things. No one has yet been able to demonstrate how to serve "the public interest, convenience and necessity" and to make a profit at the same time.

This confusion between the "ought" and the "is" in the American radio and TV industries is not unique to them, but to function at all, they simply have to ignore the spirit of the law and decide how far they need obey its letter. *Variety* made the point in 1972: "It could be no secret that the manager of a major New York TV station was speaking for a good part of the industry when he told an applicant for the post of program director: Your job here will be to protect this station's license. You'll have to take care of all that public affairs . . . (four letter word omitted)."[22]

Occasionally such a bluff is publicly called. U.S. District Judge Miles Lord neatly punctured the NCAA balloon when he pointed out that Mark Hall, a student athlete, had been "recruited to come to the University of Minnesota to be a basketball player and not a scholar. His academic record reflects that he has lived up to those expectations, as do the academic records of many of the athletes presented to this Court."[23] But in a heterogeneous society whose members cannot agree about the extent to which consumers should be protected from themselves, rhetoric and performance cannot normally be expected to match, however often Americans beat their breasts about the gap.[24] To complain that network television ought not to provide the fare that most Americans want to watch is to complain that Americans ought not to prize money and competition. But they do. And would-be immigrants the world over long for the opportunities of work and wealth the United States offers, opportunities that exist because Americans have cheerfully pursued what money can buy.

In Britain, the societal context in which the broadcasting industry grew was quite different. Hence, the purpose of and constraints upon it differed. Regular public radio broadcasting was initiated as it was in the United States, by manufacturers of radio sets. In Britain, however, there was no question of a lack of governmental authority; the Post Office assumed itself to be in charge of wireless telegraphy, because it already controlled line telegraphy. After a Post Office representative attended Hoover's first radio conference as an observer, the Post Office was convinced it wanted no part of a cacophonous ether. In May 1922, the postmaster general told the House of Commons that he proposed to call the radio manufacturers together to work out a system. Far from attempting to break up a monopoly, Post Office representatives then persuaded these manufacturers to form the British Broadcasting Company, whose income was to derive from the original stock (on which dividends were limited), royalties on receiving sets sold by members, and a license fee from all who bought sets. In 1924, the royalties were dropped.[25] From the beginning British broadcasting was set outside the context of the marketplace.

John Reith was appointed the company's general manager; he had strong views on what broadcasting should do. As he wrote in 1924, "I think it will be admitted by all that to have exploited so great a scientific invention for the purpose and pursuit of entertainment alone would have been a prostitution of its powers and an insult to the character and intelligence of the people."[26] Reith, however, was not swimming upstream; British observers such as Percy Scholes, who toured the United States between September and December 1925, came back convinced that competitive radio programming supported by advertising could not be of the quality provided by the BBC's licensed monopoly.[27] After a government committee had enquired into the future of broadcasting in 1925, the British Broadcasting Company was replaced by the British Broadcasting Corporation, operating under a royal charter. It was to be financed wholly by license fees, which were collected by a government department, the Treasury, which was then to decide what proportion of the actual fee paid should be allocated to the BBC for its operations. Once that sum was settled, the Treasury was to bow out; it became the BBC's job to use the money in any way it saw fit, within the terms of its charter.

The corporation was created in 1927 for ten years; five governors were appointed for five-year terms and Reith was appointed director-general. He insisted that while major policy decisions on topics such as the BBC's constitution did fall within Parliament's purview, no political or civil servant was to interfere "directly or indirectly in management."[28] That policy remains to this day although the degree to which the BBC is really independent of government control has sometimes been questioned.[29]

Reith had equally clear ideas about the BBC's functions. It was to cater to what was best in British life and aspirations, and by so doing, help to form public taste; by no means was it to please the greatest possible number of listeners by pandering to their whims. When Lord Reith published his memoirs in 1949 he articulated what the British establishment believed about public life. He wrote, "It was, in fact, the combination of public service motive, sense of moral obligation, assured finance, and the brute force of monopoly which enabled the BBC to make of broadcasting what no other country in the world has made of it."[30]

Reith could not, of course, have set the BBC on this path and stuck to it, had he not had public opinion behind him. American radio continued to be a whipping boy; as an "average listener" wrote in 1928, "American broadcasting is designed for people who cannot concentrate."[31] The press, popular and august, supported the policy of monopoly; as the *Times* put it in 1934, "To the British way of thinking, a service privately conducted and indirectly financed offers no attractions."[32] While there were those, particularly in advertising, who found the BBC's monopoly irksome, the nation as a whole was content with the establishment position.

For Reith conceived of his audience as a unified group, whose taste could be formed. As the *BBC Handbook* put it in 1928, the order of the day was to "give the public something slightly better than it now thinks it likes" in order to make that public "not less but more exacting."[33] But when Radio Luxembourg pirated the air in the spring of 1933, supported by advertising and by broadcasting chiefly light music on records, the British began eagerly to listen to it.[34] By 1935, the Radio Manufacturers Association was restive; it sent a memorandum to the program board, pointing out that people wanted more light entertainment than they were getting.[35] There was some truth in this contention; a survey in the same year showed that 50 percent of the British listeners heard Radio Luxembourg on Sunday, an "uplifting" day for the BBC, and 11 percent during the week, when BBC fare was more entertaining.[36]

Reith was unmoved; no serious listener research was begun until 1936, and a choice of programs for the BBC meant that one could tune to regional or national stations, both of which offered much the same variety of material.[37] Although "light" and "heavy" entertainment was available, there was no special, continuous service for either before World War II; the BBC's policy was explicitly to provide programs that were "educative," not formally but in the sense of making "life so much more interesting and enjoyable than it otherwise would be."[38]

In November 1936, the BBC put out its first television program. Always strapped for money, the corporation found the cost of the service alarming; just as the FCC did not know how to manage a technological revolution, neither did the BBC.[39] The outbreak of war in 1939 sent Britain back to radio for the duration. During the war, the BBC's reputation grew; the twenty-first birthday celebration in 1943 sparked a "round of congratulations."[40]

Yet after the war, the BBC found itself facing mounting criticism, for a number of reasons. The then director general, William Haley, pragmatically rearranged programming, starting the Light Programme in 1945, and then the Third Programme, the latter deliberately heavyweight; middlebrow music, talks, drama, and similar fare were left on the Home Service.[41] But Haley insisted that he did not wish to segregate the BBC's audience; rather, by giving people a taste of something, rather than flinging them into it, he hoped to make progress. It was, he felt, "a subtler but more indirect method of bringing listeners to move up the cultural scale.... Maybe in a few years' time the Light Programme will be where the Home Service is now and the Home will have passed on to other standards."[42] When Norman Collins became head of the Television Service in 1947, Haley instructed him to continue the BBC's radio mission, which was to "educate and entertain."[43] On the BBC's twenty-fifth anniversary, Haley made remarks on a Home Service talk that were quite unsurprising to his audience, but that could never have come from the American broadcasting industry. Haley said, "Broadcasting will not be a social asset if it produces only a nation of listeners ... It is not an end in itself.... The wireless set or the television receiver are only signposts on the way to a full life."[44] The American example was always before British eyes; as Haley asserted in 1949, Americans were concerned not with the quality of material but in performer popularity. He wanted British TV to be built "round ideas," not "around personalities."[45]

But other voices besides Haley's were being heard in the land. While the war was still on, the *Economist* published a series of articles challenging the BBC's monopoly; in 1946, Sir Fredrick Ogilvie, who had succeeded Reith in 1938, wrote to the *Times* also questioning the BBC's monopoly, on principle.[46] The BBC's charter was to expire in 1951, so in 1949 a government committee enquired into the future of broadcasting. The Listeners Association declared to it that commercial broadcasting should be set up, outside the BBC's control. The Institute of Incorporated Practitioners in Advertising wanted commercial radio and TV, but under BBC control.[47] Viewers were becoming disenchanted; the BBC had decided to extend TV coverage before putting on a new channel; and given the range of Light, Home, and Third available on radio, it was annoying to have no choice on TV. In 1950, a group of young Conservatives entered Parliament, anxious to do away with wartime restrictions; a broadcasting monopoly seemed an easy place to start.[48] Although the Beveridge committee as a whole recommended the continuation of a monopoly, one member, Selwyn Lloyd, made a minority report in which he argued for the introduction of commercial broadcasting.

The government considered the Beveridge report, but found Selwyn Lloyd's position more to its liking. In May 1952, the government suggested the BBC's monopoly should end. Public feeling ran high, and again the specter of American experience was called up. Once more, an influential ex-BBC man supported commercial television. In 1950, the BBC had belatedly raised the status of television from that of a department under a controller to a service under a director. Norman Collins, then head of TV, was not appointed director. In 1952, he wrote to the *Times* to point out that commercial radio and television did not necessarily have to follow the American pattern, because American and British standards were different. He argued that no one talked about the "commercial" press; instead, they called it the "free" press. Why should broadcasting be different?[49]

The proponents of competition won; the BBC's monopoly came to an end on July 30, 1954. Yet the new commercial enterprise set up alongside the BBC had to operate within the rules of a game that were very different from those in the United States, as the government had proposed "a typically British approach to this new problem."[50]

An Independent Television Authority was set up which consisted of from seven to ten people, corresponding to the BBC's board of governors and appointed by the postmaster general.[51] The authority was to oversee commercial TV, but its members were to have no stake in it, personal or professional. Programs were to be provided by ITV companies, for whose conduct the ITA was responsible. It was these companies, not the ITA as such, that would make or lose money. Sponsorship of programs was forbidden; advertisers could not contribute or control programs. All advertisers could do was to buy some specific airtime and produce an advertisement for it; they had no control at all over the content of the program surrounding the ad. The TV advertiser in Britain was thus required to send the visual ad into the equivalent of a visual newspaper or magazine. The timing, number, and content of advertisements was also spelled out by law, and advertisements for children were particularly strictly controlled. In fact, the Independent Broadcasting Authority (IBA) goes so far as to preview scripts of almost all commercials.

By law, programming on commercial stations was also controlled, with the emphasis on quality. Nothing was to be broadcast that "offends against good taste"; programming was to be balanced, news was to be accurate, and political and industrial controversies were to be presented impartially. The ITA was to use British programs in "proper proportions," and was required to comply with, not simply sit through, recommendations coming from special committees set up on children's and religious programs. To prevent unseemly competition in bidding for "sporting or other events of national importance," a government minister was given power to regulate broadcasting rights to such events. There is no First Amendment in Britain.

The same kind of people were appointed to the ITA as were BBC governors;[52] they were determined to see that British commercial TV did not resemble its American counterpart, for obvious reasons. What, however, they did not anticipate, was that they would have only one network to play with.[53] They had assumed that the government would allocate frequencies in such a way that several commercial services could compete with one another; but when in 1955 they requested extra channels, they were refused. The postmaster general made it clear that there would be no channel expansion at least until 1958, so that performance could be assessed and room left for technical developments such as color. Thus, although monopoly had been broken, it was succeeded not by plurality, as some supporters of commercial television had assumed, but duopoly. As B. Sendall puts it, "They [ITA] were not to know that in later years the notion of competition, except in terms of competition between the BBC and ITV, would lose favour; and that even between those two organizations competition, as distinct from planned co-existence, would come to be increasingly deprecated."[54]

The BBC took the threat of ITA competition seriously and even began circulating a house organ called "the competitor," in February 1955.[55] But in terms of what U.S. networks meant by competition, the efforts of both sides were derisory. As late as 1979, the *BBC Handbook* recorded audiences in terms such as "17½ million." It was reported after lengthy trials and negotiations that "the hope is that television audience measurement for both the BBC and ITV will be carried out by a service of the electronic type at present used by ITCA, amended to accommodate the needs of the BBC; and this will be the only source of television audience measurement data." The BBC also reaffirmed its commitment to quality, pointing out that this agreed method of audience assessment "will involve a shift of resources away from the headcounting towards qualitative and audience appreciation studies, while continuing to meet in full the audience measurement requirements of the advertisers."[56]

What, in fact, happened was that ITV's activities had brought several issues into sharp focus. The most obvious was that in spite of years of careful tutelage, British viewers lapped up such programs as "Emergency Ward 10," "Popeye," "Robin Hood," and "Saturday Night at the London Palladium" when ITV offered them. To justify receiving license fees, the BBC countered by offering equally "popular" programs. In 1956, the BBC complained in its *Annual Report* that competition did not lead to better programming, but simply the same sort of programming on different channels; what listeners really required was complementary, not competitive, offerings.[57] By 1962, the BBC had proved it could match ITV programs; but did it want its reputation to rest on such gems as the "Billy Cotton Bandshow" and the "Black and White Minstrel Show?"[58]

The Pilkington committee report on broadcasting, published in 1962, was extremely critical of ITA, saying that it had failed properly to exercise its responsibilities. The report cited poor programming, poor control of advertising, and power wielded by the few large program companies, who simply sought profits.[59] A Conservative government, however, could scarcely admit to having made a mistake in promoting free enterprise, and ITV was much too popular to abolish. What the government could do was to institute still firmer legislation for ITA and allocate a second channel to the BBC, which could be used for "minority" programming. The prospect of another channel was offered to ITV, possibly in 1965, with the provision that ITA was to ensure that similar programs would not be shown at the same time.[60]

The Pilkington report also drew attention to the high profits being reaped by ITV. The government therefore introduced a levy on them, in addition to the ordinary income tax already paid. Now it was ITV's turn to consider the disadvantages of competition, particularly as franchises were reallocated in 1967. By 1970, far from welcoming a competitive commercial channel, companies already in existence wanted what the BBC had, a channel as a complement to what was already in place. Stephen Lambert says, "They too wanted the advantages of 'try-outs,' 'repeats,' and 'cost-rationalizations,' that a complementary channel could provide."[61] In spite of the vision that sustained ITV's founders, in less than twenty years, long-standing British attitudes to competition had resurfaced.

Debate over a possible second commercial channel continued through 1970; in 1977 the Annan committee recommended that a second commercial channel should be started, but should be altogether separate from IBA. Neither the Labour nor Conservative governments found that idea acceptable; so in 1979 a new commercial channel was authorized under the IBA's control, and in 1980 its constitution became law. The home secretary, William Whitelaw, made a speech in 1979 in which the responsibilities of the IBA regarding Channel 4 were made clear. The views expressed, like Haley's in 1949, would have been confusing to an American audience, because the rules of the game were so deliberately ambiguous. Whitelaw said that the IBA would "be expected not to allow rivalry for ratings between the two channels for which it has statutory responsibility, nor to allow scheduling designed to obtain for each of those services the largest possible audience over the week." The numbers game, as such, was not to be played. What was the IBA, then, to do? It was "to add different and greater satisfactions to those now available to the viewer."[62] Channel 4 was to get its programs as much as possible from companies not contracted for ITV, so as to provide opportunities for creative people now locked out of TV program production. It was to increase the number of regional programs and provide time for educational and Welsh programs. Nor was advertising to be competitive between the channels; instead, the ITV companies were to provide the budget for the new channel, and that budget was not to depend on the revenue generated by advertisements on Channel 4. Apparently, Channel 4 was to be commercial but not competitive.

Some of the ambiguities in Whitelaw's statements were cleared up in the Broadcasting Act itself; but as Lambert points out, a great deal of interpretation was left to the IBA. Whitelaw also stated in the debate on the bill that Channel 4 would be expected to become financially self-supporting "as soon as possible." Questions were raised in Parliament and outside it as to how programming was to be both innovative and financially healthy; they were not answered.[63]

In 1983, then, British broadcasting stood in ambiguous relation to the marketplace. It still does, although a committee was set up in 1985 to examine the question of allowing advertisements on the BBC. This ambiguity was reflected in sports programming, in that the service as well as the ratings facet of the industry was given more than lip service. The existence of Channel 4, with its mandate to be different, also affected sport. Channel 4 initially planned for only two one-hour weekly sports programs,[64] partly because the BBC and ITV both already covered sport well. But in these programs, the commissioning editor decided to broadcast "new" sports such as basketball, badminton, and American football, or "old" sports played by younger or older competitors than those usually seen.[65] No one assumed that these sorts of programs were necessarily going to set ratings records; they were broadcast specifically for minority interests.

The American and British TV industries do not have quite the same purposes; the audiences they have for sport make different demands. Obviously, the most popular televised sports in Britain and the United States are different. But the scanty available evidence suggests that differences go beyond that. I have found no precisely comparable figures between Britain and the United States, but in 1979 and 1980 the BBC asked "a quota sample of approximately 1000 adults" what sports they were "interested in." (What precisely respondents understood by the words "interested in" is not clear, nor whether they thought the question referred to participation, watching live or televised events, or all three.) The combined results of these surveys indicate that *none* of the ten top-ranked sports mentioned by men were mentioned by women, and vice versa.[66] The *Miller Lite Report* gives the replies of 1,139 randomly sampled Americans to the request, "Please tell me how interested you are generally in *watching* each of the following: [sports listed]." The results show that only three of the eleven top-ranked men's sports were not mentioned by women and vice versa. Further, football was ranked first by the men and tied for second place among the women, and baseball second by the men and tied for second place among the women.[67]

Another striking difference between Britain and the United States is that the traditionally British national games are not those in which the highest percentages of people, men or women, report that they are interested. For the men, cricket ranks fourth behind boxing, Rugby League, and Rugby Union football, while soccer is ninth, behind racing in cars, on motor bikes, and on bicycles. For the women soccer ranks fifteenth, and cricket twentieth.[68] In the United States, football and baseball emerge as the two sports most people like watching, however the question is phrased.[69] The range of interest is also different. In Britain there is a difference of only 12 percent between men interested in the top sport and in the tenth; in the United States, there is range of 48 percent between men who like to watch football and those who like to watch skiing, swimming/diving, or weight lifting, the sports equally ranked eighth.[70]

The sports surveys also reveal some similarities between Britain and the United States. Although a higher percentage of women in Britain say they are interested in watching sport, the range of women's interests is similar on both sides of the Atlantic: 67 percent of British women declare themselves to be interested in skating, and 43 percent in table tennis and golf, their tenth-ranked sports; 46 percent of U.S. women like to watch gymnastics and 22 percent track and field and marathon, their tenth-ranked sports. Thus, 24 percent fewer women declare themselves interested in their tenth-ranked than in their most watched sport, in Britain and America. Also, on both sides of the Atlantic more men than women claim to be interested in or to watch sports. Boxing ranks as the sport most men in the United Kingdom are interested in, and as the third sport American men like to watch, while it does not appear in the top ten or eleven sports women are interested in or like to watch in either the United States or Britain. Further, skating ranks first among British women and second among American women, while swimming, track and field (called athletics in Britain), tennis, and horse racing are among the top ten sports in which British women are interested and that American women like to watch.[71]

The BBC also asked their respondents to say whether or not they "usually" watched on TV the sports they claimed to be interested in, and found that some sports were watched on TV by a greater proportion of those interested in them than others. (This data was not reported by gender.) If the two surveys are combined, the greatest number of people claim to watch televised snooker followed by soccer, tennis, athletics, show jumping, skating, darts, wrestling, and cricket. Not surprisingly, given these interests and the relative amount of TV coverage accorded certain sports, more than 20 percent of respondents complained that snooker, darts, and wrestling were not televised often enough.[72]

On this evidence, it appears that American TV producers can be sure that they will have an audience if they televise football and baseball, and sure that their electronic seats will be empty if they show soccer. In Britain, the BBC has a more complicated task. Men and women do not necessarily want to watch the same sports; and they do not necessarily want to watch on TV the sports they claim to be most interested in. Without better comparative data it is impossible to decide why this should be so. It seems possible, however, that the community-bonding functions baseball and football provided in the years before television, and the paucity of opportunities for the development of other sports on a national rather than a regional basis in a sprawling, heterogeneous country, may account for American choices. (Darts, for instance, have been available in British pubs for generations.) But what is clear, is that in 1980 sports preferences on each side of the Atlantic were different.

In 1984 British professional sport, while obviously in the business of entertainment, is not simply one facet of the entertainment business, as it is in the United States. While professional players and teams in Britain benefit enormously from TV, British professional sport as such is not dependent on it to anything like the extent U.S. professional sport has become. This is not simply because American TV got into the market earlier and has had more time to buy its way in. Rather it is because the economic and social structure of British and American sports is entirely different.

The sports franchise does not exist in Britain; cricket and soccer are not financed as they are in the United States. No one owns a cricket or soccer club, and while to be invited to serve on the board of directors of either is regarded as an honor, it has often been a tribute to the length of one's purse, as club directors are always expected to bail their clubs out of financial trouble. Yet there is no way in Britain for a smart businessman to use a sports franchise as a tax shelter. Losses cannot be written off against other corporate activities, because the team is not owned by its board of directors.

Through the long history of cricket until 1962, professionals were carefully distinguished from amateurs and had no part in the running of the game. Cricket clubs were organized by gentlemen for gentlemen; as the national structure of cricket began to emerge, it was the county clubs that became the focus of the professional game. A club represented its county. In 1873 (characteristically, halfway through the season) the Marylebone Cricket Club (MCC), cricket's governing body, agreed on rules to decide who could play for a specific county.[73] The counties competed with each other, but were not at all interested in profit, partly because so many outstanding players were amateurs. Even in 1930, fewer than 60 percent of cricketers playing in what the MCC classified as first-class matches were professional.[74]

Although counties had a home ground, they did not expect to play most of their matches there. Rather, they took themselves to grounds around the county, so that everyone had an opportunity to see them play. County teams still continue this traditional and hopelessly uneconomic practice, although politicians have redrawn county boundaries in recent years and professional teams themselves (except Yorkshire) no longer require birth or even residence within a specific county, rendering county affiliation more or less meaningless. Yet, as Bale points out, on average six different places were used in 1950 for important matches for each of the seventeen county clubs; by 1980, the clubs were each using an average of 8.8 different grounds. This average is the more startling when one considers that two clubs, Nottingham and Middlesex, since before 1950 have played almost all their matches at a single site.[75]

This economic folly is not as crass as it appears, for professional cricket was never designed to make money. Club patrons cheerfully supplied the difference between club receipts and expenditures as a matter of course until after World War II, when taxation made such a use of money impossible. Boards of directors now have to take different steps to avoid a cricket team's falling into bankruptcy;[76] but they are not disposed to think of cricket itself as a marketable commodity. There is, in any case, no way in which individuals could secure a return on investment; nor is it worth spending a great deal on cricket to try to enhance one's own prestige.

The American football industry is specifically organized to corner the market. The British Football Association contains ninety-two professional clubs divided on basis of skill into four divisions, and talks of expanding into a yet larger association with a fifth division. However professional soccer is run and marketed in the First Division, the very existence of some professional soccer clubs is dependent on community effort. Many Third and Fourth Division soccer clubs are normally on the verge of bankruptcy. They are kept alive by subscriptions from their directors, and by supporters, who voluntarily organize raffles, dances, and other money-raising activities. As Malcolm Musgrove, the manager of Torquay United, a Fourth Division club, wrote in the program notes of the last game of 1974, "All supporters and officials have been working hard to raise money to make sure that the club remains in being as a League side." He went on to point out that Torquay's opponents, Swansea City, "are, if anything, in an even more serious position than we are."[77] Such clubs are not regarded as the property of an owner, but as in some sense part of the local community. It is true that professional soccer is much less expensive to run than professional football, and traveling is far less costly in a country that can be fitted comfortably six times into Texas. But no soccer club board of directors could conceivably threaten to move their franchise to another city because they did not like their present supporters or facilities.

Soccer has always been more commercialized than cricket; the soccer clubs that formed the Football League in 1888 were organized by men who knew how to run soccer as a business. But these clubs were not owned by individuals, and all fell under the jurisdiction of the Football Association and Football League. As George Keeton puts it, "The articles and memoranda of association of football clubs must fill outside persons with a feeling of wonder, for they bear no relation to modern company practice, and may give the impression that they were drafted on an offday in a fit of absence of mind – as perhaps they were."[78] Some professional clubs are also private; transfer of shares is therefore restricted. Shares have often gone to people uninterested in the game, or may never have been formally transferred. This lack of interest is not surprising since many professional clubs either never pay dividends or defer dividends for years. Football club shares are not quoted on the Stock Exchange.

This cavalier attitude to finance arose because when the game was first professionalized, it was run by the upper class who wanted to preserve the local loyalties soccer had always inspired and to make sure that the game was not ruined by money-grubbing. All articles of association of a new club therefore had to be approved by the council, and without exception, clubs were required to limit dividends, which in practice have been kept to 7.5 percent, or 5 percent tax free. Although the upper class soon departed, vestiges of its outlook remained. Directors cannot be paid, either as directors or employees, so no active player or manager can serve on a board; for many years no one who had ever been a professional player was allowed to serve on a board. As Desmond Morris puts it, "The directors remain the last outpost of what might be called the amateur enthusiasm of the Victorian era. And so we have the strange contradiction of a vast, modern, sporting industry run by unpaid part-timers as a kind of hobby."[79]

The northern and midland clubs that rapidly came to dominate the professional game were organized by middle-class businessmen who paid lip service to the ideals of sportsmanship, but whose main concern was their club's prestige. They wanted professional players because professionals normally played better than amateurs; they did not, however, want to be held to ransom by talented players. So they agreed on a *maximum* wage that any player could earn, a restriction on players' opportunities that remained in operation until 1961. As the popularity of soccer grew, more and more clubs sought to join the league; directors of aspiring clubs dipped into their own pockets to buy players from other clubs (the fees for such transactions going into the selling club's coffers, not to the player's pocket), to hire managers, and to pay whatever club expenses seemed necessary to get their club into the league, and then to move up the various divisions. Paradoxically, even by the 1920s, most directors knew what kind of club they served and to what level of play it could and should aspire. To move up a division was of much less importance than to avoid moving down.

Similarly, a curious gentility ran through all the clubs' affairs. To this day, rituals remain. The home team directors may entertain the visiting team's board to drinks in the boardroom before the match; the two sets of directors then watch the first half of the match from the same box, although they sit separately. At halftime, tea is served in the boardroom, and a meal with tea after the match.[80]

For a soccer club has never been the private plaything of owners, but a community heritage. To be invited to serve as a director, therefore, is to have been given an accolade by one's peers; one cannot simply decide, as Americans do, to go out and buy a football team. Symbolically, the League and Association Cups are presented on the field, not in the dressing room, and not to the directors or manager (coach), but to the captain in the midst of his winning team. The losers, far from slinking away, are given medals; the crowd applauds them heartily also. Few British fans could name their team's board of directors; few American fans would not know their team's owner.

The structure of the British sports industry means that television cannot be used simply as a marketing device. There is no bidding war in Britain between networks to secure exclusive rights to particular sporting events; by agreement, the six major national sporting events, "Wimbledon, The Derby, the Grand National, the Cup Final, Test Cricket and the Boat Race,"[81] can be covered by both BBC and ITV, although ITV does not necessarily choose to show them all. Soccer officials are worried about what television will do to the game; in a report on sports broadcasting published in 1974, the BBC noted that the Football League's restrictions "include a ban on the 'live' coverage of matches and on the showing of recorded coverage before 10:00 pm, on the day of the match."[82] The Football League's ninety-two clubs in 1986 still do not regard television as a boon, anxious as they are to keep the party going at the gate.

This fear arises partly from the small sums, in American terms, that British television executives have to offer sports promoters. In 1974, the BBC's entire "annual expenditure on sport, both internal and external, amounts to some six-and-a-half million pounds" – at that time, less than eighteen million dollars.[83] There is no means by which the sums of money U.S. networks raise can be generated in Britain. Even in 1974, BBC officials were worried by the specter of U.S. exclusive rights to international events and their concomitant fees jeopardizing all the BBC's other sports programming. Nor can the British TV industry afford to pay very much to major sporting bodies in Britain. As the BBC put it, "If the less popular sports are to continue to get a proper look in, the major sports will have to show more realism and exercise some form of restraint in their financial demands."[84]

In using TV as their primary marketing device, American sports promoters are merely reflecting one facet of U.S. public life, its domination by electronic media.[85] Important as "the telly" is in Britain, it does not yet stand in the same relationship to public life and institutions, and probably never will. Much more important, however, is the fact that cricket and soccer are still not regarded in Britain primarily as commercial products. Those responsible for promoting professional cricket and soccer have often been ready to dig into their own pockets to support their team, and continue to do so; they have also encouraged members' and supporters' clubs. It is easy to think of ways in which cricket and soccer could be made more profitable; but even if they were, there is at present no entertainment tradition in Britain into which sports telecasting could readily be tied. The televising of cricket and soccer in Britain is done technically in ways similar to that of sports telecasting in the United States, but its purposes, rationale, and therefore its end product, are different. Cricket and soccer, then, are the subject of the next two chapters.

6

CRICKET

It has always pleased the British to pretend that no one but themselves can understand cricket. In a *Political and Economic Planning* report published in 1956 the authors wrote that cricket is "a peculiarly English game; not suitable for export and found only in places where Englishmen have taken it. Cricket is an expression of the national character and, as such, inscrutable."[1] Foreigners have aided and abetted this delusion; a book written by a Dutchman used cricket to illustrate the title, *The English: Are They Human?* In fact, cricket is structurally quite simple; had it not been, it would hardly have been chosen as a vehicle for "civilizing" Queen Victoria's overseas subjects.

Cricket's complexity lies in the skill with which it is played; one would, however, never guess it from the Marylebone Cricket Club's "explanation" of the game to overseas visitors:

> You have two sides, one out in the field and one in. Each man that's in the side that's in goes out and when he's out he comes in and the next man goes in until he's out. When they are all out the side that's out comes in and the side that's been in goes out and tries to get those coming in out. Sometimes you get men still in and not out. When both sides have been in and out including the not-outs, that's the end of the game.[2]

A more specific guide to the game can be found in the Appendix. But

112

cricket's charm lies in more than its rules, for like baseball it is steeped in tradition.

Just as Spalding was determined to provide baseball with a respectable American pedigree, nineteenth and early twentieth century Englishmen were concerned to make the ancestry of the game that was the hallmark of the British Empire equal to its station.[3] Their efforts were misguided; we are not likely to know whether cricket is in fact derived from medieval games such as "trap-ball," "stool-ball," or "cat and dog." What is clear is that what had been a boys' game in Tudor times was being played seriously by men a century later; in 1700 cricket matches were advertised and the results recorded in newspapers.[4] Brookes suggests that the landed aristocracy took up and developed the game during the eighteenth century because it "offered an opportunity to re-enact vestiges of an earlier life-style in a setting which combined the maximum of excitement with the minimum of danger."[5]

In the early eighteenth century, cricket matches were played between aristocratic teams for wagers; in 1733 the Prince of Wales donated a silver cup to be competed for between a rival team and one selected by himself.[6] Cricket was the pastime of the gentry, whose wealth was firmly based on land. The rules under which matches were to be played were first drawn up specifically for each game, then gradually codified as "laws." The eighteenth-century game was often watched by the villagers and tenants of the estates on which it was played; but the rules were drawn up not to amuse the spectators, but to ensure an enjoyable match for the players, for whom wagering on the outcome was part and parcel of the game itself. When Parliament was sitting, the gentry found themselves in London; so they began to play at the Artillery Ground. Here, they attracted swarms of spectators, ordinary workers who came to gamble, to watch the game, and to inspect their rulers' athletic prowess. By 1751 about 10,000 spectators, or about 2 percent of London's total population, were watching these London matches. Spectators were not admitted free. The first recorded admission charge of two pence was made in 1744.[7]

Cricket was patronized and played by the gentry; but it was not their exclusive preserve. As rivalries grew between patrons, some gamekeepers, gardeners, and other estate workers who showed themselves to be talented cricketers spent some of their working days playing matches set up by their employers. Independent "professional" cricketers were also ready to play for money; the game could not support anyone wholly during the eighteenth century, but it provided an enjoyable part-time summer job.

From its inception as a codified sport, cricket was tied closely to place and to class. By 1750, a good cricketer in the south of England could find estate employment that would enable him to turn out for a famous village team such as Sliden or Hambledon. Nor was the pay a small consideration. In Hambledon in 1775, players who held other jobs were paid "for practising," and for actually playing "might get between three or four shillings a day," almost three times an agricultural worker's daily wage.[8]

Besides village teams, teams loosely based on county affiliations were put together by aristocratic patrons. The patrons often played as members of whatever teams they organized; and on the field, duke and ploughman were equal, in that the patron did not expect to be tenderly treated. No doubt a duke often appeared higher in the batting order than his skills deserved; but there were plenty of other leisure pursuits open to the wealthy, and it is unlikely that ducal duffers would have been anxious to play at all. Yet equality as players did not mean that class consciousness disappeared; far from it. The tradition of "gentlemen" and "players" derived from the earliest days of cricket; dukes and ploughmen could play comfortably together precisely because both were assured of their respective places in the societal hierarchy and no activities on a cricket pitch could enhance or detract from them.

Eighteenth-century cricket did not look like modern cricket; the bats were curved, the wicket was a low affair of two sticks with a third one on top, and the bowler bowled underarm.[9] Precise rules were agreed on for each match. This is not to say the game was unformed; far from it.

In 1752 the *New Universal Magazine* published the first printed version of cricket rules, described as "The Game at Cricket, as settled by the CRICKET CLUB, in 1744, and play'd at the ARTILLERY GROUND, LONDON."[10] The length of the pitch, height of the wicket, and weight of the ball were stated, as were methods of scoring and dismissal of batsmen, and the duties of the umpires. In 1771 a match was played for fifty pounds a side between Hambledon and Chertsey; one player brought along a bat that was as wide as the wicket, which nearly cost Hambledon the match. Accordingly, the Hambledon club promptly limited the bat's width to 4¼ inches, a law included in the 1774 revisions and that stands to this day.[11]

Nothing was said in these early laws about the preparation or state of the wicket. The game was usually played on bumpy, ill-kept turf.[12] Nevertheless, cricket flourished, in villages and schools. A farmer recorded in his diary on July 10, 1778, that the Chatham Village Club had lost many of its members to the navy's press-gang, busily collecting recruits to suppress what the British called the American Revolution and the colonists the War of Independence. "No wonder they was beat," the farmer wrote of his cricket club.[13]

So prevalent was wagering on the game that from 1774 to 1884 the laws of cricket "contained special rules dealing with the settlement of bets made in connection with cricket matches."[14] To wager was the mark of an eighteenth-century gentleman; large sums were laid on one's cricket team as one would lay them on one's horse. Obviously, to win then mattered very much to the paid players because their welfare was tied closely to the approbation of their employers. But a wager was an affair of honor; the game had therefore to be played according to the spirit of whatever rules applied to the game. To wager was not, therefore, regarded as the same thing as gambling.

But by the early nineteenth century, spectators were openly gambling at big matches and frequent attempts were made to bribe players.[15] Aristocratic patronage of the game accordingly waned. During the late eighteenth century, the gentry had increasingly sought to play in private, fenced grounds, such as the one enclosed by Thomas Lord in 1787, where they would not be inspected by a rabble of uninvited guests.[16] Lord had a fine sense of Novak's "sacred space." When his landlord raised the rent, and Lord was forced to move to St. John's Wood, he dug up the old turf and moved it to the new site. When this ground was threatened by the building of the Regent Canal, he dug up the turf once more and moved it half a mile north, where "Lord's" still stands.[17] During the nineteenth century the Marylebone Cricket Club, which took Lord's as its headquarters, came to assume the role of arbiter of English cricket.

During the late eighteenth and early nineteenth centuries, cricket became a popular middle-class game, as industrialization changed the relationship between tenant and landlord. Nurtured, however, as a game for the independently wealthy, cricket retained its amateur standing, even as it gained in popularity.

By the mid-nineteenth century, to play cricket was the mark of a gentleman, but to accept payment for doing so was to put oneself irretrievably beyond the societal pale. By the 1820s the MCC was run by middle-class gentlemen, not aristocrats. These men were intent on making their status clear. By 1850 the Gentlemen versus Players match, begun in 1806, was one of the most popular at Lord's. The importance of gentlemanly, i.e. amateur, status was underlined by the raising of admission prices for this and for other very popular matches, Eton versus Harrow, and Oxford versus Cambridge, to ensure an audience of the "right sort."[18] While professionals were allowed to play cricket on some teams, it was made clear to them that control of the game was to remain in the hands of amateurs; the latter, after all, understood sportsmanship. It was in this spirit that village clergymen sponsored cricket. As the vicar of Camber in Kent wrote in 1866, "I established cricket not so much for my own amusement but because it improved the morals of the labouring classes and often kept them from places where they could come to harm."[19] The white man's burden was to be carried at home too.

It was the professionals, however, who changed the game into the one we now know, by refusing to bowl underarm. The argument about overarm bowling raged furiously in the 1820s; in 1828 the MCC allowed the hand to be raised to the elbow, and the arm to swing round outward and horizontally. By 1835, the hand could be raised to the shoulder, but full overarm bowling was still not permitted.[20] In 1846, William Clarke selected the first All-England XI organized to play a schedule of matches, a team of professionals who would play local teams, which were allowed to field up to twenty-two players to make up for their lack of skill. Local teams vied to play the best; local clubs provided hospitality.[21] The All-England XI played between twenty and twenty-five matches a season; its members could, for the first time, count on playing full-time during the summers. They made little enough money, and in 1852 the United XI of England was set up by professionals who felt Clarke had exploited them. There was opportunity for both; spectators crowded to see them. These professionals persisted in bowling overarm; by 1864, the amateurs who led the MCC had to give way before the tide of public sentiment for this overarm bowling the professionals had created.[22]

Meanwhile, county clubs had been building their teams, mostly a mixture of amateur and professional players. Problems arose in 1865 when the traditional feud between the north and south of England found expression among professional cricket players; northerners felt that for some years they had not been selected fairly by promoters of special matches and tours such as the first to Australia in 1861. In 1866, northern professionals refused to play cricket in the south of England at all. Their position was interpreted by the *Times* as a strike.[23] The MCC banned the offending northern players from Lord's.

In any case, the day of the professional elevens was done. Stronger than other teams they played, the outcome of their games was rarely in doubt; county cricket not only offered fans a geographical base for loyalty, but also matches that were less predictable. It is interesting, however, to note the nature of the charges leveled against the professional players of the 1860s.

These cricketers were accused of the sins of professional baseball players in the 1970s. They were "too prosperous," and were thoroughly selfish, caring only about their own performances, not those of the team. They turned sport into work, and behaved like trade unionists. They had none of the love of the game that dignifies the true sportsman.[24] In the 1860s, however, it was not possible to blame television for such disasters. Rather, the source of the evil was regarded as professionalism itself. The MCC drew an inevitable conclusion; the professionals were useful employees, but it would clearly never do to let them into management. Cricket, England's national game, must reflect English national character. By definition, national virtues cannot be bought, so the reins must be firmly held by those whose sources of income enabled them to regard cricket as an avocation.

Amateurs, then, controlled cricket. Employment, however, was available for professionals as the county base of cricket steadily expanded. In 1870 there were only twenty-two regular county fixtures, but by 1880 there were fifty.[25] The idea of a county championship was mooted as early as 1873, but exactly who should compete and what residence rules should be required of players was a subject of considerable controversy. In 1894, it was finally agreed that "first-class Counties" should be those whose matches against each other and some other "first-class" teams such as "the Australians" were "used in the compilation of first-class batting and bowling averages" by the MCC.[26] There was no finite number of first-class counties; the MCC had authority to add to or subtract from the list. In 1890, there were seven first-class counties, and fifteen by 1905.[27]

But while all this organization was developing, it epitomized the nineteenth-century British establishment's attitude to competition. To win was certainly very desirable, but one's team had to win within the spirit as well as the letter of the law. When in 1883 the MCC decided revision of the laws of cricket was needed, the subcommittee empowered to draft the revisions was instructed to do it "by defining terms, supplying omissions, and better wording, but without altering the spirit of the game."[28] The 1884 laws among other changes legalized six instead of four-ball overs, and introduced boundaries, but made no alterations that had a significant effect on the conduct of the game.

Eric Dunning and Kenneth Sheard suggest that the split between professional and amateur cricket players was underlined because many "gentlemen" who were products of the industrial revolution were uncertain of their status. While dukes and squires could play without fuss among their tenants in the eighteenth century, by the end of the nineteenth the social gap between many professional and amateur cricketers had been ordained by Mammon rather than God. So the professionals were required not only to know their place, but to demonstrate that they knew it, by using separate changing rooms and entrances to the ground, using separate accommodations at away matches, never aspiring to be the team captain, and seeing their initials printed on the scorecards after their surnames, to distinguish them from the amateurs, whose initials appeared before their surnames. Professionals addressed amateurs as "sir," and did odd jobs at the ground. Professionals accepted these "varieties of ritual and symbolic subordination" because playing cricket for a living was apparently preferable to most other occupations open to them,[29] and because "to know one's place" was the hallmark of English society. Further, because "gentlemen" played on the team, and "gentlemen" watched, professional cricketers had a higher status on and off the field than professional soccer players. They were part of a quiet, respectable, controlled, and leisurely game; just as servants acquired status from the master for whom they worked, so first-class professional cricketers acquired a social status by the end of the nineteenth century that soccer players never achieved.

Because amateurs played alongside professionals on the best cricket teams, cricket remained the game played by all classes. When soccer became professionalized, British boarding schools turned to rugby. When rugby became professional, Rugby Union football was carefully distinguished from Rugby League football, so that no taint of money-grubbing should smirch a game played by the upper class. It was, however, much easier to integrate professionals into cricket than into soccer, because county cricket matches lasted three days, and a test match five.[30] Although workers could and did take days off to watch particular games, the majority of spectators and almost all the club members had to have the kind of leisure only "gentlemen" could afford. Amateurs were therefore playing before their peers, rather than simply before the hoi poloi; nor was there actual physical contact in the game itself. An amateur could therefore maintain his social status although playing the game on equal footing with professionals. Further, cricket epitomized the myth of rural continuity and peace, which the gentry believed to constitute the essence of England. By 1851, less than half the population was living outside towns; but as the nineteenth century ended, the heart of England was still conceived to be in the country.[31]

While county cricket was attracting paid spectators in the early twentieth century, amateur games became the staple fare of Edwardian country-house living. Amateur games were also played on the village green, and cricket was played in every school. Few English boys, however much they despised playing hearty games, could escape using a cricket bat and ball; many took them up with delight and laid them down reluctantly. Spectators, whether family members of the village or workers' teams, or regular supporters of county matches, were quiet, orderly, and attentive. No one dreamed of shouting at the umpire or the players; a good shot or smart piece of fielding by either team was applauded, and one had to sense, rather than hear, the satisfaction that good play by the home team assured.[32]

In fact, unlike baseball and football franchises, cricket clubs were not organized primarily to attract spectators. A county match was a ritual, not an entertainment. Indeed, the game was and still is controlled by the players. The captain decides on the batting order, and may require batsmen to use particular tactics at certain stages of the game. The captain decides who shall bowl and for how long, although the bowler often places his own field, and may vary it when he wishes. Players are therefore under the authority of a man who is *primus inter pares,* with whom they can readily discuss matters between matches, not someone who does not play and whose job it is to maneuver them into a "winning combination."

Little was and is done during the game to keep the spectator informed. Football officials, for instance, early learned to communicate with the spectators, and baseball umpires' signs were large enough for everyone to see. Cricket umpires use a variety of signals that an alert fan can watch, but these signs are designed to give information to the scorer, who is out of earshot. (The scorer is required to signal the umpire before play can go on.) Cricket scoring is complicated; every ball must be accounted for. It is therefore the umpire's job to convey to the scorer what decision has been made, whenever the situation calls for it; if anyone else comprehends the umpire's signals, well and good. But the umpire makes no particular effort to communicate with anyone except the players and the scorer; the scoreboard is supposed to give the fan whatever information he may need to assess the state of play.

Cricket on these terms survived the first World War; it was a casualty of the second. The leisured class that played in and watched county cricket matches and kept the county clubs going through their subscriptions had been swept away by taxation; the distinction between professional and amateurs, virtually dead in the 1950s, was formally dropped in 1962. Even without the war, it is questionable whether cricket could have remained a game in which amateurs held their own against professionals much beyond the 1940s. In 1900 there were eighteen amateurs in the top twenty batting averages; by 1935 there were only five amateurs in the top thirty. In 1938 the Players lost to the Gentlemen at Lords; it was only their second loss there since 1914. Between 1890 and 1899, the Gentlemen had won three matches, the Players four, while three games were drawn.[33] Work, even for the young man who could afford to play first-class cricket as an amateur, had become more demanding and time-consuming after World War I; the depression had affected attitudes as well as finances.

After World War II, there was a brief resurgence of spectator interest in cricket; then it became clear that no new generation of the leisured was able or willing to support the game. Counties found it more and more difficult to pay their bills as their gate receipts dropped drastically. In 1949, 51,250 people paid £4,441 to see Surrey play Middlesex; in 1959, 45,000 paid £4,800. By 1972, 1,933 people paid £682, and in 1974, 1,401 paid £586.[34] Promising young athletes looked twice at the prospect of becoming professional in a game that no longer provided minimal security and was becoming subtly less prestigious to boot.[35]

Cricket appeared to survive by adapting. The Gillette Company offered to sponsor a knockout, one-day competition between first-class counties. The first cup was awarded in 1963; in 1964 the top five teams in the Minor Counties Championship were allowed to compete.[36] The whole point of the Gillette Cup was that only a limited number of overs could be bowled; to win, therefore, batsmen had to try to hit more or less every ball they received. Rashness does not pay in a match that lasts three days; in a limited-over match it may be the only sensible course. More hits mean more runs, more excitement, better fielding; and a result is to be had at the end of a day's match. Spectators who did not care to watch only part of a three-day match started flocking back to the grounds. The John Player Company then sponsored an even shorter match; aggressive, speedy play had come to stay. But was this new game, in fact, cricket? Or was it simply entertainment? In 1970, the founder and editor of the *Cricket Quarterly,* Roland Bowen, published a history of cricket that he considered its epitaph. He wrote, "Its rise was an accident of geography and social history, and, maybe, of one or two other local factors: its esteem during the best part of its healthy life was something quite definitely accidental as it became a kind of hand-maiden of the British Empire: and its decline was as inevitable as was the decline of that Empire." Bowen believed that the cricketing establishment had failed to grasp the nature of the social and economic changes postwar Britain was undergoing and had allowed first-class cricket to sink into a trough from which he believed it could not be rescued. He maintained that postwar cricket statistics all told the same melancholy story; fewer centuries and runs scored, fewer wickets taken, all signs of the "general falling-off of batting and bowling ability." The retention by the cricketing establishment of the outmoded, and by 1970 almost meaningless, county cricket system, had effectively banished amateurs from the first-class game; the lack of spectators at county matches, and the resulting pay scales, had ensured the employment of what Bowen considered simply mediocre professionals.[37] The new, limited-over, cricket he did not deign to consider.

By the 1970s, English cricket had a split personality. County matches still lasted three days and a test match five, but the cricketers who played in them spent a good deal of their match time in games that required quite different techniques.[38] In a forty-over match, batsmen had little practice in "playing themselves in"; that is, hitting only balls that they could hit safely until they had got the true measure of the bowler's skill and the wicket's condition. Bowlers became "solely reliant on length and line,"[39] which work well when desperate batsmen cannot wait for a loose ball, but which threaten few wickets in a longer match.

Further, the number of overs any one bowler could bowl was restricted in a limited-over match, both to provide variety and to stop defensive, and hence dull, play.[40] This offered a place on the team to a player who could bat well and bowl well, but do neither so well that he would be worth his place in a test match, which lasted so much longer. It also served to reduce opportunities for the player who was good enough for a test, but not so good an all-rounder as to make himself useful in forty overs. Cricket, in short, was becoming less specialized as it paradoxically moved along faster.

Yet in county and test cricket, the old varieties of batting and bowling were needed; so the best cricketers now required what amounted to two different sets of skills. John Arlott, however, argues that cricket has "developed" rather than changed; and "that the changes have not been fundamental but rather a matter of degree." He concedes that test-match batting is not what it was, and agrees with Bowen in thinking that lack of talent may be responsible. Arlott notes a decline in spin bowling, but he also remarks on the immensely improved fielding limited-over cricket has caused, which in itself has affected batting. His most interesting point, however, concerns changes in strategy.

Babe Ruth altered baseball because he could hit home runs. Arlott describes how Mike Smith's consistent hitting of slow left-arm spin bowling through the leg-side led inexorably to the demise of the wrist-spinner in cricket. The fast bowlers' use of the "bouncer" led to the adoption of protective headgear for batsmen. Neither of these changes is related to the needs of a forty-over match, but they have altered the game a fan sees. They are part of the continuous duel between bowler and batsman that has always been the heart of the game.[41]

Bowen perhaps represents Ring Lardner, and Arlott, James Lovitt, for certainly cricket's audience has changed. Spectators no longer gather respectfully to watch masters of an art, but wait to be entertained in a way that they can readily grasp and that is soon over. H. A. Harris, a historian who knows and loves cricket, summed up the views of the old school when he wrote in 1975, "Any detached observer has reluctantly to admit that most of what passes for top-level cricket today is the wrong kind of cricket played by the wrong kind of cricketer to titillate the wrong kind of spectator. No one would wish any aspiring youngster to imitate it."[42] But the new kind of cricket pays the bills.

Edward Buscombe believes that "one-day cricket has developed largely because sponsors were prepared to put money into it on account of the advertising it would bring them in television."[43] The MCC accepted limited-over cricket because the other means they had taken to bring back spectators, such as shortening boundaries, limiting the number of fielders on the leg-side, allowing no more than 100 overs in the first innings of a county match, and fiddling about with bonus points, had singularly failed. In 1974, Surrey County Cricket Club's gate receipts for eleven days of one-day home matches amounted to £9,609; thirty-three days of cricket in eleven home county matches raised only £5,831. Throughout the country, John Player League gates doubled from 1969 to 1976.[44] Professional cricket in Britain now lives by one-day matches.

Whether or not the sponsors have got their money's worth is a moot point. After ten years of sponsorship only a very few people questioned in a market research study "associated Gillette products with cricket's Gillette Cup." While BBC audiences for one-day matches climbed steadily, the total remained small;[45] we may soon see cricket only on Channel 4, the channel devoted to minority interests.

In May 1977, an Australian businessman, Kerry Packer, forced cricketers throughout the world to consider what their sport actually represented.[46] He signed contracts with thirty-five world-class players and offered contracts to others to play cricket on a circuit he would control. The matches would be shown on his Australian television channel, and the cricketers would be handsomely compensated. Packer's "circus," as it was soon dubbed, would perform without benefit of the International (formerly Imperial) Cricket Conference, cricket's governing body. Public uproar greeted Packer's proposals, and the positions taken revealed quite clearly what values were attached to cricket.

The establishment stood firm. Members of the International Cricket Conference and of the boards of national cricket associations affiliated to it held that Packer's proposals would reduce the game to a shambles. He intended to play games by floodlight so as to attract people who worked all day, to use a white ball, which was more easily followed than the conventional red leather one, to allow bowling that would be dangerous to the batsman but exciting for the spectators, and generally to enliven the game. He also proposed to arrange World Series Cricket matches with total disregard for the existing national and international fixture lists, banking on the fact that his higher pay scales for the players would induce them to play for him rather than for national associations. Many British fans backed the ICC's stand; in their view, one-day cricket had already sufficiently altered the game, and they had no desire to see it emasculated still further. They were also concerned lest the historic ties between counties and cricket, already tenuous, be snapped altogether, because they doubted that cricket could survive as a mere spectacle.

Many players regarded the situation differently. Since the end of World War II, the mystique of being a professional cricketer had been steadily eroding; one-day cricket had taught all players to regard themselves as entertainers. If their primary function was to please crowds, why not sign up with a man who proposed to pay them five times as much as their present employers, give them much greater TV exposure, and put them before bigger crowds at the grounds?

Further, the professionals had been simmering for years. Fred Trueman, one of the best fast bowlers ever to play for England, summed up in his autobiography what many of them felt. Trueman was born in 1931; as he said, "The kind of person dominating cricket throughout most of my career came from a wealthy family, played cricket for his university and then a county without ever proving much. The game was full of people like this, relics from the Victorian era."[47] Although the distinction between amateur and professional had been finally abolished in 1962, it remained in the minds of those who governed cricket. Members of the national and international boards simply could not grasp what the fuss was about; not dependent on the game for economic survival themselves, they had no inkling of the feelings and aspirations of those who were. They had never learned to examine criticism; in 1960, for instance, the Surrey committee withdrew Jim Laker's pass to the Oval, their ground, because he published *Over To Me*,[48] a book in which he made some very forthright comments about the game. The MCC subsequently withdrew Laker's honorary membership. At the same time, player contracts were tightened up so as to prevent publication of such materials in the future, in the name of not harming the game. In 1960, the gulf between management and player was already ominously wide.[49]

The chairman of the Australian Cricket Board, Robert Parish, pointed out in a speech in May 1978 that the pay of Australian first-class cricketers had substantially increased since 1974. He was quite right, but failed to mention that compared to the rewards of international soccer or tennis players, cricketers' earnings could only be considered derisory. He also overlooked the fact that however interested Australians have been in cricket, the attitudes of Australian fans have not necessarily been those of the British. As early as the 1890s, Australians were in the plebeian habit of shouting to the players during matches.[50] In 1914, cricket in New South Wales was in a parlous financial condition; suggestions were seriously made that the rules should be changed to force the batsmen to score at least once an over, and that the bowlers should bowl two overs from the same end, to eliminate the waiting about after every over.[51] During World War I, in fact, the class differences between the workers who wanted sport to be fun and the middle class who thought of sport as a means of character building were clearly articulated in Australia.[52]

For Parish, as for members of the cricketing establishment worldwide, money was not really the issue. For them, cricket had a transcendent value; as in the 1930s, "cricket symbolized the cultural hegemony of British social values and their successful transfer from generation to generation throughout the Empire."[53] Board members, from international to county levels, many fans, and some professionals found it hard to conceive that men who had grown up in traditional cricket, a game steeped in ritual and sportsmanship, could lightly turn their backs on it.

Many professionals, however, saw no reason why they should not regard their cricketing skills as a marketable commodity. They felt quite capable of playing in Packer's "circus" when it was functioning, and playing in test matches as well; in their view the ICC was simply acting to restrain trade, and was concerned less with the "purity of the game" than with the existing power structure.

Packer ran his "circus" in 1978 at a heavy loss, but was estimated to have broken even in 1979. He stopped it from January 1980, because in 1979 the Australian Cricket Board granted to Packer's Channel 9 exclusive TV rights for test and other Australian matches. The board had previously announced that these rights would be put out to tender; they also offered Packer more than the contract. They "agreed to consider favorably the introduction of the 30 yard circle in limited-over matches, day/night matches, and on an experimental basis, the use of colored clothing in Benson and Hedges one-day limited overs international matches."[54]

In a sense, both sides had won. In 1978-79 the England-Australia test match series had lost money for the first time in Australia's history because many cricketers were playing for World Series Cricket (WSC) instead, and the public did not choose to pay to watch any but the most representative sides. But cricket was only one of Packer's many business ventures; he was quoted as saying that he would probably not have started WSC had he had to do it all over again.[55] He had got in 1979 what he wanted in 1976; exclusive TV rights for cricket as it was run and presented by the ICC.

Certainly Packer's intervention had shaken up the cricketing world. But what the whole brouhaha demonstrated was not merely that some professional cricketers and the ICC were poles apart, but that money talks. Those who played in Packer's "circus" knew well that they were not playing the game on which they cut their teeth; Packer may have had a very shrewd suspicion that while spectators might flock for a while to what E. W. Swanton called "blood-and-thunder cricket which will have a curiosity value to some,"[56] their easily attracted attention could be as easily diverted by the next marketing specialist with capital and a gimmick.

The ICC was glad to let the dust settle, although some member countries felt that the Australians had let them down by agreeing to experiment with innovations. Gordon Ross, writing in *Wisden,* was able to assure British readers that even one-day international matches would not be wrecked, for "England would refuse to play in colored clothing and suffer any of the other intolerable gimmicks of WSC television presentation."[57]

Television came to cricket at a time when its traditional place in England was already being supplanted. After World War II, increased mobility and increased disposable income for many members of the working class, coupled with increased taxation and decreased leisure for the upper class, had fundamentally changed the public attitudes that supported cricket. When cricket was televised, it proved excellent for the fan, but less enticing for the spectator.

At first sight, cricket would seem to possess structural features that make it excellent for TV. The camera crew knows where to start; the bowler must deliver six balls from one end of the pitch to a batsman defending a fixed wicket. Close-ups can show not only the bowler's and batsman's action, but the work of the wicket keeper and the fielders close by, the "slips." The total pitch can also be shown so that the position of the fielders is made clear. The small ball is large enough to see on the screen, and can be delivered fast or slowly and hit in a variety of ways to a number of places.

Statistics are frequently superimposed on the picture, including the state of play, the performance of individuals batting and bowling in past and present test matches, team batting and bowling averages, and whatever else can be wrung out of a computer. The scoreboard, itself a mass of numbers, is usually shown between overs.

Thanks to the information presented visually, and the close-ups and replays, the most subtle features of cricket can be seen much better by a TV viewer than at the ground. But cricket, as a TV sport for the uninitiated, possesses some fatal flaws.

There are few predictable crises in cricket. Unless one stays glued to the set throughout a match, one may miss most of the "events" that influence the final result. No one can foretell when a bowler, toiling away over after over, will suddenly take a wicket. If he then dismisses the next batsman on the following ball, there is the possibility of his getting a third wicket on his next ball, a "hat trick." But this does not often occur; the tension it produces is palpable, but there is no equivalent of a third down and long yardage, or two balls and two strikes with two outs.

The outcome of the play is also unpredictable. While everyone knows where play begins, in that the bowler must deliver the ball from a set place, there is no movement equivalent to the way in which the quarterback takes the snap that will help the camera crew decide in what form the cricket play may develop. Further, to follow the ball when it is hit is to miss the placement of the fielders. There is no problem for fans, who have the field set in their mind's eye, because it has been shown to them several times by the camera. But for spectators, who did not know what they were supposed to be concentrating on when they saw the whole field in a long camera shot, the ball now appears to be traveling over an unmarked expanse of grass in a completely random fashion. Yet if the ball is not followed in close-up, any good hit will result in camera shots of the whole or most of the field, on which pigmy white-clad figures are mysteriously moving or standing still.

There are gaps in the game. The action stops after every six balls are delivered and there is no huddle from which players are coming and going, or bullpen action. Even after a ball is bowled, nothing may happen, as the batsman may decide not to attempt to hit the ball, or merely block it.

Spectators like action; they always have. In an 1886 test match, a batsman scored just thirty-four runs in 3¾ hours. A verse appeared later in *Mr. Punch:*[58]

> And the clock's slow hands go round,
> And you still keep up your sticks,
> But, oh, for the lift of a smiting hand,
> And the sound of a swipe for six.
>
> Block, block, block,
> At the foot of thy wickets, ah, do!
> But one hour of Grace or Walter Read
> Were worth a week of you![59]

In test matches, the pace is so leisurely that it is almost impossible to translate it to a living-room setting, except for fans who are settling down exactly as they would at a game. On August 1, 1977, on the fourth day of a test match, an average of one minute and thirty-seven seconds elapsed between the early overs, and fifteen seconds between the time a ball was hit and it was bowled again. During this time no action was taking place except that of the bowler walking back to take his run, rubbing the ball on his trousers to make it come off the pitch with a little more movement. While action replays of batsmen can be shown in such moments, it can't be done on every ball; and fast bowlers move fast only when they are actually delivering the ball. Often as much as thirty seconds elapsed between one ball's delivery and the next. Test cricketers apparently ignore the preferences of spectators, as test matches are now even slower than they used to be. As Arlott points out, in a test match between England and the West Indies in 1957, bowlers managed to average 110 overs a day. In 1980, in one match the West Indies bowled an average of only 75 overs a day, while in 1981, in one match Australia and England averaged 84 overs a day.[60]

In these circumstances, the most skillful use of TV may produce few spectators. Thus far, British TV producers have not even made the attempt; the TV viewer is not a spectator who could become a fan if properly handled, but a person who just could not get to the ground.

For such a one, a televised test match can be a joy. On June 7, 1980, as play was about to open on the third day of the test match between England and the West Indies, the "sacred space" was identified and the start of "sacred time" indicated as a shot of the central clock at the Nottingham ground showed that play was beginning precisely at 11:30 A.M.

The text was translated exceptionally well. Distance shots of the field showed fielding positions; several times a set piece, such as the wicket keeper and the slips, was shown in close detail. Visual variety was assured by showing close-ups of the bowler at the beginning of his run or of the batsman awaiting delivery of the ball; on other occasions, the bowler was followed close up throughout his delivery. A well-struck ball was occasionally followed in close-up to a fielder; more often its path across part of the field was shown. Camera angles were varied, so that viewers sometimes saw the field from behind the bowler or wicket keeper, sometimes from the side. Replays of the fall of a wicket or of a particularly spectacular shot were shown from several angles. Yet at no time was the flow of the play, or the pattern an experienced cricketer needed to see, disrupted by fancy camera work. It was assumed that the viewer was there to experience the match, not to be titillated by a jazzed-up version of it.

Statistics were frequently superimposed over a background shot when pauses occurred in the action. Individual as well as team records were shown when these were relevant; a bowler's record in past test matches would be shown at the end of the over, and the viewer given sufficient time to look at it, rather than simply glance at the score.

The commentators assumed that viewers thoroughly understood the game and had no need of instruction; their comments were those of friends sitting at a match, chatting spontaneously to each other. Ted Dexter, an international cricketer, was perfectly content to keep silent for a minute at a time (an unheard of period for an American commentator), and then to say something like, "A lovely piece of fielding," in tones of deep satisfaction.[61] To American viewers this remark would appear inane; American commentators are supposed to mediate a televised event, not talk to friends. But it *was* a lovely piece of fielding, and had one been sitting at the ground, that is precisely what one would have said. Ted Dexter was indeed clearly aware of his duty; cricketers do not wear numbers or names on their backs, and Dexter knew that people come and go from their TV sets. So he obligingly spoke up: "For those of you seeking identification, Marshall is wearing a sleeveless shirt." No American commentator would so innocently separate the sheep from the goats; Dexter had no intention of being patronizing, but was simply realistic. He also offered instruction on the American model; the breeze, he said, was not assisting the bowler's natural swing. The instruction, however, was not consistent, and it was never sought overtly by another commentator, prodding the man who is supposed to be instructing his audience so that they will come to understand and care about the game. Dexter was talking largely as he would to someone already sufficiently interested to attend the match in person.

It is not that British camera crews and commentators are unaware of the possibilities of their medium. On June 5, 1980, the West Indian captain, Clive Lloyd, split his hand fielding, and needed three stitches between his second and third fingers; yet the following day he came out to bat. The viewers were given a close-up of his grip, while the commentator explained what the consequence of such an injury might be to Lloyd's batting skill; in any case, viewers were left in no doubt that whatever happened, the hand was "bound to be mighty sore." This, however, was no series of remarks made to get the spectator's interest; they were both a tribute to Lloyd's courage (no substitutes are allowed to bat or bowl in test matches) and an explanation that one knowledgeable friend might give to another. Televised cricket in Britain is for the fan.

Yet while the BBC is wisely translating cricket according to its time-honored tradition, viewers quickly become aware that the behavior of spectators is not what it used to be. West Indians have always watched cricket exuberantly; when they emigrated to Britain, they continued to follow the game and celebrate it in their own way. At county cricket grounds chants reminiscent of soccer began to be heard; horns and whistles were blown during play. Even Lord's began to resound with strange noises.

The cultural gulf between the English and West Indians, even those born in Britain, was demonstrated clearly in the final of the Prudential World Cup played at Lord's on June 25, 1983, between India and the West Indies. During this limited-over match, the West Indian spectators were blowing whistles and trumpets, shouting even during play, and jumping up and down in excitement. No TV viewer could miss their exuberance. The English authorities, however, never gave up. As Stephen Pile, the *Sunday Times* correspondent, wrote the next day, "By 7 o'clock India were poised to snatch victory from the jaws of expected defeat. 'Please,' said the wearily polite English voice, 'don't invade the pitch when the game ends. Do let the players off first.' All afternoon he had been telling the overexuberant, hooting, waving, and singing fans to sit down, or get behind the boundary, or consider others or move cars or generally behave themselves." Pile contrasted that behavior with what went on in the "members' enclosure [where] ties and moustaches rose up to clap with polite restraint . . . 'If you raise your voice in here you get thrown out,' a member explained, barely making himself heard in the enclosure above the Caribbean din." This contrast in acceptable behavior has nothing to do with television; or, indeed, with the game itself. As Pile explained, tongue in cheek, cricket was never intended to be exciting; as it always has been, "it is just one perfectly pleasant afternoon tea sandwiched by an awful lot of standing around."[62]

Yet if spectators have became unruly, the BBC camera crew and commentators were clear about the standards they intended to uphold for cricketers themselves. The West Indian bowler M. A. Holding was bowling to India's last batsman; Holding's first ball was a legal but intimidating bouncer, which hit the batsman's helmet. The camera swung to the umpire, H. D. Bird, who was clearly annoyed with Holding and had words with him; the commentators pointed out that such bowling was "unnecessary" and contrary to the spirit of the game, not least because no one would be sent in as number 11 if he could do much with his bat. The commentators commended the umpire for rebuking Holding, and when his next ball was well hit, suggested that everyone in the ground, including the West Indian spectators, would be happy to see the Indian batsman stand up for himself. There was no question here of using the incident to underline the palpable tension of the match, or the deep rivalry between the teams; viewers were obviously expected to deplore what was considered unsportsmanlike (although quite legal) behavior.

In translating their text, then, the BBC attempts to continue the traditions of play established in cricket by the "Gentlemen." As an elderly cricketer wrote in a curious little book on cricket etiquette, "Probably in no game do the unwritten laws play so prominent a part as they do in cricket, nor in other games are they anything like so comprehensive." E. Gerald French would have been appalled by the crowd's behavior at Lord's in June 1983, for he wrote, "Cricket is not a game that is improved – indeed it may suffer from serious degeneration – by unbridled behavior either on the part of the players or of spectators. The hysterical throwing up of hands at moments of crisis; the raucous, belligerent bellowings of appeals, supported by glaring insistence; the whistling, cat-calling, and yelling of onlookers – all such excesses may be considered not unsuitable for other games, but in cricket, all who indulge in them transgress the game's unwritten laws."[63] The behavior of spectators at matches is now "not cricket," but the players in Lord's international matches, limited-over though they may be, are still supposed by the BBC to conform to nineteenth-century codes.

How long those codes will be upheld even on the field is questionable. Richard Cashman describes a series of incidents in Australia and New Zealand during the March 1979 to February 1980 season that demonstrate "the rapid decline in accepted conventions in first-class cricket." Batsmen smashed down stumps when they disagreed with umpires' decisions, players took advantage of the letter of the rules in clear defiance of the game's spirit, delayed the game, deliberately ran into the umpires, and generally acted like louts. Cashman suggests that cricket is passing through the first throes of full-fledged professionalism;[64] if so, it will take more than television coverage to enable the game to survive. Such behavior disgusts cricket fans and there are plenty of other more exciting sports waiting to attract spectators.

For what delights fans about televised cricket is that TV enables them to see more clearly the nuances of the game. As Arlott puts it, "The television watcher now has the most perfect cricket spectator service that has ever existed."[65] The subtle duel between bowler and batsman, as between baseball's pitcher and batter, is much more closely revealed on TV than at the game itself. Instant replays can demonstrate exactly what the players did that was right or wrong, and the skills of individual players are revealed in all their glory. But in cricket as it used to be played, skill often resided in not doing something, just as it does in baseball. One does not flail all over the water for a big trout; one tempts him. In June 1980, a commentator praised Geoff Boycott's test match batting by calling it "watchful, careful and very well constructed." Such activities are satisfying for the participants and the initiated viewer, but not terribly interesting for those who are watching casually. Packer knew what he was doing in trying to transform cricket; as it stood, it was not a game ideally suited for people trained to watch the clock.

Limited-over cricket is much faster than the test match game, and requires rather different, if not less demanding, skills from those who play it. But county cricket was already in difficulties before limited-over cricket was devised. It could be argued that it was the amount of money available in other professional sports because TV existed that diverted exciting young athletes from cricket and made those who remained ready to barter the game they knew for one less subtle and time-consuming. That argument, however, ignores the fundamental economic, social, and cultural changes through which Britain has passed since 1945, of which the emergence of TV is but one. As a director of the Notts County Cricket Club explained in a between-innings 1980 interview, cricket now has to be a business. The old press box had been converted into boxes for rent at £3,500 a season (in 1980 about $7,000); women had been invited to take out full club memberships at £150 a year; attempts had been made to get families to come to the ground. The interview demonstrated that cricket of the 1970s was being nudged toward baseball of the 1880s. But when test match play resumed, it was equally clear that these matches, at any rate, were being televised for the aficionado.

Those who could afford to sustain cricket as an avocation no longer do so. It was, however, not television that separated them and their pocketbooks from the game. Rather, television has been to cricket what it has been to other sports, a boon to those fans who cannot physically be present at the match. For cricket still means to some Englishmen what it meant to Denzil Batchelor in 1947. He wrote, "When I watch it for an hour, or a day, or a season, I am catching a glimpse, a halcyon flash, of a great pageant which stretches far back in our history."[66] Cricket has survived by adapting; but in Britain it adapted to attract spectators to the ground, not primarily for the benefit of the TV camera. And until the chief aim of British television is to make money, and that of the MCC to maximize cricket's audience, TV in Britain cannot be used as cricket's primary marketing device. TV has "caused" none of cricket's present ills, all of which stem from societal changes brought about not by electronics, but by World War II.

7

SOCCER

Few soccer matches are televised live in Britain, because the Football Association has never tried to use the "telly" as a marketing device. Given the history and structure of professional football in Britain, the FA is probably wise; if soccer is to survive as one of Britain's national games into the twenty-first century, it will not be because soccer games were televised.

Soccer has a long history; but the game was not commercialized until the end of the nineteenth century. A form of soccer was played all over England as early as the twelfth century and probably before that; but like all folk games, its rules varied.[1] In 1862 a master at one of England's public schools codified a set of rules, which were modified in 1863 by members of Cambridge University who had played the game.[2] Their work led to the formation of the Football Association. The fundamental feature of the game played by members of this association was that the ball could not be moved by the hands, and players had to aim their kicks at the ball, not each other. In 1871, when the Rugby Union was formed, the split between the two games was clear; soccer was to be a game for the feet.

But like rugby, soccer was a game sponsored by the elite. The first Football Association secretary, C. W. Alcock, was a master at one of Britain's oldest public schools, Harrow; in 1870 he worked for the establishment of a knockout competition between clubs, based on the tournament played in his school. In 1871 the Football Association Cup competition was begun; and in the first four years it was dominated by teams made up of players who had been to public school. Public-school traditions determined the conduct of the game. High value was placed on sportsmanship; to win was certainly desirable, but only by playing within the spirit of the game. Umpires were not officially recognized until 1873–74; the playing team captains ran each match.[3]

But soccer did not long remain the province of the leisured. As Steven Tischler has convincingly shown, middle-class British businessmen quickly realized that money was to be made out of organizing sport for a working class whose leisure time became greater after legislation in the 1860s reduced working hours.[4] In the late 1870s, working men took up soccer enthusiastically; schoolboys played it wherever they could find a space. Men with free Saturday afternoons could be induced not merely to play soccer but to watch it, particularly as the shortage of public playing space in the rapidly growing industrial towns was severe. By the 1880s, local businessmen had begun to organize teams, which played inside fenced areas to which admission was charged.

It soon became clear that crowds would flock to good matches, which were those between the best players. Many good players were working men, who could not afford to lose wages by traveling and playing at times they should have been at work. Clinging to the amateur tradition, but recognizing a working man's dilemma, the Football Association's Rule 16 allowed players to receive payment for "actual expenses and wages actually lost." However, match promoters looking for a profit were not trammeled by public-school ethics of sportsmanship and tradition; the new clubs quickly began to induce good players to appear by paying them illegally.[5]

Only working men needed to be "shamateurs" and they took full advantage of their opportunities. They played, of course, for whoever paid them best. Television had not been invented when soccer club-hopping became rife, epitomized by one "Jones, formerly of Walsall, next of Great Lever, late of Blackburn, and now of Great Lever again."[6] The public-school men who governed the Football Association were deeply affronted by this professionalism; as one group of them wrote in 1882, "In some districts the *summum bonum* of life is abbreviated and spelt C-A-S-H."[7] In 1884 the whole matter of professionalism was brought up by the Football Association; its pros and cons were discussed at length in the newspapers and sporting press.

The amateur faction believed that games ought to be played for their own sake or not at all. Sport should not become a trade. To play for money was not merely to ruin the activity itself; it was also to open the floodgates to the hoi polloi. Amateurs wanted to play with members of their own social class, not with plebeians paid by the hour whose special athletic skills allowed them to transcend their station on a Saturday afternoon.

Those who supported professionalism were equally clear in their minds. The best players brought the best gate receipts; yet no stability of fixture lists, of club membership, or of player performance could be ensured when every good player could hock his services illegally to the highest bidder.[8] The game was already professional; to legalize professionalism would simply be to recognize an accomplished fact.

In 1885, the Football Association bowed to the inevitable; the ban against professional players was withdrawn. Professional players had been engaged chiefly by soccer teams from the industrial towns in the midlands and north of England; quickly these clubs got on with organizing themselves to field fully professional teams. In fact, 1885 was the last year in which an amateur club ever reached the Cup Final.[9] In 1888 the Football League was founded by professional clubs that undertook to play matches with each other on advertised dates, regardless of cup or other competitions. The games themselves were to be played according to the rules of the Football Association, but league membership, fixtures, and all other matters pertaining to the league's running were to be governed by the Football League executive. The *Birmingham Daily Mail* alleged that the motive behind the league's formation was "commercial, pure and unadulterated"; yet, as Tony Mason points out, "It is clear that professional football clubs were not primarily profit-making institutions and what profits were made were usually ploughed back."[10] But the taint of money was there; so while the amateur game flourished, it became progressively more the province of the working class.[11]

The league's directors rapidly moved to exert control over players. By 1890, no player could transfer from one league club to another without the written consent of his first club, for as a journalist wrote in 1895, it was "all very well for people to chatter about buying and selling players. . . . Teams must be comparatively level to sustain the interest – if they are not, receipts fall off, and without receipts players cannot be paid wages."[12] Rozelle could not have put it better. By 1900 a maximum-wage rule was passed; by 1909 even the wealthier clubs had realized it was in their own best interests to abide by it. Their stance prompted the Players' Union to threaten a strike.

There was no television to act as a scapegoat in 1909, and life-styles in Britain in that year and in the United States in 1982 were vastly different. Yet the arguments put forward by the owners, players, sportswriters, and public concerning the 1982 NFL strike were astonishingly similar to those expressed by club directors, players, journalists, and public concerning the threatened soccer strike in 1909.

Before the 1982 strike began, Rozelle, the NFL commissioner, pointed out that the demand for 55 percent of NFL gross revenue was "not realistic because the owners don't want the players in their business."[13] In 1909, William Pickford, an official of the Football Association, stated that the strike issue "comes down to the question of who is to be master, the clubs who pay the wages or the players who receive them."[14] An angry fan wrote of the high salaries NFL players were making, of their six-month work year, of their college scholarships, and asked why such favored young men were contemplating a strike. A poll, reported on the 1982 strike's twenty-fourth day, showed that 36 percent of those responding favored the owners and 35 percent the players.[15] A sportswriter pointed out in 1909 that soccer players traveled first class, worked only eight months and had "£4 per week coming in all the time. I think most Trades Unionists would put up with the little grievances for such treatment."[16]

In 1982, Ed Garvey, executive director of the NFL Players Association, addressed trade union meetings and got AFL-CIO support; the *Conservative Digest* published an article enquiring whether Garvey was trying to socialize football.[17] In 1909, the Players' Union secured the backing of the General Federation of Trade Unions, who saw the struggle of directors and footballers as one between master and man.[18]

In 1982, in spite of pressure from owners, professional football players organized two games themselves; both flopped.[19] In 1909, the Players' Union secretary hoped to arrange matches between players who were loyal to the Union. Club directors and press alike were hostile to the idea; *Cricket and Football Field*'s editor expressed clearly the terms under which soccer was being marketed. It was best done "with men at the head who in the main have plenty of this world's goods and give their time and consideration to football's welfare as a diversion and as a tonic."[20] Similarly, the editor of the *Northern Athlete* pointed out that supporters were not concerned with random collections of good players per se, but in rivalries between teams that stood for something.[21]

In 1982, some sportswriters and owners were anxious to show that players either were not solidly behind the strike or had been misled. In September, before the strike began, a sportswriter for the *Denver Post* averred that the Broncos did not want to strike, would not vote for it, did not support the 55-percent gross revenue idea, and did not understand the proposals either of the union or of the owners.[22] In 1909, club directors and the press labeled those calling for a strike "firebrands" and "agitators" who were leading the gullible into dangerous paths. It was confidently declared that the soccer careers of those who supported a strike would be over.[23] In 1982, as the strike dragged on, a hostile fan enquired where else football players could earn the money they were being offered;[24] in 1909 a writer enquired whether any footballer would be foolish enough to want to exchange his four pounds a week for a forty-eight-hour week at thirty shillings.[25]

The 1909 story ended differently; the soccer players decided not to strike. The clubs agreed to allow claims for workmen's compensation to go though the courts instead of being adjudicated by the Football Association; the Players' Union dropped its trade union affiliation.[26] But the transfer and maximum-wage rules remained in effect;[27] players remained chattels. In 1982, that issue was not in dispute; the NFL Players Association wanted better compensation, not true free agency. In both cases, however, the players gained very little; but it is probably true that the British soccer players stood to lose more had they struck. There was no shortage of good and willing soccer players in Britain in 1909. What the events of 1909 settled was that professional soccer players were workers; as such, soccer was a game played by the working class for the working class.

Thus, within forty years, soccer had become an organized business. In so doing, it had lost its upper-class sponsorship; soccer's class origins were quickly forgotten, and soccer became Britain's national sport for the masses. Even so, soccer did not become a business like football because the restraint of trade applied to soccer players was never applied to the spread of clubs. As a result, an organization emerged that by American standards is chaotic.

Professional soccer in Britain developed as a local game, based on local community support, and has never been reduced to anything like the order imposed by the NFL. In 1891, two clubs were added to the original twelve in the league and two more in 1892, when twelve more teams were made into a new Second Division. By 1919, there were twenty-two clubs in each division. In 1920–21, twenty-two clubs mainly from the south of England made up a Third Division; a northern section was added the following year. By 1951, each of the sections contained twenty-four clubs. In 1958, the Third Division was broken into the Third and Fourth Divisions, based on the clubs' record.[28] As each division was added, the model of the First Division remained; each of the ninety-two clubs now plays every club in its own division once at home and once away. Each match winner gets two points; a draw (tie) earns one point. At the end of the season, the lowest two to four clubs in the First, Second, and Third Divisions have to drop down a division, or are "relegated"; the top teams in each division below are "promoted" to take their places.[29] The divisions are not geographically distributed; in the days when few working men had cars this mattered very little, because people who wanted to watch professional soccer simply went off on a Saturday afternoon to their local club.

Further, the league continued to be part of the Football Association.

The League Cup went to the First Division team that had the most points at the end of the season. The Association Cup, however, continued to be a knockout competition, open to all comers, professional, semiprofessional, or amateur. To this day, a semiprofessional or even an amateur side can excite national attention by knocking out a league team, especially if the team is in the Second Division. The links between the professional and amateur game were thus firmly secured.[30]

Professional soccer in Britain is still largely run as if it were a local amateur sport rather than international show business. No attempt is made to reduce the number of professional clubs, much less to upgrade the weaker ones. Any player may be traded during a season, and there is no limit on transfer fees or anything like a draft system. The skillful clubs, richer because they attract more fans because they play quality soccer, can therefore buy up the best talent.

The aim of every First Division club's board of directors has always been to win the Cup; in lower divisions, directors hope for their club's promotion. But if a club cannot head its division, at all costs it must not end the season at the bottom; it must not be relegated. Most boards of directors therefore fight hardest not to lose; actually to move up a division and stay there may involve expenditure on players and other costly measures that neither gate receipts nor the purses of the directors and supporters' organizations can sustain. In the 1980s, few directors concern themselves with the day-to-day running of the team, but it is the directors' business to see that the club suffers no loss of prestige. Relegation is a club catastrophe.

British soccer fans have always taken their sport seriously. They did not expect comfort; the majority were quite prepared to stand throughout a game, leaving the few stadium seats to those who could afford them. Although women went to matches in the 1880s, as the sport was professionalized and lost its social status, their numbers declined. There was no question of soccer being a family activity; working-class women had too much to do to go to football matches and so did their daughters. Although women and children might be taken to special events such as the Cup Final, and a few might go to local matches, professional soccer was a man's game, played for men; because leisure time roles were clearly differentiated in Britain by the turn of the century, few women expected or wanted to go to soccer matches.[31]

In Britain, no tradition of the game-as-spectacle developed. Working men had little money to spare, so ground facilities for spectators were of the cheapest; even today, the majority of spectators attending professional soccer matches expect to have to stand. When violence among spectators increased during the 1970s, clubs put in more seats as a measure of crowd control; they did not do it to increase the comfort of the patron. While the local unit of a military band may march halfheartedly up and down the pitch before the match begins, there is no music during the match, no invocation, color guard, or national anthem. Players are not introduced. No vendors ply their snack and cold-drink trade during the match; beer and cups of tea are usually available from a centrally located refreshment stand, which few people visit except before the game and at halftime. Spectators have not come to a happening, an event; they have come to watch a football match.

Nor is there any tradition of instructing the ignorant, so prominent a feature of all American public life. No commentary at all is given while the match is in progress; spectators are supposed to know what is going on. The programs contain none of the personal details about players of which NFL programs are full; British soccer programs are like newsletters. U.S. football referees turn to each side of the stadium to signal the precise nature of a rule infraction that is to be penalized. In soccer, while some signals exist, mainly to ensure communication between the referee and linesmen, the referee most often just blows his whistle to halt the players and award a penalty; frequently spectators have little idea of what went wrong. Sometimes the solitary referee (aided only by two linesmen whom he may chose to ignore) loses control of the game momentarily because the ball moves so quickly from one end of the field to the other that he cannot keep up with it. But the referee's word remains law; and he is there not to instruct the spectator, but to control the game. Spectators must learn what they can from their peers; professional soccer is a ritual for the initiated.

Soccer is a fluid, continuous game, and is in no sense episodic. Coaches are prohibited from directing the game from the sideline; but the game changes so rapidly, it would be impossible for them to be of much use in any case. Apart from the goalkeeper, no modern soccer player is a true specialist, and all players have to be able to attack or defend depending on whether their side has or has lost the ball. The change between defense and attack occurs in the players' minds and often takes place so rapidly that spectators have no time to savor the change or consider its consequences. In the Cup Final replay in 1983, for instance, in the space of a few seconds, an indirect free kick by Brighton was deflected by a Manchester United player who dribbled the ball straight up to Brighton's goal, where S. Gatling, a Brighton player, put the ball off the field for a corner. Brighton got the ball on the corner kick, and took it straight down the field for a shot caught by the Manchester United goalkeeper. In this very short space of time, Brighton had actually been attacker, defender, and attacker again. In a good match, this is often how the play goes.

Spectators also have to keep their wits about them because goals are often scored unexpectedly. Spectators must watch the players' movements to savor a change or consider its consequences. All players, except the goalkeeper, can expect in an evenly matched game to spend as much time in their opponents' half of the field as in their own.[32] Coaches (known in Britain as managers) may instruct their teams to play in rather general patterns such as the 4-2-4 or the 4-3-3 systems (that is, four strikers, two or three link men and four or three defenders), but every player must concentrate on the ball and the spaces on the field that open and close as the game develops. He must be aware of his teammates, but no one can tell him exactly where to go or what to do at any given point; he must work that out for himself.[33]

Soccer is fundamentally a simple game. The excitement of watching it derives from watching the consummate skill of individual ball handling, and from the ball sense and timing through which individuals organize themselves into a team. The best soccer player is not merely the one who has superb ball control, but who can make opportunities for his teammates' timing and positioning. He is not doing simply what his coach told him to do, and for which he will be praised or blamed in filmed postmortems; he is his own man, cooperating with, and competing against, other supermen.

The importance of the individual carries over into rules governing substitutes. Until 1970, no substitutes at all were allowed, even if players were injured; the team simply had to get on as best it could, even in a Cup Final. In World Cup competition two substitutes were allowed in 1970; England followed reluctantly by allowing one.

Yet in spite of the seriousness that still underlies British soccer, style in the field and in the terraces (stands) began to change during the 1960s. Until that time, British soccer had remained stubbornly insular. International soccer competition burgeoned after World War II as transportation improvements made travel quick, easy, and cheap. But league clubs had no intention of releasing players for international matches if by so doing they jeopardized their club results. Sir Matt Busby, Manchester United's manager, was one of the first influential members of the British soccer industry to see the advantages of playing abroad. In the 1960s, the exuberant displays of overseas players when they scored a goal were being imitated by British players, who had hitherto contented themselves with a handshake or pat on the back. An extended playing season and overseas opponents made British players fitter, faster, and more fluid. On the terraces, the cloth-capped men of the thirties in their best suits were replaced by wildly garbed and decorated fans who had the money for display and societal approval of festive dress whatever the occasion. The fans began to entertain each other with clapping and chants. A soccer match became a more boisterous and uninhibited occasion than ever.

None of this affected the attention paid to the game. As Morris put it, "To turn this symbolic event into Disneyland fun may be to destroy its essential dignity. To succeed, it may always have to be an intensely serious and male-dominated activity."[34] Morris wrote that in 1980; yet by the early 1970s, it was clear that British soccer was in trouble. Men were no longer flocking to soccer matches as they once had done; newspaper articles began to appear with such titles as "Have the Crowds Gone for Good?"[35] The decline in spectators had, in fact, been going on for some years. In the 1948–49 season, about 41.27 million people attended league matches; by 1966–67 attendance was down to about 29 million,[36] and by 1974–75, to 25.48 million. Significantly the greatest loss over ten years had been sustained by Fourth Division clubs; their supporters were now financially able to go to watch better matches or do something else entirely. Many clubs were in deep financial trouble. To save some clubs everyone pitched in; Crystal Palace's laundry was done "by the groundsman's wife and his sister-in-law," and local firms began sponsoring individual players by paying their salaries. At Burnley, the club began collecting five pence (about twelve cents) weekly from supporters in their homes and in ten years raised £1 million.[37]

In all the discussions that went on during the seventies, it was taken for granted that revenue would have to come from the gate and supporters, with help from other sources such as the pools promoters, who run by mail the weekly legalized betting on match results that millions of people take very seriously. Each club got about £25,000 a season from this source in 1976.[38] No one suggested that TV was a likely savior of the sport, partly because it was clearly recognized that TV was only one of the elements in the decline of attendance at soccer matches.

Not that directors had ever thought very kindly about television. The first league game was televised in 1960. In 1964, the league allowed the BBC to screen an edited fifty-five-minute version of one league game each week, the edited version to be shown not less than two hours after the game. The Football Association succeeded in cutting the time down to forty-five minutes.[39] Quite clearly, directors were afraid of the effect of TV on the gate; in the 1972–73 season the program inset distributed by the league contained an article entitled "Ban the Box," in which the author pointed out that Third and Fourth Division clubs simply could not stand comparison with the first-class soccer that fans could watch in comfort in the evening.[40]

It did not occur to those in charge of professional soccer in Britain to let the weak go to the wall. The Cup Final has been admirably televised, full-length, in Britain over the years; "Match of the Day" could technically resemble "Monday Night Football" if the BBC and ITV were allowed to transmit live, full-length matches. To do so, however, would bring about the demise of many professional clubs, and no one officially connected with soccer is prepared to trade TV time for the best clubs for the death of the rest. Soccer clubs in Britain are not U.S. franchises.

Nor did British soccer clubs take the obvious commercial decision Americans had made in the nineteenth century, which was to move a faltering club to a more profitable location. As John Bale points out, the British football industry "is characterised by locational inertia." Bale also demonstrates that nine of the ten clubs that have dropped out of the Football League since 1920 are in areas that have been depressed economically; clubs that have joined the league since 1920 are in more prosperous areas. But this has not been the result of taking thought; market forces have simply been allowed to operate in local communities. Bale also shows that better geographical distribution of league teams could improve their profitability; but, as he says, "football is not run with profit maximisation in mind."[41]

This dogged determination to hold on to tradition survives even when the problems it presents are well known. The author of the "Ban the Box" article, for instance, admitted that a great deal of the football seen at any professional soccer ground was not particularly entertaining. Other writers made the same point. As David Lacey, a *Guardian* sportswriter, pointed out in 1974, "Football began to lose its audience the moment that apprehension began to replace the uncertainty that has always been part of the game's appeal as a spectator's sport."[42] There is no rule in soccer that ensures that the ball will ever go the other side, unless a goal is scored. This means that a team may be trying not to attack, but simply to hold on to the ball to prevent the other side from scoring. This defensive soccer is dreary in the extreme; but as long as there is no incentive to increase the number of goals scored by a winning team it pays members of the team to pass the ball aimlessly among themselves, back to the goalkeeper, or to do anything, in short, to prevent action. For the players, this strategy is mere common sense; why jeopardize the two points for a win by putting the ball somewhere where one's opponents might turn the game around? Even the one point for a draw, especially at an away game, where the spectators are on the opponent's side, is better than no point for a loss. A soccer team determined simply to defend is extraordinarily hard to beat. Players and managers do not care that the drama has gone out of the game, killed by movements designed only to waste time.

League rules ensured that it was safer to play and not lose than to play to win; safer for the team, but quite deadly for the fan, much less the spectator. But those in charge of soccer did not take the route U.S. entrepreneurs of baseball and football had done; to alter soccer rules simply to attract spectators smacked of sacrilege.

John Arlott, a sports commentator and writer of vast experience, in

1973 put his finger more surely on the root of soccer's problem. He pointed out that in the immediate postwar years, fans came to the games by bus and train, not in cars, which they could not yet afford. Not until the 1956-57 season were league games allowed to be played by floodlights; it was assumed that fans would come straight from a Saturday morning's work to the match. Twenty years later all that had changed; people no longer worked on Saturday mornings and a car took one anywhere.[43] Christopher Brasher, an Olympic athlete, had made it clear in 1972 that the "clothcapped fan" had gone forever. "Instead, modern man is more likely to be out shopping, gardening or cleaning his car on a Saturday afternoon, watching 'Match of the Day' in the evening, and then going out on Sunday morning and playing himself." Brasher urged clubs to use their grounds productively, by building sports centers into the stands. Brasher suggested that while the number who attended soccer matches was going down, the number who played it was going up, and wondered why clubs could not capitalize on men's need for playing space.[44]

Violence also played its part; some fans ceased to attend when soccer matches, particularly in urban areas, became sites for violent disturbance during the 1960s.[45] Whatever the cause of violence on the terraces, it did not result from TV; but it did alter the nature of the stadium experience. Security fences were built to keep fans wearing clothes advertising their desire for trouble (the "aggro outfit" as it came to be called) separate from the rest; "dry moats" were dug between the terraces and the pitch; police with fierce, trained dogs patrolled the ground. Some of the young men whose behavior invoked such measures were using the soccer match as an occasion for aggression; as one informant put it, "Butley and Phil and Stevie and them: they're not interested in football. They just want the aggravation. That's what it is with a lot of the [National] Front lads at Chelsea."[46]

Nor could violence on the field itself be ascribed to television. Sportsmanship as the upper classes understood it was by no means always demonstrated at a prewar professional soccer match; but the anger and rough play that players allowed themselves in the sixties and seventies was related to a general breakdown of civility during the same period. British university student riots were a pale copy of those in the United States, but the traditionally law-abiding behavior that still allows most British policemen to go unarmed was changing throughout British society during this period. Without close analysis of game films it is difficult to substantiate, but the violence on the soccer field seemed less related to the need to win than to the refusal to control one's own impulsive behavior or to accept unfavorable decisions by the referee.

As professional soccer began to lose its audience, even First Division clubs began to look at their balance sheets. Steven Tischler has shown that businessmen organized league soccer; but he did not attempt to show how profitable their ventures actually were. By the 1970s, certainly, most businessmen connected with soccer were losing money.[47] Richard Redden and Hugh Hebert, sportswriters, suggested that part of the problem lay in the fact that soccer clubs are not businesses in the conventional sense, for British soccer teams are not supposed to make a profit. Their bottom line is to play well, if possible well enough to move into a new division. They are competing for prestige, not cash. As a result, conventional business techniques may appear inappropriate. Tradition counts; as the chairman of Crystal Palace, whose personal guarantee covered £260,000 of the team's £624,000 overdrafts in 1975, put it, "It [the club] will be there when we've all gone, won't it?"[48] So directors do not try to exploit share issues, much less negotiate properly with pools promoters or television companies.

Yet there is some money to be made from televising soccer if the best games were regularly to be televised. If one is at ease with the game's inherent structure, as the British are, translation to a TV screen presents few problems for experienced directors and camera crews. In the first place, the variety of movements within soccer is considerable. The ball can, for instance, be dribbled, passed short between several men, forward, sideways or backward, heeled, headed short or long, kicked long and high, thrown by the goalkeeper, or thrown in from the sidelines. The pace of a game can alter dramatically as a single player cuts loose and races for a shot, or as a group tap the ball slowly between them, trapping the defense while waiting for others in their team to move into position. A player can barely move the ball as he plays cat and mouse with a defender; then he can send a mighty pass out to another who races over the turf, or finally outfox the defender and tear off downfield. A team that knows each other's play can work the ball around defenders, however well they mark, by placing the ball fractionally ahead of each attacking player; a mistake in timing, and the attackers abruptly become defenders.

Even though these movements are often unpredictable, cameras can be shifted speedily enough to capture a good deal of drama. In one five-minute segment of the 1983 Football Association Cup Final, for instance, the BBC showed close-ups of individual players dribbling, kicking, passing, running (two), and a group of players vying for the ball. What might be called actionless close-ups were also shown of players preparing for a corner kick (four), of a player waiting to head the ball, of another getting up and walking, of a player's back, and of a player standing. The chairman of the Brighton club and both coaches in the stands were also shown in close-up. In the 1983 F.A. Cup replay, a five-minute segment contained close-ups of individual players kicking the ball, dribbling and kicking it, throwing it in from the sideline, playing cat and mouse with another player and then dribbling the ball (three), passing (two), and heading the ball; and of the goalkeeper taking a goal kick. Actionless close-ups included players placing the ball for a free kick, waiting for a throw-in or other action (five), running or walking into position (five), running or walking as the commentator mentioned them (three), the goalkeeper holding the ball, and the goalkeeper following the ball as it went over the sideline.

Camera angles on these close-ups can also provide visual variety. In these instances, the whole body was usually shown from above (fourteen), but close-ups of head and shoulders, or head to knees, were often shown from the side, and one shot, of the goalkeeper taking a free kick, was shown at eye level from behind. Which angle was used appeared to depend on the situation; when it was important to see where and how the player was moving the close-up was usually shown from above. These close-ups were very brief if it was necessary to see how the pattern of the game was developing; more time was taken over the set pieces such as a throw-in.

A variety of focal lengths and camera angles was used during the game as a whole, to hold the viewer's interest. The 1983 Cup Final replay contained a typical sequence of such shots. G. Pearce, of Brighton, was shown running into position after a block had sent the ball off-field for a corner; then part of the field was shown from further away, to show how the players were positioning themselves for the corner kick. The relevant part of the field was shown as the camera followed the ball from the corner kick and as it was cleared and passed. A close-up from above was shown of a tackle and pass, then part of the field was quickly shown as the ball went back toward the Brighton goal; after a defensive play, there was a close-up of a kick, then the ball was followed at a longer distance, then close-ups were shown of a Manchester United player running and a Brighton player standing still. Short shots were shown of the part of the field where the players were positioned for a free kick, a close-up of the three closest players was shown, and then came a longer shot of the players farthest from the ball as the free kick was taken and the ball passed.

This speedy change of focus is absolutely essential to soccer coverage, for without it, even the most knowledgeable fan is apt to lose track of the game. Viewers can watch the ball being passed between several players or dribbled by one; but if they cannot see where the rest of the players are or how they are moving, they cannot know whether the team is passing slowly because it needs a breather, because all players are not yet in position, because they're sitting on a lead, or because they're not concentrating. Further, viewers need to know exactly where the ball is on the pitch. In football, the markings on the field make it abundantly clear exactly where the teams are at any given moment; the huge numbers are even marked with a minus on one side of the field, lest anyone should be confused. A soccer pitch contains relatively few markings, and unless the camera keeps the geography up to date, it is easy to look at the screen and see only a group of men running about on an indeterminate stretch of grass that bears no immediate relationship to either goal.

Soccer also requires unremitting attention, which the British have been trained to give to it. Soccer contains few predictable crises, yet paradoxically goals may be scored at any time. Even the camera crew may not have time to get the shot in close-up. They cannot afford to zoom in while the ball is within shooting range, because the ball might be popped in by almost anyone. A commentator can be caught napping. Toby Charles was discussing attendance figures during a 1978 match broadcast on PBS and suddenly broke off to say, "Oh, it's a goal again." Nor can replays be much help; there are no ballcarriers on which cameras can be reliably focused to provide viewers with close-ups of the scoring play. Even with a battery of cameras around each goal, set up only to provide replays, it is hard to see how the pattern that led to the goals could be discerned quickly enough to produce the close-up replays to which football viewers have become so accustomed.

The British do not require predictable and recurrent crises in their national sports; a corner is a crisis, as is a free kick, but a sudden brilliant move on the part of any player can make any soccer game memorable. It does not bother the British that the referee alone keeps time, so no one knows precisely when the final whistle will be blown. As players are independent once they are on the field, the fateful decisions that have to be made by American coaches are missing from soccer, but not missed by soccer fans at the grounds or in front of the screen.

In translating the 1983 Cup Final, the BBC not only made use of all the technical expertise it had, but also concentrated on conveying the mood of the crowd. In so doing, it reinforced what British audiences wanted to see from their equivalent of the Super Bowl.

The commentator reminded viewers that on this very date (May 21) sixty years before, the first F.A. Cup match was played between Bolton Wanderers and West Ham United. The shots of the flags waving in the breeze, of the crowd singing the traditional Cup Final hymn "Abide with Me" (when the camera relentlessly skipped over individuals who were not singing), and of the military band playing on the pitch, reminded viewers of the "pageantry and sense of occasion with which we watch the Cup Final." The Cup Final's "sacred time and space" were faithfully translated.

Everyone watching the match at home or at the grounds knew the two teams playing; Manchester United, the proud, historically mighty club, pitted against Brighton and Hove Albion, a team whose home is in south coast seaside towns, who that very season had been relegated to the Second Division, and who were assumed to have no real chance against their famous opponents.[49] Yet as the commentator pointed out, the managers (coaches) of both teams were "each born in a working class district of Liverpool just before the war."

The "bond of brothers" was early underlined; the captain of each team introduced each of his players to the duke of Kent, the president of the Football Association, on the pitch. Yet while the last names and numbers of players were later flashed on the screen, these introductions were not made over the microphone. This was a private ceremony, translated on the air exactly as it was done at the grounds. There, the assumption was that no one needed to be told who was playing because supporters would obviously know their teams. Another break with American habits of mind was the casual shot of the two team managers sitting side by side. Everyone knew, of course, that their only function was to decide when and if to send in their one allowed substitute, and to talk to their teams at halftime. And however important it was for their teams to win, the British did not expect the coaches to fight the team battle off the field.

Before and during the game, the BBC showed the crowd entertaining itself. But no viewer could have thought he was at an American game. There were of course no cheerleaders, and there were far more hand-held team flags than banners. The banners did not address the commentators, if only because soccer is so rarely broadcast live that the British equivalent of "Dandy Don" or Howard Cosell does not exist. The banners therefore were often puns on the teams or their managers: "All Things Brighton and Beautiful," "Maggie May But Norman Will," "Seagulls Make a Melia of United." Supporters of both teams also roared their chants and sang their own songs, learned on their home ground.[50] These were spontaneously sung, full-throated and unmistakably carried by male voices. "Rooting" was evident throughout; these teams each had a genuine community history.

There was also a clear rhythm to the sounds. Behind an NFL game commentary, there is often a general buzz, which erupts into collected sound only on rare occasions. The BBC faithfully allowed the viewer to hear the ebb and flow of sound as the fans, keenly alert to every important move in the game whether or not it resulted in a shot at goal or a goal, gave appropriate tongue. These fans thoroughly understood what they were watching. In this particular Cup Final, Novak's concept of "agon" could hardly have been better epitomized. Brighton, the underdog, refused to concede defeat. Taking advantage of a soggy pitch, they outplayed themselves time and time again, to the point that the game ended in a draw.

Everyone in Britain knew what would happen next, however shocking it would seem to Americans. The equivalent of the Super Bowl would simply have to be played again, on another day. Never mind that the BBC was broadcasting the Cup Final to over fifty countries; when lawful overtime was ended the match had to be replayed. There was no difficulty in arranging the replay for the following week; the premier British soccer match does not need the commercial lead time required by a Super Bowl. In the replay, there was no mistake; Manchester won by 4 goals to 1. But nobody suggested that the teams should keep playing on May 21 until a result was reached; in Britain, teams that have played the requisite, legal amount of overtime are deemed equally matched and must meet again if a winner is to be determined.

The seals of "competing" and "self-discovery" were also evident. BBC sports commentators are under no obligation to persuade their listeners that the game they are watching is better than it is. Players can therefore be evaluated realistically. Indeed, why should a commentator make himself look foolish by failing to note shortcomings or by overpraising a star, when he assumes his listeners are quite capable of making their own judgments? Of course, millions of viewers watching the Cup Final do not habitually watch TV soccer programs, which are heavily edited. On January 3, 1976, for instance, "Match of the Day" included parts of three matches, as well as interviews and other material. But BBC commentators do not assume it to be their duty to hook occasional viewers to soccer, whereas Super Bowl commentators continue their usual practice of entertaining and instructing the uninitiated.

There is no advertising on BBC, so concentration on the event in itself could be total. As the camera ranged the ground, it did, of course, pick up the permanently fixed advertisements attached to the low fences that surround any F.A. soccer pitch. But the camera neither focused on them nor sped past them; a viewer could notice or ignore them just as he could notice or ignore the heavy, high iron fencing separating the front rows of spectators from the pitch. (Violence has come to Wembley as it has to almost every British professional soccer ground.)

For the BBC, as for the British, the game is not over when it has been won. The teams did not rush for their changing rooms when the final whistle sounded at the end of the replay. The cup was presented to Manchester United's captain on the field, and the team ran a lap of honor around it, waving the cup as it went. The losers got their medals. The crowd applauded happily, savoring the fact that they had seen a game played, not only an event won. Naturally, Manchester was delighted with the result; but Brighton, wanting so much to win, was cheered to have acquited themselves creditably. The point of this competition, faithfully translated by the BBC, was to compete, as well as to win.

It is unfortunate that the soccer that Americans have seen on their TV screens has rarely been well translated, even when it has been well played. The PBS games, even edited as they are, do not demonstrate the quality of camera work the BBC exhibited in these 1983 Cup Final and replay telecasts. In a typical PBS televised game (July 5, 1982) seventy-five close-ups were shown before halftime. Of those only twenty-four were action shots, including eight of dribbling, six of vying for the ball and two of a throw-in. Fifty-one close-ups were static, including eleven of a goalkeeper. It is safe to focus on the goalie, because while the ball is off the field, or while the goalkeeper holds it, the camera crew can relax yet give the illusion of focusing in on the play at the same time. Other close-ups focused on fouled or fouling players (seven), on groups of players standing around another or running back for a set piece (five), and miscellaneous shots of the referee (four) or captains (four). Yet the heart of a soccer game is its action, the very part of it that PBS viewers did not see very often in close-up.

As soccer players wear only numbers on their shirts and are not always clearly seen, Toby Charles, a British commentator, spent part of his time simply saying things like, "X to Y or Z coming up to tackle – oh, look at that!" The lack of communication between referee and commentator becomes painfully obvious to an audience used to American football. As Toby Charles remarked cheerfully in a match between Hamburg and Cologne broadcast on February 19, 1978, the referee gave a "free kick, but I don't know what that was for." To the American viewer, soccer must often appear as a game in which half-sized men rush aimlessly up and down a stretch of turf, occasionally getting their feet to the ball. Of such stuff, gripping TV is not made.

When American soccer was shown on network TV the same problems occurred. The format ostensibly matched that of football; a Dallas Tornado match against the Fort Lauderdale Strikers on August 9, 1980, was announced by Ray Gaskin and Ken Cooper, who tried to inform their audience as well as entertain them. The Tornado starting lineup had faces as well as names in it; there was a constant stream of chatter about such matters as coaches, past plays, statistics of goals scored; a replay of a tricky obstruction call was shown so that Cooper could explain it. Some propaganda for soccer as opposed to football was thrown in; Cooper remarked on the grand play of a small man who had made his way into a professional team, and suggested to youngsters that one didn't necessarily have to be "big and strong" to be a professional soccer success. Advertisers, however, had to be accommodated; one goal was seen by TV viewers only in a replay, as it was scored while the advertisement was in progress. The unpredictable nature of soccer could hardly have been more clearly demonstrated. Further, on several occasions a commentator would ask the viewers to notice something that their screens did not show them, such as the strikers all being within thirty-five yards of the goal. These patterns are an inherent part of soccer, but the translators evidently lacked the skill and experience to transmit them properly.[51]

It has frequently been suggested that football became so popular a TV sport in the United States because it epitomized values respected by many Americans. It is dependent on teamwork, but the individual can show his paces; it is organized, specialized, makes use of a bewildering array of electronic technology. Football is also violent, and its conduct and language have been compared to warfare. It is a corporate industry, in which management and workers are clearly differentiated, yet it contains aesthetic and mystical elements that transcend normal industrial activity. The fact is, however, that it became overwhelmingly popular in the 1960s, precisely during the period when it was most intelligently marketed. Spectators were systematically taught how to appreciate it, while TV producers capitalized on its structure. At the same time, the NFL made certain that the product would live up to expectations.[52] Professional soccer will not lack spectators in the United States because it is primarily individual, spontaneous, unspecialized, and requires a minimum of technology, but because unless one has played the game from one's youth up, and/or developed loyalty to a particular professional team, soccer is hard for Americans to understand. Soccer depends primarily on process, rather than result, and as such it runs counter to the very deep-seated American tradition of winning; its structure and trappings are quite unlike those of any sport Americans value.

Promotors of professional soccer in the United States have had a hard row to hoe, because the amateur game did not take root when it was introduced.[53] Although the first famous college football game played in 1879 resembled soccer, football itself quickly supplanted soccer. There have been sporadic attempts to get professional soccer going in the United States; before 1914 the president of Bethlehem Steel had spent over $125,000 on a soccer field and facilities and continued to import Scottish pro players to stiffen teams.[54] In 1930 the United States sent a team to the World Cup, and in 1950 the United States beat Britain in the same competition. But no great popular enthusiasm followed these international successes.

Ironically, it was the televising of the 1966 World Cup that led promoters to try to set up a national professional soccer league in 1967; typically, two leagues emerged whose differences led to an $18 million lawsuit.[55] As everyone in both leagues had lost a great deal of money, the differences were composed, and the North American Soccer League was founded and internationally recognized. But again, teams lost money; in 1969, with only five clubs as members, it was doubtful whether the NASL could continue. The crisis was weathered; but although by 1975 the

NASL contained twenty clubs, professional soccer in the United States was by no means financially sound; in 1980, the NASL commissioner, Phil Woosnam, admitted that after ten years no NASL team was making money. In 1982, the then fourteen teams of the NASL lost collectively $25 to $30 million dollars.[56]

Down to nine teams, the NASL in April 1984 signed a collective bargaining agreement with the Players Association, which stipulated that each team would reduce its overall payroll for players by 10 percent in each of the following three years. The NASL, using this and other means, hoped to be spending a maximum of $825,000 on players by the third year.[57] The fundamental difference between soccer in Britain and the United States is illustrated by the fact that of the twelve clubs that formed the Football League in 1888, all except one (Accrington, which went backrupt in 1974) are still playing.[58] In the United States the last charter member of the NASL to survive under its original name, the Dallas Tornado, went out of business in 1981. The NASL collapsed entirely in 1985.

The NASL did its best to fit soccer into the conventions that NFL fans have come to accept. First, the game was regarded as a spectacle; promotions were arranged to draw spectators, while cheerleaders, halftime shows, mascots, vendors, and announcers were all on hand. Brian Glanville's remarks epitomize the difference between British and U.S. expectations. Pelé "played his farewell game at Giants Stadium to the accompaniment of an orchestrated furor which may have nauseated the true lover of soccer, but appeared to satisfy the crowd."[59] Second, the NASL put into effect rule changes designed to conform to American views of what makes professional sport worth watching.

American spectators require that one team win and the other lose; a draw, especially a goalless draw, is entirely unacceptable. In 1974, the NASL therefore introduced a penalty-kick contest to decide drawn games;[60] the winner of that got three instead of the outright winner's six points. In 1975 even a "draw-win" got six points, and in 1977 the NASL abandoned international rules entirely and devised a "shoot-out" between the goalkeeper and one designated opponent at a time, to decide draws. In the shoot-out, a player started with the ball on the thirty-five-yard line, and had five seconds to rush the goalkeeper and make his shot. The teams alternated shots, using different players, until each had had five shots or until one team got a 2-1 advantage.[61] That team was then awarded the goal and the match. The shoot-out was obviously inspired by the mythic wild-west gunfighter duels, but was more than that. It was an easily understood test of prowess, in which a team's fate hung on the skill of recognizable, and therefore accountable, individuals. There was no equivocation, no anomaly in the situation, and the element of chance had been almost wholly eliminated.

Americans also dislike concentrating throughout a game. At a British soccer game, people remain more or less in their seats or in one spot on the terraces throughout; an American crowd seethes. Americans therefore want to watch a game in which they are not likely to miss the only score because they are momentarily not attending. So the NASL tried to alter the rules to increase the possibility of scoring. They proposed widening the eight-yard goal, and reduced the area in which a player could be offside by moving the line from midfield to the thirty-five-yard line. The whole object of the offside rule (which since 1925 has required that two defenders be between an attacker and the goal when he gets the ball) is to keep down the score. What would be the point of the game if a couple of players could simply stand by the goal mouth, waiting to receive a long pass from the backfield, to pop the ball into the net? Further, instead of merely awarding points for a win and a draw, the NASL awarded additional points for goals scored.

All this scrambling about to alter the rules is reminiscent of baseball of the 1880s; it was not done to please TV producers, who have never been particularly interested in soccer. It was done to attract to the stadium the paying customers, those who have no knowledge of or interest in the game, but who might be induced to watch it if it could be made to fit their predilections.

To the purist, the essence of soccer is that goal-scoring is extremely difficult. Of course the result matters; but the joy of soccer resides in the game as played. The NASL was, however, convinced not only that a result was required, but that the competition should be as tension-filled as possible. In 1978, for instance, the Cosmos lost the divisional play-off away and won at home; but in the two games they scored only six goals and had nine scored against them. According to soccer tradition, they should have proceeded no further; but the NASL had decided that a game is a game is a game, so the Cosmos immediately played another minigame, which they won 1-0 on a shoot-out and were therefore declared the overall winners. All the tournament play was thus negated by a tiebreaker. This kind of thing disturbs British soccer fans, not only because it is new, but because it substitutes the victory of the moment for the long, hard slog of the "proper" game.[62]

The Fédération Internationale de Football Association, the international soccer authority, was surprisingly tolerant of NASL vagaries.[63] But it finally cracked down. In 1978 the NASL was warned, and for the 1981 season the NASL was instructed to move the offside boundary back to midfield and to allow two instead of three substitutes. These instructions did not sit well with American coaches. As Mike Renshaw of the Dallas Tornado was quoted as saying, "In my way of thinking FIFA has a behind-the-times and stick-in-the-mud attitude typical of European soccer. They just can't realize that we are in the entertainment business."[64]

The problem about the entertainment business is that it requires novelty. Soccer cannot provide it. This is not to say that techniques of televising soccer could not be improved. It is to say that however much money the U.S. television industry were to pour into promoting soccer in order to attract spectators, the ratings could never be high. Soccer is a game for fans, those who have knowledge of and interest in each game's progress and outcome. To teach Americans, who are used to controlled games, which apparently "consist more of talking about what to do than actually playing,"[65] to enjoy an unpredictable and hence essentially uncontrolled game in which the action is fluid and continuous, is an almost impossible task. Television alone cannot achieve such a transformation. Not until a generation of boys and girls who have played soccer themselves and who have watched good teams play in person is old enough to want to watch soccer on TV will there be a U.S. television market for it.

Cable TV may provide a market for U.S. professional soccer; but as it stands, the international game does not fit American preconceptions of what professional sport ought to be. Indoor soccer, an American invention, could capture American imagination, but television alone cannot give spectators the incentive they need for learning to look at a sporting event, a soccer match, in a wholly new way.

Nor could TV be called on to save British soccer. Even though women have begun to play soccer as amateurs particularly in the south of England,[66] it remains a male-bonded activity in a society where sex roles are changing. Soccer's old audience has also changed; the professional game was crafted with the working class in mind, and it cannot suddenly become the kind of sport upwardly mobile spectators of either sex embrace.

Yet because professional soccer was necessarily tied to particular communities, many professional teams now survive in places that are not primarily working class. These teams may never become famous, but they are the focus of some community pride. Torquay United, a Fourth Division club, and one that I often watched, can never hope to move even into the Second Division. But the team will go on playing for as long as its local supporters continue to think of it as their team and do more for its financial health than simply buy tickets to the matches.

The administrators of British soccer are ambivalent toward TV because their sport is not first and foremost an industry. Rather like TV's Channel 4, soccer is commercialized but not commercially competitive. Until what the British want from soccer changes, the Football Association's use of TV will be quite unlike the NFL's relationship with U.S. networks.

8

TENNIS

Different conceptions of what is desirable in sport, and the knowledge required to translate properly a particular sport from stadium to screen, are perhaps most clearly demonstrated by examination of U.S. and British televised tennis. The 1987 CBS telecast of the U.S. Open Men's Finals was refreshingly free from gimmicks, but U.S. networks have often translated tennis in ways that fit tennis into the preconceptions of what a sportscast should be, regardless of the requirements of the game itself. British tennis broadcasts, stodgy by American standards, reflect the fact that Wimbledon tennis was first televised in the 1930s as a national event. Wimbledon tennis is therefore still not in competition with other sports broadcasts, as any tennis match shown on American network TV must be. The BBC has no mandate to tempt casual spectators to sample whatever tennis it broadcasts; ITV knows it is pointless to try. The BBC's output must therefore conform to what constitutes the best seat in the stands for the fan who understands the game and who has absorbed its tradition.

This is true although lawn tennis itself has been metamorphosed in the last fifteen years. What transformed it, however, was not television, but American money. In 1968, in the first major tournament in which professionals and amateurs were allowed to play together, the top prize was $7,200. In 1971, Rod Laver had to win just one match in the $210,000 Tennis Championship Classic to earn $10,000.[1] In 1982, Lamar Hunt's World Championship Tennis circuit offered $8 million in prize money in twenty-two tournaments in direct competition with the Grand Prix circuit, which offered $300,000 in 1970 and ten years later provided $17 million in eighty-eight tournaments.[2] Some of this bonanza came from television, more of it came from sponsors.[3]

There is no way to disentangle the symbiotic relationship between TV and the newspapers and other print media that advertise televised tennis events and comment on them afterward, nor to gauge the effect of both media on stadium ticket sales. It seems unlikely that any sponsors would now put up money for a tournament if they thought their products would not get at least indirect TV exposure as a result. What corporate sponsors know, however, is that they will gain tax and other advantages as a result of their funding tennis tournaments, whether or not the tournament itself is nationally or locally televised. Unlike for baseball and football, no predictable level of television funding is available, and even without television, tennis players would not be on the breadline. However, had Lamar Hunt not interested himself in tennis, it is doubtful whether professional tennis would today be the money-spinner for the top players that it is.[4]

Lawn tennis was originated by Major Walter Wingfield and played by guests on his Welsh estate.[5] Wingfield's game, first played on a grass court in the shape of an hourglass in 1873, bore little resemblance to the French *paume* played indoors and out, or to court tennis or "real" tennis, now played indoors, save that a net and rackets were involved. Wingfield wanted to patent his game, but was given a patent only on the court's shape; he then copyrighted the rules.[6]

Wingfield's "Sphairistike," as he called it, caught on, but within a few years the shape of the court was changed and new rules were devised. Wingfield's version, patented and copyrighted as it was, nevertheless quickly lost its following. On June 9, 1877, the *Field,* the English sporting magazine for the affluent, announced a "lawn tennis meeting open to all amateurs" at "The All England Croquet and Lawn Tennis Club, Wimbledon." The court and rules used were not Wingfield's. This, the first lawn tennis championship, was not of great significance at the time; no play was even scheduled for the first Friday and Saturday of the "meeting" because of the Eton-Harrow cricket match being played at Lord's.[7]

Wimbledon's lawn tennis met many needs. Upper-middle-class Englishmen owned houses that had plenty of room for a court on the lawn; almost anyone could hit a ball back and forth over a net, and the game was more exciting than croquet, but could easily be played by ladies. The style of play was then, of course, quite unlike modern tennis; the game that went on in people's gardens was often "referred to contemptuously as 'pat-ball.' "[8]

But while a genteel, restrained game could be played casually, lawn tennis offered opportunities for hard, speedy play by those who took it seriously. In 1880, sixty players entered the Wimbledon Championship; by then, twelve courts had been built and stands put up. That year, the admission price went up from a shilling to half a crown, a 150 percent increase. In 1884, the first women's tournament was held.[9]

After a set of rules and equipment had been brought from England, members of the American Dwight and Sears families were responsible for popularizing lawn tennis among their friends; they held a tournament in 1876. But the Outerbridge family staged the tournament on Staten Island in 1880 that was to lead to the founding of the United States Lawn Tennis Association and a National Championship held at Newport in 1881. In 1887 the first U.S. Women's Tournament was held. By 1890, seventy-five clubs and one regional association were part of the USLTA; within five years, 106 clubs and ten associations had joined. Then membership dropped off; by 1902 the USLTA had only forty-four clubs and associations. After that, growth was slower and steadier.[10]

On both sides of the Atlantic, tennis was played by the affluent. The court had to be reasonably flat; it could not be used by too many people too often if the grass were not to be trampled flat.[11] A maximum of four people could play at once; everyone needed rackets and balls. This was no game for the poor packed in the industrial slums of England or the United States. But just because the Wimbledon and U.S. Championships were contested and watched by the socially prominent, newspapers reported them in detail, just as they did the Oxford and Cambridge cricket matches and Ivy League football.

Tennis soon spread beyond England and the United States. The first Davis Cup match was played in 1900 between Britain and the United States; in 1904, France and Belgium entered, joined in 1905 by Australasia (Australia and New Zealand). The International Lawn Tennis Federation was formed in 1913.[12] Everywhere, however, tennis was played and supported by the upper class; everywhere, therefore, its spectators were decorous and its championship players held to a code of impeccable court conduct. Each national association required its players to be amateurs, in spirit as well as letter.

It was not long, however, before players began to chafe at these restrictions. In 1920, Bill Tilden won the U.S. National Singles title, and went on to win it another five years in succession. He played in Davis Cup matches – and submitted huge expense accounts. He wrote about tennis – for pay. In 1924, the USLTA revised its rules to forbid players being paid for writing about tennis; an uproar followed. The rules were amended in 1925 to forbid players using their tennis titles or reputation when they wrote about tennis for pay, and to forbid players to write for pay about any match in which they were competing. Tilden was probably making

$25,000 a year from writing about tournaments he was playing in; immediately after the 1925 rule was made, he wrote, for pay, about a tournament in which he was competing, in open defiance of the USLTA's authority. The USLTA warned him; Tilden was unrepentant.[13]

The dilemma the USLTA faced is one with which every tennis promoter since has struggled. Tilden was enormously popular; to refuse him the opportunity to earn money as a journalist seemed somehow un-American. Then in 1927 the United States lost the Davis Cup to France. In 1928, Tilden wrote about Wimbledon while he was competing; the USLTA suspended him, and he was pulled off the Davis Cup team sent to play Italy in August. The U.S. team beat Italy; but without Tilden were very unlikely to beat the French. The French themselves wanted Tilden to play; without him, they feared for the gate receipts. The State Department was pressured to appeal to the USLTA. The American press was solidly behind Tilden; he was, they felt, a journalist as well as a tennis player, and had every right to be so compensated. The USLTA caved in; Tilden played in the Davis Cup matches and was then suspended.[14]

In a team sport, a recalcitrant player can be replaced; in tennis, the individual player constitutes the game. Whether the rules the player flouts involve activities on or off the court, to suspend a star is to dilute a tournament. The USLTA was in a particularly difficult position, because in refusing a player the right to earn money by writing, they appeared to be extending their authority well beyond court boundaries. Tilden solved their problem for them by turning professional in 1930.

The problem of the tennis "shamateur" refused to go away. On both sides of the Atlantic, tennis during the 1930s drew its audience as it always had done, mainly from the affluent. Tennis was not taught or played in schools for the hoi polloi; it had no popular following. The official promoters of the game therefore had a stranglehold on players; to turn professional was to put oneself outside all the official tournament apparatus and hence beyond most media coverage.

In 1926, Suzanne Leglen was the most famous woman player, having won the Wimbledon and French singles six times each, as well as women's and mixed doubles championships. A U.S. promoter, Charles Pyle, persuaded her to tour America for a guarantee of $50,000. So little was tennis known as a spectator sport in the United States that Suzanne Leglen demanded her money in advance; for, of course, once she had accepted any money for playing tennis, she could no longer compete in the only tournaments that then counted, the amateur ones. Pyle recruited one other woman and four men to play on the tour; which, to everyone's astonishment, made him a profit of $80,000.[15]

In spite of such success, and the formation of the United States Professional Lawn Tennis Association in 1927, Tilden in 1930 was allying himself with a struggling group. It was much simpler for players officially to remain amateurs, and with the connivance of tournament sponsors to accept outrageous expenses or in other covert ways to circumvent the rules. By the 1940s, most top players were professionals in amateur clothing, but provided the cash did not show through, the ILTF could continue to pride itself on the integrity of tennis.

Professional players were free of ILTF control, and therefore free to make money openly if they could. But as Jack Kramer, the world's best amateur player in 1947, best professional player in 1948, and best-known professional tour promoter until 1962, points out, "No matter how you cut it, a tennis tour was a tough way to make a buck." Kramer recalls playing in "the opera house in Saratoga, New York once, where the back wall was eighteen inches from the baseline. Near Springfield, Massachusetts we played in a gym where baseball stanchions were set two feet behind the baseline so you had to run around them to get from one side of the court to the other." As a promoter, Kramer learned to check the number of tickets printed against the number sold, to arrange for a portable court to be driven from one arena to the next, to alter the rules to try to bring in spectators, and on some tours abroad to trade on the black market to change local currency to U.S. dollars, then smuggle the dollars through customs.[16]

Professional players who could stand the pace often did make money (although they sometimes lost it too), and Kramer was not by any means the only man who organized professional tennis tours. As amateur tennis was an upper-class sport, prestigious newspapers gave it space; and as tennis is an individual sport and only a very few players could win the most prestigious tournament or even represent their countries in the Davis Cup, the names of top amateur players were well known in tennis circles. When, therefore, an amateur player turned professional, or looked as if he might, the news went beyond the sports pages; even editors took a public interest in the decision. As more money for sport became available in the postwar world, amateurs began to turn professional more rapidly, in spite of the adverse publicity that attended their decision.

As Kramer points out, the rift between the amateur and professional game had harmed both by the early 1960s. The amateur game was bled of its talent just as those players became worth watching; the professionals had no recognizable tournament format, little prestige, and a public image of players who had bartered glory for personal gain. During all these years, the BBC had faithfully televised Wimbledon; but it was a BBC executive who suggested to Kramer that he find eight players for a professional tournament to be played at Wimbledon in 1967, two months after "The Championships." The BBC provided the singles purse of $35,000.

The tournament was extremely successful, and demonstrated all too clearly how attenuated the amateur game had become.[17]

A few months after this Wimbledon professional tournament, a U.S. sports promoter, Dave Dixon, began to look about for sports that might fill the proposed New Orleans Superdome. He was shocked to discover how little tennis had been exploited and persuaded Lamar Hunt to underwrite 25 percent of a new enterprise, World Championship Tennis. The professionals under contract to WCT would receive guarantees against prize money in tournaments WCT promoted.

At the same time, George MacCall, the U.S. Davis Cup captain, was forming the National Tennis League; besides one good amateur he signed some of the professionals Dixon wanted, so Dixon looked at other amateurs. For his "Handsome Eight" he got five of the best amateurs, three of them Wimbledon semifinalists in 1967. Within the same year, therefore, six of the top ten male amateurs were out of the ILTF game, which gave forward-looking officials their chance.[18]

For the world had changed between 1945 and 1968. While Britain remained a class-conscious society, increasing affluence and mobility had emptied the "Downstairs" portion of the "Upstairs, Downstairs" world and therefore made life "Upstairs" entirely different. The hypocritical cult of amateurism in tennis had begun to look not merely old-fashioned but silly. Now that such wholesale defection from the male amateur ranks had taken place, Wimbledon officials were better placed to put tennis on an honest footing. In 1968, the first open tournament was held; the day of the amateur, as well as of the "shamateur," was over.

Rod Laver played through the transition period from amateur to open tennis; his book, *The Education of a Tennis Player,* is refreshingly frank. In his first year as a professional in 1963 he beat Ken Rosewall in the final of a tournament, but there was no payoff because the promoters were broke. This is not to say that Laver's first professional year was a disaster; he had agreed to join a group of Australian players who were in effect running things themselves while they played, for a figure of $110,000 over three years. To earn such sums, this professional group played anywhere, on anything; in Nottingham, England, on a court a yard wider and two feet longer than it should have been, on another English court that was so slippery from condensation dripping from the ceiling that the game had to be abandoned; in Boston Garden where the court was laid not on the ice but on rough planks over it, so that the surface was a series of bumps.[19] From 1968 onward, Rod Laver could play on the kind of courts and in the conditions that had enabled him to become a professional in the first place.

Open ILTF tournaments by themselves, however, would not necessarily have changed the face of tennis very rapidly. There were not enough of them, and they were run in the genteel fashion the ILTF had brought to perfection in the decades of shamateurism. Dave Dixon's idea did not at first look important; WCT lost almost $100,000 in three months, largely because Dixon knew too little about tennis to organize a tour effectively.[20] But Lamar Hunt's appetite had been whetted; he bought Dixon out. Working through Mike Davis, a Welshman who had turned professional in 1960 after being ranked Great Britain's number 1 for five years, Hunt in 1970 signed thirty-two of the top male players in the world. He thus ensured the existence of an international tennis circuit whose members were responsible only to the WCT. Henceforth, professional tennis was to be run internationally as a business; the power of the ILTF had been, if not broken, at least seriously undermined.[21]

As long as ILTF's game was the only one in town, players had to play it. In 1970, from January to May, WCT players were engaged in WCT tournaments; the ILTF's own Grand Prix circuit was organized to avoid those months, leaving WCT players free to enter such Grand Prix tournaments as they wished. (Significantly, the Grand Prix tournaments themselves were sponsored by an American bank.) But WCT players were in fact under contract year-round; in 1971, WCT demanded $24,000 expense money for sending its players to Wimbledon. In 1972, the ILTF refused to pay. Hunt's players did not appear at Wimbledon, in spite of the tournament's prestige; if the ILTF did not care to know where the best players got their money, the players themselves were well aware of it. Hunt did not want to remake tennis in his own image; he did want to remind the tennis establishment that he who pays the piper calls the tune. In the negotiations that followed the 1972 debacle, Hunt was reasonable; he had, however, shown decisively that it was neither sentiment nor tradition that now controlled international tennis, but money.

Lamar Hunt regarded tennis as a business; a first-class business, true, but one that had to operate in the black. If spectators were to be attracted to tennis matches, they had to be given the kind of game they wanted to see. In WCT's first and disastrous season, Hunt had allowed Dixon to shake up the game by cutting out let serves, putting players in bright clothing, and encouraging noise from the audience.[22] These attempts to create an instant new sport drove tennis fans away without bringing in spectators. Hunt quickly learned not to go beyond the bounds of fan tolerance, but was by no means unwilling to promote innovations that would make the game more appealing to Americans who were new to it. WCT therefore welcomed changes that postwar economic and social conditions had already brought to the ILTF's attention.

One of these was the tiebreak. For more than eighty years, the winner of any given set had to be two games ahead of his opponent; lawn tennis spectators were ladies and gentlemen of leisure who were happy to sit through epic battles in which a player might need to win fifteen games before settling a single set. Increased affluence and mobility after the war brought more people to tennis matches; but they were people who had to work for their living. After professionals took over the game, the ILTF reversed itself and in 1970 permitted experiments with tiebreaks,[23] which meant that when a set reached six games all, the winner of it was the player who could win a finite (and usually small) number of points, such as best of thirteen, or seven points provided the player was two ahead. Tiebreaks fundamentally altered the rhythm of the game, increasing tension and putting a high premium on serving and concentration.

While the WCT was attacking the ILTF on one front, the Association of Tennis Professionals, formed in 1972, attacked on another. A Yugoslavian player had been suspended by his national federation for failing to play in his country's Davis Cup matches. The term of his suspension prevented him in 1973 from entering Wimbledon, a tournament under ILTF control. The ATP members announced that they would boycott any tournament from which Nikki Pilic was banned, in protest against the arbitrary nature of the ILTF's powers. The ILTF would not yield; neither would the ATP. In 1973 Wimbledon proceeded without most of the world's top male players.[24]

Even five years previously, such an action on the part of tennis players would have been unthinkable. The ILTF, through its national organizations, told players when to play, where to play, and how to behave, on and off the court. The autocratic and often unenlightened nature of ILTF control is well illustrated in Margaret Court's autobiography,[25] but players had the choice of conforming, being suspended from the only tournaments regarded as official, or turning professional, the latter choice one that provided very little opportunity for women in the 1960s.[26] In 1973, both male and female players could be independent. While the WCT had been organized for men, and the 1970 ILTF Grand Prix circuit had ignored women altogether, Billie Jean King's energy, Gladys Heldman's clout, and Joseph Cullman's financial backing had provided what became the Virginia Slims women's tour. The ATP was concerned with men's rather than women's tennis, but the fact remained that players were no longer going to starve if they refused to accept ILTF authority. Dixon's and Hunt's activities had made tennis a marketable product; players could therefore act singly or as a group, according to their own inclinations.

Billie Jean King's insistence on the equality of women tennis players had less to do with the sport itself than with changing times. Perhaps no other sport could have been so acceptable a vehicle for women's aspirations, because in tennis it is possible to look feminine and graceful while winning. There is no bodily contact, so the deeply entrenched stereotypes of woman as civilizer and man as protector are not attacked. And in the early 1970s, affluent Americans were ready for a new game that could be played by men and women, separately and together. The craze for physical fitness sweeping the United States included women, who were now allowed to sweat in public. Tennis was an ideal new activity. It was complex, but could be played at almost any skill level; it was not physically violent, but allowed players to be fiercely competitive, even hostile, and full of guile. It was not particularly time-consuming, and needed only a couple of players, not a whole team. An American woman could therefore acceptably speak out on behalf of all women players, in a country where women's rights were a public issue, and in which one measure of public worth is money. Further, women's tennis was not regarded by male players as a threat. Having played with women all their lives, the best male players knew there was no contest; if women's tennis succeeded, it was not going to take the bread out of men's mouths.

All this had very little to do with television. In Britain, Wimbledon tennis was televised as early as 1937 as a national event, along with such events as the Lord Mayor's Show, and the laying of wreaths at the Cenotaph on November 11, Armistice Day.[27] After the war, Wimbledon was again televised, but there was no attempt made actively to promote tennis as a spectator sport. By the time television executives in the United States were becoming seriously interested in tennis, fundamental changes had already been made in the game, which by intent or chance created a sport that was more attractive to a newcomer than the old lawn tennis. Before 1970, for instance, all matches had to be played with white balls; after that, the ILTF allowed experiments with colored balls because white balls were hard to follow at indoor matches under lights.[28] The visual combination of white and green is dull on television; a new element of color had been introduced, which suited the medium, but which had not been provided specifically for it.

The pace of the game had also changed. After World War II, Americans began to develop a style of play that depended not on grace, but power. Bobby Wilson was one of Britain's better postwar tennis players. In his autobiography he explains why he did not turn pro in 1960, and his reasons now seem almost quaint. He also believed, however, that the postwar athleticism had put him at a disadvantage, because he was a "natural" player, relying on innate rhythm rather than raw speed and strength.[29] Power and speed are fascinating to watch and, provided the ball is large enough to follow on screen and the action sufficiently predictable for the camera to follow, are doubly exciting on television.

Power and stamina do win matches. And as the early rounds of tournaments are often not televised, viewers may miss what is a very important aspect of the game. It is not that the text here has been altered; it is that viewers do not have volumes 1 and 2 translated for them; they have to start with volume 3, the final.

Cliff Drysdale's consummate artistry in the 1977 WCT quarterfinals was called a "brilliant performance" by the *Dallas Morning News* sportswriter the next day, but also a "loose and crafty challenge"; his shots were "sly responses."[30] At thirty-five, Drysdale could not hope to outrun Dick Stockton; he had to outplace and outthink him. Drysdale knew he had nothing to lose; his delicacy and sense of style were a delight to watch. He varied his pace, serve, and placement, and demonstrated exquisite manners while apparently enjoying the whole match. Stockton's irritability and doggedness began to seem out of place; but it was Stockton who went on to the finals and who was nationally televised as he lost it.

This may be one reason why women's professional tennis is popular; the game is slower, more varied, less explosive than that of the men. Viewers, whether they can articulate it or not, become aware that they are watching a different dimension of the same game, and respond accordingly.

There were other changes in tennis. Although three of the four Grand Slam tournaments were played on grass, there was a long-standing tradition of hard-court play. Struggling bands of professionals had often played indoors, where rain and poor light could not result in ticket holders demanding their money back. Whether the game is to be televised or not, hard-court surfaces can be painted so that it is easier to see whether the ball is in or out; on good hard-court surfaces there is none of the unpredictability that comes from grass,[31] which is fast, wears out unevenly during a tournament, and is affected by humidity. It is undoubtedly true that tennis played on grass possesses a smell, a texture, and a certain degree of spontaneity that hard courts cannot give; all this is replaced on a hard court by concentration on a ball that behaves unpredictably only if it is mishit. Grass courts, however, are practicable only in a country where grass grows readily and well, and where the pressure of population on the courts is not great. Once tennis became a game for more than the elite, hard courts were inevitable.

The move from Forest Hills to Flushing Meadow is a case in point. As Sally Wilson pointed out, U.S. tennis by the 1970s had "outgrown the private club in size and definition." Now the U.S. Open "embraces New York itself – its size, noise, spectacle and prices."[32] The move was not dictated by television. Indeed, had it been, more care might have been taken in choosing the site. The noise from La Guardia airport is deafening at the stadium, but is much more distracting on TV both in its volume and irregularity. Wilson reported that negotiations to reroute airport traffic had been undertaken during the peak coverage hours, but in 1980 I found the intrusion of aircraft noise almost intolerable. The site, in fact, had not been thought of primarily as a studio, although of course it could serve as one.

While televised tennis in the United States probably helped to popularize the game (and such a claim is extremely difficult to document because the physical fitness craze and U.S. television coverage coincided), the move from grass to hard courts and from outdoor to indoor matches can hardly be said to result from TV coverage. Human beings like to be comfortable, and there seems to be no point in enduring the outside when the inside is available. The "back to nature" movement on both sides of the Atlantic has spawned an array of camping equipment whose sole function is to civilize the experience of the primitive. The steady erosion of play on grass courts and a nationwide movement to playing indoors is merely part of a general trend toward using available technology to make playing and watching sport more attractive and accessible to everyone.

Nor can television be held responsible for the breakdown in mannerly behavior on the court. The ILTF had enforced rigid standards; by 1973, no one else possessed the power to do so. Player's groups such as the Women's Tennis Association drew up their own codes of conduct, but enforcement of them has proved exceedingly difficult.[33] Elite sports are marked by restrained public behavior on the part of both players and spectators; sports for the masses on both sides of the Atlantic involve noise from the spectators, loud comments on the official's conduct of the match, expressions of frustration on the part of the players, and lively movement on everyone's part. It is extremely difficult to play good tennis in a turbulent atmosphere;[34] but for TV spectators, the roar of the crowd behind the football or baseball commentator is in comforting contrast to the eerie sound of ball on strings. A player's antics may upset his opponent's concentration, and provide welcome relief from the quality of attention courtside spectators are expected to maintain. It is a small step from clowning to outright discourtesy; all too many players have now taken that step. Sponsors, however, do not want to see a player thrown out of a game, because it then stops. The ATP makes noises, but is not very interested in applying sanctions, because, like car drivers on a jury, any one of them may fall foul of the rules. Yet when a game is not in progress, the rules are slavishly applied.

Bjorn Borg, a five-time Wimbledon champion and outstanding court gentlemen, was barred from the 1982 tournament by the ATP because he had not entered the required number of Grand Prix tournaments. No precedent would necessarily have been set had he been allowed to play; television cannot be blamed for ATP's failure of vision. Manners palpably no longer count; obeying the letter of the law clearly does. As long as tickets can be sold for matches in which notorious troublemakers are scheduled to appear, so long will petulance and boorishness continue.

In fact, American television came to tennis when the metamorphosis of lawn tennis was well under way. It came after the power of the ILTF had been broken, at a time when players themselves were ready for experiments. Ironically, the fact that so much professional tennis activity took place in the United States created a difficulty of governance that the players, at least, had not anticipated. In 1965, the professional players had formed the International Professional Tennis Federation and declared that only members would be allowed to play in professional tournaments. Pancho Gonzales refused to join, was barred from a tournament, and filed an antitrust suit for $250,000. The federation was dumbfounded; Gonzales was promptly allowed to play wherever he wanted.[35] The players who formed the Association of Tennis Professionals in 1972 hoped to run tennis in much the same way as the Professional Golfers Association runs golf; but it was too late. Hunt had established WCT as a business; players therefore could not function as management and labor without falling foul of the antitrust laws.[36] No governing body emerged in tennis to replace the ILTF, so anyone who wanted to exploit tennis was free to try. World Team Tennis was organized in 1974; spectators were encouraged to behave as if they were at a football game. The clubs lost an average of $300,000 each during the first year and by 1978 were out of business. Team tennis was revived in 1982,[37] but on the opening night at Reunion Arena in Dallas a tiny group of several hundred spectators turned out. The franchise failed.[38]

With the power of the ILTF broken, it was in the players' and entrepreneurs' interest to promote a game that would draw spectators to the stadium, viewers to their sets, and hence sponsors to underwrite the game. And while the introduction of color made a tremendous difference to the attractiveness of all televised sport, it perhaps affected tennis more than most, because as anyone knows who has tried it, the effort of following a tennis ball on a black and white screen requires the kind of concentration only a dedicated fan is likely to give. In 1970, 95 percent of U.S. homes had TV and 39 percent of these had color sets; by 1972, 64 percent of sets were color.[39] Color sets were more expensive than black and white, so were likely to be owned by the affluent, precisely the audience televised tennis seemed likely to attract.

For what U.S. television executives saw was an opportunity to reach a market that was demographically appealing because it was affluent, educated, upwardly mobile, and trendy.[40] Tennis was much cheaper to televise than football or golf,[41] and it was novel. In the early 1970s, it was also clear that the power base of tennis had shifted to America because of the money players could make. As no governing authority ruled the game, individuals from any country in the world could make their way into the top tournaments ("top" in prestige or in cash), and America became their Mecca. Without a central governing authority, tennis was ripe for TV exploitation of all kinds; Wimbledon could be shown live, in Britain and the United States, but so could television spectaculars such as the $100,000 winner-take-all match between Jimmy Connors and Rod Laver in 1975.[42]

Structurally tennis, in its old and new forms, suited television fairly well. The best players in all major tournaments were so placed in the draw that they did not knock each other out in the early rounds; an unpredictable final should therefore theoretically result, because if a seeded player was out of form a lesser player could beat him or her before the finals were reached. Tennis is also a game of continual crisis; John McEnroe saved seven match points in the 1980 Wimbledon finals to get himself into the fifth set. Visually, the game offers great variety, not only because of the difference between strokes such as a volley and lob, but because similar strokes can be played differently; a serve can be angled or sliced, delivered fast or slowly, and placed differently within the service court. The pace of the game can change within a single rally. Cameras can easily follow the ball, not only because the court itself is small enough to be covered without reducing the players to midgets, but because every point must begin in the same way. The number of lines in the court means that a viewer can interpret the significance of each player's moves, even when the whole court is not shown on the screen.

Tennis lacks the violence of a contact sport, but there is a drama inherent in individual sports: no one can help the players when they are actually on the court. Although they may have mapped out their strategies with coaches beforehand, while they are playing they battle alone. If they are injured or exhausted no one can replace them; they are, for the duration of the match, indispensable. Viewers watch not a specialist assembly line, but young supermen and superwomen who are each one of a kind.

Yet while tennis possesses some characteristics that appear to make it a successful TV sport, it is sadly deficient in others. To begin with, matches are unpredictable in length, which causes scheduling problems. Although baseball is unpredictable too, at least its cast of characters changes frequently; unless a tennis player defaults, the same faces and bodies are on the screen every time one looks at the court. Unless the match is very close, such constant exposure can become tedious.

Much more fundamental is tne fact that there is no large popular base of spectators waiting to fill electronic seats. It is one thing to arrange a spectacular such as the 1973 "Riggs-King Battle of the Sexes," quite another to build a stable viewing audience. The Riggs-King event tapped into a highly emotional topic, built on the publicity engendered by the Riggs-Court match, and was therefore heavily publicized for weeks beforehand. But the event obviously could not be repeated, and to stage it, its sponsors had tossed aside the seals of "sacred time and space." Matches played on courts that have no particular history or reason for being lack an important dimension of "sacred space." Although the outcome of few tennis games can be predicted with certainty until the last ball has been played, "sacred time" requires a rhythmic, seasonal pattern for its fulfillment. It is ironic that not even casual viewers would have watched the Riggs-King event had not the players earned their way to it by means of tournaments that depended on just those seals of "sacred time and space."

What is also ironic is that once the game started, the hype was cast aside, and two players became locked in a contest that could be won only by their ability to play tennis. Both were heirs to a tradition, and even if they were prepared to use it as a means to an end, they could not destroy it on court. Perhaps viewers who watched a woman in her prime beat a man well past his nevertheless caught a glimpse of the fascination of tennis, especially if they had never seen it before.

Yet to build a tennis audience from spectators who are more or less ignorant of the sport is an almost impossible task, because the game is inherently cerebral, rootless, now lacks seasonal rhythms and a meaning-ful tournament structure, and is plagued by irresponsible court behavior.

Tennis is a game not of the hand but of the head. Those who do not understand the game may be captivated by the brilliant, athletic shots, but fail to realize that most winning strokes have to be set up, and that a viewer needs to watch the shot before the one that ends the point to understand how it was possible for the winning shot to be made. Where was the ball placed, to draw the opponent into an untenable position? What known weaknesses of the opponent were being tested? How was the pace varied so as to catch the opponent unprepared? To watch a tennis match requires a level of concentration few spectators are accus-tomed to bestowing on their TV sets, and makes the experience for the beginner rather hard work.

Team-sport players are attached to a city. It is true that key individuals may be traded so often that home fans have some difficulty in distinguish-ing between their own and an opposing team, but the team itself remains an institution. Even if one team player is injured or exhausted during a game, the game goes on; in tennis the players are irreplaceable, so the match collapses if a player does. If one player happens not to be playing particularly well that day, there is no means of substituting another who may inject some life into the affair. The players represent no one but themselves; as a viewer I cannot think "we" won, or feel any kind of thrill about the standard of play my city or town managed to achieve. Because of the individual nature of the game, team tennis is a contradiction in terms, as fans and spectators have made clear.

Further, apart from preseason games, teams play to achieve pennant or other place standings in a comprehensible and traditional seasonal contest, which will all comfortingly be repeated next year. The Australian Open no longer attracts the field its position as one of the Grand Slam tournaments should bring; sponsors can be found the world over for tournaments that mean nothing to the American or British publics. Even international matches such as the Davis Cup have been rendered meaningless, because many players would rather be using their skills in remunerative tournaments than representing their country for a pittance.[43] No one, and certainly not the ILTF, can now compel any country to field a representative team. Tennis players are usually competing for nothing that seems significant to a viewer; to improve one's computer standing or win a nameless tournament may be important for the player, but is unlikely to set the viewer's pulses racing.

In 1982, Lamar Hunt tried to give WCT tennis a format that would make sense to people used to rhythmic and understandable competition. Having confined WCT's activity to five months of the year since 1978, he withdrew from the ILTF's Grand Prix circuit and announced a men's Triple Crown of Tennis, divided into three playing seasons with championship finals at the end of each. He also made a stab at guaranteeing name recognition, by cutting down the number of players eligible for WCT events. But Hunt could not be certain that famous players would always appear in the televised finals, nor could he even advertise beforehand who those finalists would be.

Further, televised tennis is merciless to the players. We see not only consummate athleticism and extraordinary levels of concentration, but querulousness and glumness. When McEnroe lashed out at and damaged a CBS microphone on court, on the grounds that what a player says under his breath is not audible or even visible to fans in the stadium and should not therefore be taken into every living room, he wanted to eat his cake and have it, too. The text has to be writ large for me in my living room. I want my supermen supersized. Obsessive self-interest can remind me not of the godlike qualities of a superb player and the transcendence of the event, but of my own sordid humanity. Boorishness was not engendered by television, but the clarity with which television reveals it may yet destroy professional tennis on the screen.

U.S. television executives quickly became aware of the problems of translating tennis. What they might have done was to look carefully at the text and consider how it could best be annotated so as to make it comprehensible to people who lacked experience of tennis. What they actually did was to try to translate tennis into language with which Americans were already familiar; the result was often a botched translation.

No one watching the old lawn tennis thought, for instance, of counting such things as "unforced errors," "service aces," or the percentage of first serves in relation to the number of points won. These statistics, however, not only reflect an attempt to provide the plethora of numbers that Americans expect in their sport, but also serve as subplots. How fast does X serve, and is it faster than Y or Z? Whether these things matter, in the sense that they have a bearing on the outcome of the match, needs investigation. Tracy Austin, for example, won the 1981 U.S. Open Women's Singles Championship although her serve was at least 10 mph slower than Martina Navratilova's; but then Navratilova served many more double faults. The significance of all these things would be fascinating to compute; but as matters stand, the illusion of precision is being not merely maintained, but fostered, and provides something for the viewer to focus on besides the players and the ball. Conditioned as they are to quantification in sport, Americans look for the kind of measurable success in tennis that the game itself is hard put to provide.[44]

Many of the camera angles used during the play are also characteristically American. The viewer is often placed behind the receiving player at eye level, so that the ball appears to be coming directly into the living room. Camera angles will sometimes change during a point, and throughout a game the viewer is spirited about the court in the quest for visual variety. In the semifinals of the Men's Singles at Wimbledon in 1981, in the second game of the second set, televised by NBC, the viewer first was placed behind and above the receiver, then was given a close-up of both Borg and Connors in turn. Viewers were returned to a view behind the receiver, then got a close-up of Connors, went back behind Borg, then got a close-up of him, before returning behind Borg, but this time at eye level. A shot of Connors's wife in the crowd was shown before a close-up of Connors's serve, then the viewer went back behind and above the receiver. And so it continued. Visual variety was clearly the key to the broadcast.

The effort to involve the viewer, however, is self-defeating because it leads to gross distortion of the text. Few people at the stadium are behind a player receiving the ball at eye level, and even they are not so close that they cannot see the pattern of the game unfolding. Tennis is above all a game of strategy, in which each player is attempting ultimately to place the ball at such a speed and in such a position that the opponent cannot return it. It may take several shots, each gradually creating a free space on the court, to produce the winner; it may, if the opponent is unwary, unskilled, or has a lapse of concentration, take only one. To put the home viewer directly behind a player, at eye level, is to deprive that viewer of any chance of discerning the pattern of play.[45] The spurious sense of speed and tension is seen to be spurious by viewers who understand tennis, and the technique does not sufficiently overcome the other disadvantages of tennis as a sport for the casual viewer to hold attention for long. What is happening here is not that TV producers are creating a new game, but that they are simply providing a poor translation.

Similarly, much attention is given to varying the camera angle on the serve. In a 1980 U.S. Open match between Brian Teacher and Roscoe Tanner, there were close-ups of the face of the server, presumably to show tension and effort; the same technique was used in other matches. Half the torso was sometimes shown, or the face and arm; it was almost as if the producers were afraid to let the viewer see a whole serve very often, for fear that repetition would stale the palate. Such tricks as these, however, are not enough to attract the casual viewer, and a few of them go a long way with viewers who want to watch a game they cannot physically get to. Again, this is a problem of translation; there is no substitute for understanding the text.

Rarely have I seen such a bizarre translation as the CBS mangling of the 1983 Wimbledon Men's Singles Final. The visual tricks began early, in the third game of the first set, when the score was at deuce. The viewer was placed behind and on eye level with Connors through the first serve fault, and remained there for a few shots of the rally that developed after the second serve. Suddenly the ball was followed close up all the way to Ivan Lendl, then the viewer was whisked back behind and on eye level with Connors as he hit the ball. We then followed the ball close up again to Lendl, but were whisked back again to Connors. We traveled close up with the ball again toward Lendl; mercifully it went out. That is, for much of the play of this point, the viewers had been left with no idea of what was happening; there was no way in which they could supply the pattern of play in their minds' eye, because they had no idea of the positions of either player on court and no way of judging the pace or angle of the ball. It was as if the camera crew had gone mad and thought they were following a kickoff return or a long bomb.

And so it continued. It began to seem as if CBS feared to let viewers settle down and watch the game; whenever the rally threatened to last for more than a few strokes, the disorientation started again. Admittedly, this final was not one that will go down in Wimbledon annals; but that was no reason to give American viewers hack work.

In the battle to keep a spectator's wandering attention, TV executives may inadvertently trap themselves. The 1982 Wimbledon women's final was played between Martina Navratilova and Christine Evert-Lloyd. On another court, John McEnroe was playing Tim Mayotte in the rain-delayed men's final. During breaks in the women's match viewers were taken to the men's game, and if there was something exciting going on, were forced to remain there. While McEnroe was finishing off a set, viewers missed the whole of the first game of the women's second set, as well as part of the second game, and were returned late to the women's match on several other occasions. The women's event could not be treated as an event in itself, when so well known a male player as McEnroe was performing elsewhere; again, in an effort to secure visual variety and to sustain viewer interest, it was deemed perfectly reasonable to omit part of what viewers had ostensibly tuned in to see.[46]

All of this could, of course, be construed as evidence that television, as a medium, changes what it transmits. My point is that American TV producers deliberately chose to try to alter the essence of tennis to fit it to what they believed American perceptions to be. There is nothing intrinsic about the television apparatus itself that forces its users to do violence to the game. Translators of football and baseball come to the game with an experiential base, whether they are aware of it or not, and understand the language in which they are working. The translators of tennis either misunderstood the game or believed they could create a more interesting text.

For techniques used in other sports to hold viewers' attention do not necessarily distort the tennis text. The split screen provides interesting visual variety, as do shots of the umpire, linesmen, and prominent people in the crowd. Replays show isolated shots or the development of a whole point. The camera can flow back from a section of the crowd to a long shot of the whole court. Slick coordination between the commentators and camera crews can be accomplished, as an apparently casual remark about the number of spectators can instantly produce a shot of the packed stadium.

It is not merely U.S. camera crews who have difficulty with tennis, but commentators too. They seem quite unable to break out of the mold set by baseball and football. American sports audiences demand a flow of information; yet, traditionally, no one talks during tennis play itself. The breaks between games are occupied by advertisements, so commentators have to keep their remarks short and squeeze them in even if it means talking across a point. In the 1982 Wimbledon women's finals, in the second and third games of the first set, the longest pause Dick Enberg and Bud Collins allowed was twenty-two seconds, and the average pause between remarks was seven seconds. They talked across the umpire, and even across play, although they usually stopped as the racket actually hit the ball. Industrious as they tried to be, they talked only 29.8 percent of the total time players were on court. Almost half of what they had to say was in some sense an analysis of the game; that is, they explained such things as why a player's moves were appropriate or inappropriate, how a ball had been played and with what aim and effect. This information was rarely very technical; it was designed to help spectators understand the game better and to affirm what fans already knew. Remarks having nothing to do with the actual game in progress, referring to spectators, to Wimbledon itself, even to Prince William's birth, made up 21.4 percent of the commentary. Only 15.7 percent of the commentary was spent on the background of the players, their records, and such matters. (There is obviously a limit on what can be said about two people, however eminent.) A mere 15.6 percent of the comments were purely factual, giving the score or state of play; much of this sort of information was printed on the screen, and the umpire could often be heard, even through a commentator's remarks.[47]

What the commentators were doing was to annotate the text for the benefit of the uninitiated. Professional tennis has no history to speak of; amateur tennis in the United States is still largely confined to the affluent.[48] If spectators are to be wooed to the set, they must know what they are watching; U.S. commentators do their best to provide help.

There is a striking contrast between U.S. and British commentary on this particular game. A British audience had no particular interest in McEnroe except to denigrate him; but, in any case, the women's final is always given the honor it deserves, by being treated as an event in itself. There are no advertisements on the BBC, so Dan Maskell, Virginia Wade, and Ann Jones had about twenty-one more minutes of airtime to fill than Bud Collins and Dick Enberg. In fact, they actually talked for about eight minutes less. In the second and third games of the first set where Enberg and Collins chatted, Dan Maskell allowed one pause of one minute nineteen seconds; there was another of one minute eight seconds. The average pause between comments was forty-eight seconds. Nor is this paucity of comment unusual. In the men's semifinal match between Connors and Mark Edmondson, the longest pause of the first two games was one minute twenty seconds, and there was another of one minute seven seconds. The average pause between comments was about forty-two seconds.

Just over 70 percent of this sparse commentary on the match was given to analysis of the game. Much of this was quite technical and brief; longer comments were made between games and sets, although even these commentators clearly felt themselves under no obligation to fill in the silence by informing or amusing viewers. This commentary was for the friend in the seat, the person who would have been at the match had it been possible. Every utterance of the umpire was clearly heard; the BBC, unlike CBS, took the viewer to the game by allowing the umpire to be heard instead of talking across or around the courtside announcement of the score. As a result, a mere 5.4 percent of the commentary was spent on the state of play. Only another 9.8 percent was given to spectators or to other matters extrinsic to the event itself. The background of the players took 14.2 percent of the commentary. That is, very little of the commentators' efforts went into making the spectators feel part of the spectacle; rather, these were the sort of comments one friend might make to another sitting at the match. Further, relatively few comments were made by Virginia Wade, and Ann Jones spoke only between sets; Dan Maskell said what it was deemed necessary to say, and the gossipy byplay so much a part of U.S. commentary was never in evidence. Most of the time Dan Maskell referred to the players as "Mrs. Evert Lloyd" and "Miss Navratilova," although he occasionally called them by their first names. Bud Collins referred throughout to "Chrissie" and "Martina." For the BBC this match was an event, as it always has been, not a spectacle.

British commentary by American standards is sparse; the BBC translation of the visual tennis text is by American standards dull. On June 30, 1983, Martina Navratilova was to play Yvonne Vermaak in the women's semifinal. No names were shown on the screen as the players walked onto court, nor did the commentator mention them. As play commenced, a close-up behind Navratilova zoomed to a half torso just before the serve, but before the serve was delivered, the whole court was shown from above and behind the server; the angle remained the same throughout the play of the point. A close-up of Navratilova was shown after she lost the point, and as she prepared to serve; then the view returned to the whole court from above and behind as before. A close-up of Vermaak was shown after she won the next point; then viewers again went back to the whole court. This, in brief, was the established pattern; sufficient close-ups of players between points, showing the full head and shoulders, or sometimes the whole body, but when play was in progress the court was shown from above and behind either the server or receiver. In the first four games of this match there were no crowd shots, even when the players changed ends, and no replays, although the scoreboard was shown.

Precisely similar coverage was given to the other semifinal match between Billie Jean King and Andrea Jaeger. In the sixth game of the second set, Billie Jean King's face was seen in close-up before she served, then the court was shown from above and behind her throughout the point. Another close-up of Billie Jean King was shown as she walked back having lost the point. Again, the court was shown from above and behind her during the play of the point, and a close-up of Jaeger after she had lost the point. Then the court was again shown from behind the server. Visual variety is given through these close-ups, which often involve zooming in and different angles, but it is obviously assumed that viewers want to see the match from the equivalent of a good stadium seat, without gimmicks.

The BBC thus seeks to translate the text as faithfully as possible, for viewers who are already interested. ITV treats Wimbledon similarly, as an event for the initiated, not a spectacle to which everyone can be enticed if it is only made sufficiently exciting. Given the quality of play in these two particular matches,[49] it is probably as well that no false hopes were raised, but good or bad, what was evident at the court was also made evident on the screen. It is assumed that viewers are knowledgeable and interested, and so no attempts are made to attract or hold their attention beyond what the text itself demands.

On one channel or another, play at Wimbledon can be followed almost continuously. For Wimbledon is the last bastion of lawn tennis, and while electronic bleepers have been let into the grass to aid line judges, the old standards of lawn tennis are still self-consciously enforced. In 1981, Connors was reproved for grunting on court; nowhere else in the world would such a warning have been given. Shouts of "Come on Jimmy" may now float from the stands, and cushions rain down on the court when a crowd is disgusted, but the officials still behave much as they did before professionals were allowed to set foot on the hallowed turf. Unlike other British sports, which have feared television,[50] Wimbledon has always welcomed it, but the televising of the sport has not in the least altered conceptions of what is desirable there.

The contrast between American and British conceptions of the desirable on the tennis court was most clearly revealed in their reaction to McEnroe's tantrums during the 1981 Championships. The British press, from popular papers like the *Daily Mail* and *Daily Mirror* to the staid *Times,* universally lambasted McEnroe; no TV commentator supported him. Some American papers also deplored McEnroe's behavior, but Bud Collins, who introduced "Breakfast at Wimbledon" and who has continued to be a TV tennis commentator, took a different tack. Commenting on the finals in the United States, he referred to Wimbledon officials as the "fustian fathers" of tennis, and suggested that they had been unduly pained by what was simply boyish behavior. McEnroe's exemplary restraint when the umpire overruled a linesman's close call to put McEnroe two set points down was evidence that he could, when he set his mind to it, simply play tennis; his comments when he reached New York indicated that he saw no reason why he should be so imposed upon. McEnroe won his 1981 title worthily, surviving publicity and match calls that would have destroyed a lesser athlete. But the international attention paid to McEnroe's progress through the tournament was significant not simply to the player himself, but to professional tennis.

For professional tennis cannot survive in a vacuum. Lacking as it does all the characteristics and customs of mass spectator sports, it must survive in Britain and America on the devotion of those who understand it. Television remorselessly reveals self-interest, churlishness, and pettiness. When Novak's seals of sport, "competing" and "self-discovery," are violated, the inner life of tennis dies, and there is nothing left for which to root. When players begin to classify tournaments solely in terms of money, and by their behavior indicate that the French Open, say, is just another clay court tournament, the historic threads of the game are loosened, and some of its transcendence is lost. For the "bond of brothers," Novak's third seal, in tennis must consist of past and present champions, because it is not a team sport. Symbolically, this is represented at Wimbledon by an invitation to the champion to become a member of the All-England Club. Such gestures are far from meaningless; and if champions them-selves do not distinguish one money-making event from another, their fans will be hard put to do so.

Professional tennis will not live or die in the future on its television contracts, but on the perceptions of those who govern, play, and watch it. Television, per se, does not create those perceptions, but it reveals them. Television cannot break professional tennis, nor can it make it; the health of tennis in the future will therefore depend on those who write the text, not on those who translate it.

9

TELEVISED SPORT
IN CONTEXT

In 1950, 9 percent of American homes had TV sets; by 1955, 65 percent did, and ten years later, 93 percent. In Britain, 5 percent of homes had licensed TV sets in 1951; by 1966, 81 percent did.[1] Between 1950 and 1965, fundamental economic and social changes took place on both sides of the Atlantic that were not caused by TV, and whose precise relationship to the new medium is extremely difficult to determine. But these changes not only altered attitudes and perceptions toward sport as such, but also made an enormous difference to the actual conduct of sport as an industry. TV did not operate on sport in a vacuum; rather, it was one technological innovation among many.

Watching sport on TV became much more interesting when color sets replaced black and white. In 1965, only 5 percent of American homes had color TV; by 1972, 64 percent did. In 1971, when 91 percent of British homes had TV, only 9 percent had color sets, but their numbers increased rapidly.[2] By the time, however, that color sets were widely viewed in American and British homes, the pattern of telecasting sport had already been set, and the sports industry on both sides of the Atlantic was dealing with a vastly more affluent, mobile, and uninhibited audience than in 1950.

It was not television alone that created a "global village." In July 1929, Transcontinental Air Transport inaugurated a New York-Los Angeles air-rail link that took a record forty-eight hours but cost between $337 and $403 one-way. In June 1933, a United Airlines Boeing 247 established a coast-to-coast record of nineteen hours; but the aircraft could carry only ten passengers. By 1946, a Constellation could get from coast to coast in eleven hours. But it was not until jets permanently replaced the older, slower, and more expensive forms of propulsion in 1958[3] that professional sport in the United States could be anything but regional. In 1930, Horace Stoneham could not have moved his Giants to San Francisco nor Walter O'Malley the Dodgers to Los Angeles, whatever the state of their original ballparks, or however few fans went through the turnstiles, because their teams could not have traveled fast enough to play any other major leaguers. In 1958, the move made perfect sense. It was not TV alone that "nationalized" American sport and internationalized world sport; it was technological advances in transportation.

Before World War II, ballparks and stadiums had to accommodate some cars. Even in 1929, there was one car on the road for every five Americans. The depression and war curtailed the curve of growth, but in the postwar boom, "wheels" became ubiquitous. By the end of 1966, there was more than one car for every three Americans; Los Angeles had more cars than families. Road construction paralleled the increase; in 1939, there were 1,063,000 miles of paved road in the United States, and by 1950 this number had almost doubled. In 1956, the Interstate and Defense Highway Act created an interstate highway system; by 1964, there were 2,730,000 miles of paved road.[4] Journeys that had been unthinkable for a fan and unbearably tedious for a team became relatively fast and easy. Improvements in road building and in design of cars and buses also made for swifter, more comfortable travel.

The world actually experienced by most Americans was rapidly expanding just at the time when TV was bringing them an electronic version of that world; after World War II, many had the affluence to break out of the local confines imposed by the poverty of the depression and the restrictions of wartime. Families flocked to suburbia, seeking their "Little boxes on the hillside,/Little boxes made of ticky-tacky . . . And they all look just the same."[5] Downtown ballparks and stadiums in deteriorating neighborhoods, now a long drive from home, lost their appeal. As Roger Kahn put it in *The Boys of Summer,* "The Dodgers deserted Brooklyn. Wreckers swarmed into Ebbets Field and leveled the stands. Soil that had felt the spikes of Robinson and Reese was washed from the faces of mewling children. The New York *Herald Tribune* writhed, changed its face and collapsed. I covered a team that no longer exists in a demolished ballpark for a newspaper that is dead."[6] By the time, therefore, that almost all Americans could watch sporting events on their own TV sets, they were already in a position to ignore local professional sport. Attendance at minor-league baseball games demonstrates the changing habits of American baseball fans.

In the midwar years, only about 5.5 million people attended minor-league games, down from about 18 million in 1940. Just after the war, the figure shot up to about 37 million, reached a high point of about 38 million almost five years later, and then after about 1952 began to slump precipitously. In 1955, the figure was back down to about 18 million, and to about 10 million in 1960.[7] By no means were all of these missing fans watching major-league baseball on TV; with better roads and more money to buy the better cars to drive on them, and more leisure, fans were no longer tied to their local ballparks.

In the 1950s, comparatively few fans could get to a major-league ballpark, but they could exercise discrimination in the play they did watch. Having seen better play, they obviously preferred to do something entirely different from looking at the fumblings of the local hopefuls and has-beens they had had, perforce, to be satisfied with during the depression and the war.

For as attendance at the minor leagues went down, attendance at major-league ballparks went up. In 1956, approximately the same number of people attended minor and major-league baseball games; from then on, minor-league attendance waned and major-league attendance waxed. The major leagues expanded; by 1977, attendance at the major leagues had just surpassed the best attendance the minor leagues had ever managed.[8]

Baseball was not the only sport to benefit from postwar American affluence. In 1935, Americans spent less than $125 million on all sports for which admission was charged; by 1947, they were spending about $250 million. They continued at approximately that rate until the mid-1950s; by 1965, they were spending about $650 million to get into live sporting events. Perhaps seeing sporting events on TV inspired them to go to watch games in person; whatever the cause, by 1975 Americans were spending more than $1.4 billion for such entertainment.[9]

While it is quite impossible to know exactly how sports fans traveled to watch their teams over the years, the overall trends in traffic between cities, at least, can be discovered. In 1939, roughly two-thirds of those who bought tickets to travel between cities went by train; twenty years later, only a third did. Over 40 percent of travelers between cities who did not drive themselves were now going by air;[10] 52 percent of the U.S. rail network had no passenger trains.[11] Obviously, most of those paying passengers were not traveling to sporting events; but if Americans were willing to spend increasing amounts to attend sporting events, it is reasonable to assume they were also willing to pay to get to them.

And by 1960, air travel was not restricted to scheduled flights. In 1954, North American Airlines, an unscheduled carrier, flew over 329 million passenger miles, which was more then "any of the three smallest U.S.

Domestic Trunk Airlines." This unscheduled airline traffic grew to such an extent that in 1962, Congress confined the "supplemental" airlines to charter work; the revenues of these airlines almost doubled by 1966. In that year, only a fifth of their revenue came from purely commercial sources; by 1968, that proportion had risen to almost a half.[12]

Now, many of these charter planes were carrying passengers who had no interest at all in sport; nevertheless, rapid, relatively cheap, custom-tailored air transportation was available during the 1960s for players and fans alike. Had TV not existed, NFL supporters could easily have been gathered up to fly to any stadium where their team was playing, as fans fly to the Super Bowl. Just as postwar affluence forced the expansion of the NFL, so the increased disposable income that Americans were willing to spend on sport would have forced much greater expansion of the NFL in the absence of TV. That TV did enormously increase the number of football spectators is obvious; given, however, the combination of affluence, mobility, and interest in professional sport beginning after the war it seems equally clear that the NFL would have prospered mightily in any event.

While the British did not experience anything like the degree of affluence Americans enjoyed after World War II, their standard of living shot up comparably. Shorter working hours, car ownership, and greater affluence freed workers from dependence on their local soccer teams for Saturday afternoon entertainment. Third and Fourth Division teams lost their audience just as the minor-league baseball teams did; TV had little to do with it. County cricket lost its monetary base along with its leisured audience for reasons that have nothing to do with TV. Amateur teams had played limited-over cricket for years; well before 1980, the professionals would have adopted it.

To get from Britain to a European country in 1950 involved a tedious journey by boat and rail; the technological changes in aircraft, as well as the network of motorways that spread through postwar Europe and the development of very fast passenger trains, made it simple for clubs from different nations to play each other. World Cup cricket was made possible by jet travel. British TV simply broadcast matches that were organized and played primarily with live audiences in mind. The extended season that British cricket and soccer players enjoy in the 1980s evolved from changed social and economic conditions, not electronic wizardry.

Technology and increased affluence also affected dress. When American troops arrived in Britain during the war, the nylons they brought caused many an international incident. With the invention of stretch fabrics, game uniforms no longer had to be loose; as plastics came into use for boots and shoes, the clodhopping soccer player in his flapping shorts was transformed into a ballet dancer. Football players began to look less like gladiators than spacemen; as artificial turf replaced the real thing, their uniforms remained outwardly pristine to the end of the game. TV did not cause any of these changes, but viewers certainly benefited from them; athletes were no longer swaddled in their heavy-duty clothes, but outlined by them. Technology inadvertently added an aesthetic dimension to professional sport; baseball, football, and soccer players began to look as civilized, as expensive to the untutored eye, as cricketers and tennis players always had. As the market for casual clothes developed, stadium fans altered their wardrobes too. TV, on both sides of the Atlantic, showed crowds clothed for the occasion because they could now afford a specialized wardrobe.

Increased affluence in the postwar world also meant there was more money for athletes themselves. TV has undoubtedly poured huge sums into the coffers of American sport; these bonanzas, however, have not trickled down to players proportionately. Historically, what has increased player salaries most in the United States has been the presence of rival leagues. In baseball, the existence of the American and Federal Leagues both led to an upsurge of wages as players either jumped to the rival leagues or threatened to do so.[13] Football salaries increased through the activities of the All-American Football Conference and took a huge leap with the formation of the American Football League. As O. J. Simpson pointed out, "That was the generation gap in pro football. Since the big-money era had started with the war between the two leagues, many of us had been able to use bonuses and salaries to set up enterprises that would aid us throughout our lives."[14]

The NFL Players Association representatives complained in a 1981 report that average NFL salaries were half those of baseball and basketball, and even below those of hockey, a sport that had no national TV contract.[15] The 1982 strike did not get the players what they were asking for. But in 1984, the association announced that the average base salary of NFL players had gone up by 25 percent; Gene Upshaw, the executive director, admitted that the United States Football League had made the difference.[16] Without the USFL, the Cowboys would certainly not have had to pay Herschel Walker a sum that distressed many of his new teammates.

Other factors have also increased salaries. Long before TV's advent, superstars raised the level of journeymen salaries; as Voigt points out, Babe Ruth's salary pulled others after him.[17] Arbitration awards in baseball, based on comparisons between players, have also tended to increase salaries. As James Dworkin points out, "Player salaries [in baseball] have gone up in recent years for a whole host of reasons, including the right to employ salary arbitration, the right to demand and veto trades, inflation, and others."[18] Baseball was televised long before 1974; it was not TV, but union activity that made possible the final-offer salary arbitration that went into effect that year. Union activity has been less successful in football, not because of owner intransigence alone, but because very few individual players can transform a football team in the way that, say, a Vida Blue could transform the Giants.[19]

It is also easy to forget that even in the years before TV, some players did very well for themselves. The 1916 World Series check was almost $4,000,[20] which represents at least $36,000 today and was free of income tax. In that year a telegrapher was making less than $1,300. But pre-World War II professional players did not have the agents, the unions, and above all the human rights movement on their side. Chattels they were, in fact, but they were marketed as heroes, dedicating themselves to the good of the game. Heroes do not concern themselves with cash.

In Britain, TV did not pour money into sport; increased player affluence was fueled from other sources. Consonant with the removal of barriers between master and servant in other spheres, the maximum-wage restriction in soccer was struck down in court in 1961. It is hard to live a stylish life on twenty pounds a week; the dress and behavior of star British soccer players altered when they had more cash. As they became more flamboyant they became better media copy, and hence attractive to advertisers. Cricketers are much less well paid, and as their game has lost much of its appeal, its stars are less in demand for lucrative off-field opportunities. What TV has done for all professional athletes in Britain is to bring their faces into the living room. Yet because of the way in which sport, particularly soccer, is televised, players may be recognized less from their performances on the field than from their appearances in talk shows or magazinelike programs.

In the days before TV, stars made money from endorsements, banquet speeches, and the like.[21] But their faces were not seen daily in the living room peddling after-shave lotion; their opportunities for making extra money were not thrust under their fans' noses. When players' incomes were apparently linked to the stadium, fans could believe that men were dedicating their lives for a chance to excel at a game, or envy the athletically talented youth who had escaped the life of manual labor that was theirs. Since sports have been televised, players are known to barter their talents for money; the joy of sports seems to have been reduced to a business deal.

According to the *Miller Lite Report,* 76 percent of the people questioned strongly agreed with the statement that professional athletes are overpaid. Only 42 percent agreed that professional athletes are more dedicated to the game than to their own gain.[22] On both sides of the Atlantic, newspaper reports of players' incomes deal with figures quite beyond the earning power of all but a few readers. For so long were professional sports in the United States marketed as a facet of the American dream that it is hard to accept the reality behind the myth; had all players in the past been working for love of the game, no one would ever have needed a reserve clause. In Britain, professionals were suspect until well after World War II, but their salaries were kept until the 1960s at what fans could regard as a decently low level.

In the period between the two world wars, America's sportsmen were marketed as the epitome of middle-class virtue. Lardner's Jack Keefe[23] was a successful character not only because he was consummately created, but because he was set against the hero-worshiping imagery other sports-writers were purveying. After 1943, Dick Young began to suggest that some baseball stars might be less than perfect; but as a fledgling sportswriter, Roger Kahn had not the heart to tell his father, a devoted baseball fan for fifty years, that "his imaginings were fluff."[24] It is tempting to suggest that sportswriters turned to denigration when TV deprived them of the chance to describe to readers games they had not already watched; but it was during the 1960s that repudiation of authority, iconoclasm, and what one might call the smear and snarl conduct of public affairs became the rule in both the United States and Britain. Babe Ruth's public image was lovingly burnished; the life-style of a Joe Namath, a Bill Walton, or a George Best was wallowed in. The American and British publics enjoyed their antiheroes; a player like Roger Staubach became, for many, a goody-two-shoes.

In the 1950s, no one thought of arming British policemen; when the railroads first ran special trains to take soccer fans to matches, no one envisaged the vandalism and hooliganism these trains came to represent. As the cult of amateurism and the veneer it laid on professional sport waned, and as civility departed from public life off the field, unheard-of behavior became commonplace on the field. This had nothing to do with television. In fact, British television has often tried to uphold standards of decorum reminiscent of the early twentieth century.

On June 7, 1980, for instance, the schoolboy international match between England and Scotland was unexpectedly interrupted by three spectators who ran onto the field. Immediately, the cameras swung away from what the commentator called the "louts." As he asked rhetorically, "Why should we glorify them?" Calling the interruption "scandalous," the commentator verbally described proceedings as the intruders were "marched off the field, and good riddance to them." The cameras pointed anywhere but at the disturbance. No viewer could have thought this incident was part of the "entertainment" being offered; rather the com-mentary and camera underlined the violation of "sacred" time and space.

But in the 1981 U.S. Open Women's semifinal match at Flushing Meadow, a similar disruption was treated quite differently. By mutual agreement, Evert Lloyd and Navratilova stopped playing until a spectator who had been shouting was removed from the stands. Neither player made a public fuss; they simply rallied gently until officials took action. The cameras focused on the spectator, then on the hapless employees sent to remove him, and followed his ejection from the stadium. The shouter was given a full measure of the attention he craved, for with no play going on, the cameras had automatically focused on the "action."

British cameras do, of course, follow protesting soccer players to the referee and tennis players to the umpire's chair, and try to transmit the subsequent conversation. This is part of the event itself, and if players themselves do not habitually reflect self-control, that is not something to be concealed. Athletes cannot, however, be expected to transcend the temper of their times. If, indeed, TV publicized and glamorized the newly rebellious, it did so in contexts having nothing to do with sport. The sportsmanship of the fifties was simply one casualty among many.

In 1950, few parents of college students had ever worried about their children's use of drugs. By 1965, when most Americans had TV sets, parents had begun to worry; by 1980, parents who had never worried about drugs, licit and illicit, were a dying breed. In 1950, few aspirants to fame in baseball, football, cricket, or soccer would have smoked heavily; for generations, tobacco had been known to be bad for the wind. Alcohol was another matter entirely; it was perfectly permissible, either side of the Atlantic, to be paralytically drunk in celebration or to drown one's sorrows. To play with a hangover was not uncommon; but few players believed they were at their best if they were intoxicated on the field itself. Steroids, however, were something else; they appeared to give one a competitive edge if taken consistently. Mind-altering substances reduced the pain of body contact or simply became habitual. Drug addicts needed their fixes to play at all, much less to play well; drugged in college, they took their addictions into the professional game, where increased income allowed them to pay for steadily increasing consumption.

Druggies are unlikely to be concerned with sportsmanship. Had nothing else altered in American or British society between 1950 and 1986, the availability of drugs and their use by athletes would have affected standards of conduct in practice and play. Yet it is hard to see how the televising of sport can be held responsible for athletes' drug consumption. With or without TV, the necessity and desire for winning would have been present; whatever rationalizations athletes make for drug use would have been made had no TV been present in any American or British home.

Nor can TV be held responsible for the squalid mess that American school and college teams often represent. TV may have provided vivid role models for blacks, but it was the colleges who prostituted themselves in recruiting athletes rather than students from the ghettos. It was high schools looking for a winning team who encouraged students to believe that sport was more worthwhile than study, and happily offered up illiterate players, black and white, to the colleges. The NCAA's debates on its belated attempts to reform recruiting made it obvious that colleges wanted athletes on campus solely for what they could get out of them.

Schools in the United States resisted the children's soccer revolution as long as they could. They were finally overwhelmed by the students' interest, the fitness craze that swept America in the 1970s, and, in part, the dissemination of knowledge about sports medicine, a speciality that was scarcely known before 1950. Parents who were delighted to see their sons tough it out on the school football field in the 1950s could not know of the lasting damage being done to young necks and knees; even in the 1970s, few parents were aware of the dangers of head tackling. No parent can now plead ignorance; and parents who are themselves jogging, playing tennis, or working out at the Y are less and less likely to be enamoured of the "leadership qualities" that sitting on a bench in football uniform supposedly engenders.

This change in attitude alone could account for diminishing numbers of spectators at school team events. But other changes have also occurred since 1950. Mothers have increasingly entered the work force. In 1950, 12 percent of married women with children under six years old worked outside the home; in 1980, 45 percent did, and 54 percent of all married women with children under eighteen held an outside job. Parents have less time in the 1980s than in the 1950s to attend school sports events.[25] The nonschool soccer leagues sprouting up all over the United States have also absorbed the time and attention of many parents who once attended school events because there were no others.

In sparsely populated areas, school sports teams will probably continue to provide a focus for community pride in the United States. They can do so, however, only as long as the team sports represented matter to the outside world, and as long as the formal educational system gives such sports its wholehearted support. The mind-set that produced this community phenomenon antedated TV; it will decline or survive for reasons having little or nothing to do with sports telecasting.

The range of sports facilities open to everyone in Britain has always been greater than in many parts of the United States, particularly sparsely populated rural areas. Public indoor swimming pools, for instance, are open winter and summer; they were even kept open during World War II. Dart boards are on the walls of every pub; no working man's club is complete without snooker. Games are not put away in Britain with other childish things, and for so long has amateur and professional sport existed side by side that televising "the best" has not put the amateur leagues out of action, any more than televising baseball has affected softball. Professional snooker players on the telly have not diminished interest and activity in snooker at the lower levels.

But if TV has not led to less participation in amateur sport, TV has not integrated sport in Britain, any more than it has done in the United States. In spite of the BBC's efforts to preserve traditional standards of decorum at cricket matches and to avoid racism in soccer, public perception of the real state of affairs is as clear as Americans' perception of NFL drug problems. TV can neither set nor uphold conditions that do not exist at the stadium; sports telecasting is rooted in actual experience.

It seems to me that the harshest critics of televised sport have failed to recognize that what TV has done is to show us more of professional sport's reality than we really wanted to see. Televised sport has undoubtedly destroyed illusion. In ruthlessly exposing the fundamental relationship between a commercialized sport and its audience, stadium fans have been forced to realize that their sense of control and of community are little more than a fantasy.

Not everyone who goes to a stadium is a fan; gate receipts have always gone up when a well-known player or famous team came to town,[26] and a team that consistently loses, on either side of the Atlantic, can expect to see its ticket sales slump. But to go to a stadium at all requires a degree of commitment to the event as such, and the person who buys a ticket makes a direct transaction with the ball club.

Before sport was televised, entrepreneurs were satisfied if the stadium seats were more or less full. When attendance slumped, attention was given to improving the grounds, changing the rules, playing night games, or doing whatever was considered necessary to attract the patron. The changes made affected equally everyone who saw the game. People who believed a particular sport or team was deteriorating stayed away; their absence gave the stadium managers an immediate and unambiguous message. Radio, exciting as it was, could be no substitute for stadium attendance. Those who bought tickets had a distinct advantage over those who stayed at home.

When games began to be televised, the stadium walls were suddenly blown outward. Now entrepreneurs were concerned to fill an infinite number of seats, and while filling the stadium remained economically important,[27] the members of the stadium audience were forced to realize that they and their team were no longer taking part in a community rite. Without their permission, their rituals had been opened to any Tom, Dick, or Harry who turned on the TV set. Rule and other changes could now be made not only to woo people to support a particular team, but to catch the wandering attention of the viewer who might push up the ratings. Stadium fans became merely one pillar in support of commercial sport, not its cornerstone.

Worse, the very object of the fan's devotion had been transformed, at least in the United States, from an end to a means. Even if a fan realized that professional sports had always been industrial enterprises, in the age before television the promoter of a stadium event was selling a fan an identifiable product. Commercial TV network executives simply use the sports event so that they can sell something else – advertisements. The money now available from TV has also attracted into sport entrepreneurs who know little about the specific game they are underwriting, but do not hesitate to meddle with their employees who do. Commercialized sport was always played for profit; but it was not publicly discussed as a commodity to be packaged and merchandised like chewing gum. Before games were televised, stadium fans thought they sustained their clubs; now they know that their interests may well be sacrificed to those of people who have not bothered to buy tickets. Their psychic investment has been spurned, while the ball club continues to exact payment; in their eyes their status has been reduced from that of partners to consumers.

Roger Angell has written eloquently along just these lines. He complains that the World Series of 1976 was played at night, too late in the year, so that players battled the cold as well as each other. The series was played on artificial turf, which altered the conditions of play. A designated hitter was used. For Angell the sport of baseball had been violated in the name of Nielsen, and he recoiled in horror from the idea of moving the World Series permanently to a domed stadium and transforming it into another Super Bowl.[28]

What, however, Angell wants to preserve is not the sport of baseball, which has undergone countless changes, but the stadium fan's sense of community. Technology has made it possible for us all to witness the marvel of the World Series, and the time may well have come to create a "sacred space" worthy of it. When the best baseball began to be played only in urban ballparks, the game was severed from its rural beginnings; that happened long before the advent of television. Now that we have the technology, why should we not construct a stadium to insulate players from the vagaries of the weather, as properly prepared ballparks insulated our forefathers from the vagaries of the meadow? There is nothing "sacred" about the time spent sitting under the umbrellas when the skies open, as they did in the 1982 World Series; in fact, the rain may deprive us of seeing a player at the height of his powers because he has lost his momentum.

Changes in bats and balls, much more significant than changes in turf, were made long before baseball was televised. These changes were made to draw people to the stadium, and the whole strategy of the game altered as a result. Artificial turf should be dispensed with if it shortens a player's working life or decreases his repertoire of skills, but not because it requires changes in strategy. Baseball has lived through many of those.

Moreover, wholesale attempts to change the rules of any sport are self-defeating; attempts to make soccer palatable to U.S. audiences have drawn neither stadium nor electronic support. More subtle rule changes may, in fact, work for the benefit of both players and fans. The tiebreak in tennis puts a premium on coolness and concentration, rather than on stamina; it requires players to command a slightly different set of skills when their "normal" tennis strategies have been demonstrated to be roughly equal. Stroke instead of medal play in golf makes every player complete the whole course, with each unique hazard; if anything, the game has been made more testing and subtle, rather than less.

Yet we are shocked when college basketball authorities openly admit that new foul rules have been drawn up with an eye on the TV audience.[29] We forget that rules were being altered to attract spectators to college football games in the nineteenth century. What has changed is the rhetoric, not the substance.

But the joy of sports has not changed. National sports in the United States are owned and organized by businessmen, as part and parcel of other enterprises. The marketing of those sports is therefore conducted in an ethos quite different from that of countries where national sport is not conceived primarily in business terms. There must, however, be a product to market; as soon as sport becomes a mere entertainment, it loses its audience. At Super Bowl XX the introduction of the Most Valuable Players of all the previous Super Bowls demonstrated how conscious the NFL is that professional football must be more than a game; it must have a history, a tradition, a liturgy, even a calendar of saints.

In Britain, neither soccer nor cricket is conceived of as primarily a business. Nor is television – yet. In Britain, therefore, TV cannot reinforce the sports industry to their mutual commercial benefit. As radio in Britain was perceived from its inception as a service, so TV's Channel 4, the latest addition to the British TV industry and a commercial channel, is legally required to provide for "minority" interests in program contracting and presentation.

For British TV, therefore, to translate any particular sporting text in such a way as to deliberately increase spectatorship for that event would be to fly in the face of heritage and tradition. In the United States the opposite is true, for it has never been enough in the United States to keep the pot simmering; it must overflow. In both Britain and the United States, TV has thus been used in sports telecasting to reinforce existing tradition, not to undermine it.

In short, what we believe TV has "done" to sport depends very much on the rest of our personal cultural baggage. What we can all agree on is that a televised sporting event gives a common experience to far greater numbers of people than ever could enjoy it at any given stadium. Based on her work in Brazil, Janet Lever suggests that televised sport can, because of its shared properties, act as a sort of social glue.[30] This idea needs far more exploration. Fans may well be equally moved by watching their soccer teams on "Match of the Day," or by seeing two teams with which they have little emotional involvement play the Cup Final, or by following a World Cup match between teams from countries they do not care about. So long as the soccer is interesting, these fans will be absorbed. If, however, they watch "Match of the Day" only when they seek identification with their own tribe, they will not bother to switch on the set for the World Cup, unless their own nation's team is competing. The ratings for the World Series and Super Bowl suggest that interest can be aroused that goes well beyond local loyalties. So it may be that a sports telecast can help human beings enlarge their sympathies, as well as keep them in touch with their teams. We do not yet know.

A host of other questions about the relationship between TV and sport awaits examination. It seems to me, however, that we shall not discover much about the matter unless we set it in a broad context.[31] What I hope I have shown is that particular sports can be televised well or badly; that simply to televise a sport will not ensure its popularity; and that the form and structure of a sports telecast will reflect traditional perceptions of the nature and content of the event itself, as well as of the taken-for-granted nature of what constitutes a sporting event. In Britain and the United States, TV producers want viewers to see an event they will watch and then wish to watch again. The telecast will reflect producers' beliefs, examined and unexamined, about what a sports contest is and represents. If we wish, therefore, to understand a sports telecast, our first task must be to abandon our myopic concern with the medium itself, and examine the telecast within, and not apart from, its cultural context.

APPENDIX

The Game of
Cricket in Brief

As in baseball, one team fields while members of the other team bat. The difference is that two batsmen in a cricket team are on the field at once, one at each end of the pitch, which is twenty-two yards long.

Instead of bases, there is a "wicket" at each end of the pitch that consists of three sticks called "stumps" stuck in the ground. Across the top rest two other small sticks, in grooves, called "bails." To get a batsman out at the wicket, it must be "broken"; that is the bails must be knocked off the stumps by the ball, either on its own, or held by a fielder.

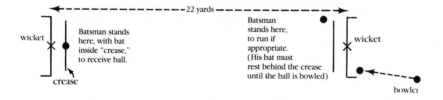

FIG. 1. Diagram of cricket pitch. All lines are marked in white on the grass. (Broken lines in the diagram indicate distance.)

The bowler delivers the ball overarm to a batsman at the other end of the pitch. The ball usually bounces once on the ground before it is hit. The batsman can hit it or not, as he chooses. If he hits it, he can choose whether or not to run; that is,

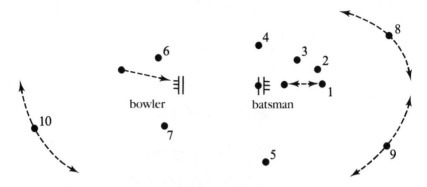

FIG. 2. Diagram of a field for a right-handed batsman and right-handed bowler. (The eleven fielders can be placed in a number of different positions depending on the state of play, whether the bowler is fast or slow, etc.) 1. Wicketkeeper (Moves back or close up to wicket, depending on bowler's speed of delivery). 2. and 3. Slips (Number depends on conduct of game). 4. Point. 5. Square leg. 6. Mid-off. 7. Mid-on. 8. Third man. 9. Long leg. 10. Long-off. After the bowler has bowled his over he will field somewhere, usually in the outfield, replacing the bowler who has been fielding for him.

to run to the other end of the pitch. The batsman there runs at the same time, so that they can cross. Every time they cross one run is scored. They can cross up to three times on one ball, if it has been hit far enough. A "four" or "six" (runs) can be scored by hitting the ball across the boundary line (an ellipse drawn at some distance around the pitch), rather like a home run. A four is scored if the ball hits the ground before crossing the boundary; a six if it clears the line before touching the ground.

While the batsmen are running, the fielders chase the ball, as in baseball. A fielder can return the ball to either end of the pitch; if the ball breaks the wicket before the batsman reaches the "crease" (a line in front of it) with his feet or bat, the batsman is "run out."

The batsman can be "caught out," as in baseball, or he can be got out in a number of other ways. Each batsman who is out is replaced by another, until ten men are out; the eleventh batsman has to retire, but is marked in the score book as "not out." Unlike baseball batters, batsmen stay in the game after they have hit the ball; they must be got out or retire.

A bowler bowls six balls from one end of the pitch, then another bowler bowls six balls from the other end. Except in limited-over cricket, a bowler goes on bowling his six balls, an "over," as long as the captain allows; but when each bowler is relieved, he does not leave the field, as a pitcher does, but goes on fielding as he did during the over he wasn't bowling.

When the whole side is out, or in limited-over cricket, when one team has run out of overs, the teams change over. The game ends when time runs out (five days in a test match, three days in a county match) or when all the overs allowed have been played in a one-day match. The winner is the team that has scored the most runs, provided that in a test or county match, one side has lost all its wickets; if one side has not lost all its wickets, the match is drawn. In test or county cricket each side bats twice or "plays two innings."

NOTES

Introduction

1. The case against televised sport is most decisively set out by Benjamin Rader in *In Its Own Image: How Television Has Transformed Sports* (New York: Free Press, 1984).

2. Fans should not be confused with spectators. The *Miller Lite Report,* which claims to be "the most comprehensive sports study ever conducted," adopts a purely quantitative approach to fans; no attempt is made to measure the quality of anyone's involvement in sport. "Avid fans" are considered to be those who report frequent watching, listening, reading, and talking. On these grounds, an avid fan could be one who reads the sports pages and watches TV sports news every day, watches "Monday Night Football" and one other sports program, and gossips about sport to spouse and colleagues. The avid fan, in other words, need know very little about any particular sport, and care about none. This definition won't do.

True fans have devoted themselves to a game. They know the rules, remember great plays and players of the past, watch the progress of the current crop with an informed and dispassionate eye, read about sport, and take their children to the game. A fan is one who, as an Englishman put it, is "football daft." Miller Brewing Company, *The Miller Lite Report on American Attitudes toward Sports* (Milwaukee: Miller Brewing Co., 1983) pp. 1, 207-8; Michael Parkinson, *Football Daft* (London: Stanley Paul, 1971).

3. David Halberstam, *The Breaks of the Game* (New York: Knopf, 1981), p. 14.

4. Not all professional athletes necessarily receive proper and prompt medical attention; but they are increasingly knowledgeable about their rights, and no

promoter can give athletes the cavalier treatment nineteenth and early twentieth century athletes received.

5. These traditions may change as spectators change. West Indians attending cricket matches have brought their ebullience with them, which has completely altered the genteel somnolence that was traditionally associated with professional cricket.

6. Riochi Okabe, "Cultural Assumptions of East and West: Japan and the United States," p. 22. In *Intercultural Communication Theory: Current Perspectives,* ed. William B. Gudykunst (Beverly Hills: Sage Publications, 1983), pp. 21-44.

7. Edward Buscombe, ed., *Football on Television,* (London: British Film Institute, 1975).

8. Ibid., p. 6.

9. Unlike *TV Guide, Radio Times* (BBC) and *TV Times* (ITV) are initiated by the broadcasting organizations.

10. Buscombe, *Football on Television,* p. 6.

11. As Allen Guttmann puts it, "Why then *do* people watch? No matter how complex the response to this five-word question, no answer will be universally valid." Allen Guttmann, *Sports Spectators* (New York: Columbia University Press, 1986), p. 176.

12. R. S. Rait Kerr, *The Laws of Cricket: Their History and Growth* (London: Longmans, Green and Co., 1950). The only work on baseball rules, John D. Allen's "The History of Professional Baseball Rule Changes (1800-1970)" (M. S. thesis, University of Wisconsin, 1971), is sadly misnamed.

13. Daniel Snowman, *Britain and America: An Interpretation of Their Culture 1945-1975* (New York: New York University Press, 1977), pp. 8-9, 11-13.

14. J. A. Mangan, *Athleticism in the Victorian and Edwardian Public School: The Emergence and Consolidation of an Educational Ideology* (Cambridge: Cambridge University Press, 1981), p. 3.

Chapter 1

1. Michael Novak, *The Joy of Sports: End Zones, Bases, Baskets, Balls and the Consecration of the American Spirit* (New York: Basic Books, 1976) pp. 252-53.

2. The first book-length treatment of televised sport was William O. Johnson's *Super Spectator and the Electric Lilliputians* (Boston: Little, Brown and Co., 1971). Comments about TV's relationship to sport were made in books on other topics, such as Roger Angell's *The Five Seasons: A Baseball Companion* (New York: Popular Library, 1978) and Leonard Schecter's *The Jocks* (Indianapolis: Bobbs-Merrill, 1969), but the next book on TV and sport was Ron Powers's *Supertube: The Rise of Television Sports* (New York: Coward-McCann, 1984). This was quickly followed by Benjamin G. Rader's *In Its Own Image: How Television Has Transformed Sports* (New York: Free Press, 1984), the personal statement of a historian who believes that TV has "trivialized the experience of spectator sports" (p. 5).

Articles in which questions are raised about TV's malignant effect on sports include the following: David L. Altheide and Robert P. Snow, "Sports versus the

Mass Media," *Urban Life* 7, no. 2 (July 1978): 189-204; Michael Arlen, "The Bodiless Tackle, the Second-Hand Thud," *New Yorker,* Apr. 29, 1967, pp. 159-64; Russell Baker, "Please Turn Off the Sports," *New York Times,* Apr. 20, 1975, p. 31; Jennings Bryant, Paul Comisky, and Dolf Zillmann, "Drama in Sports Commentary," *Journal of Communication* 27, no. 3 (Summer 1977): 140-49; Jeffrey Goldstein and Brenda J. Bredemeier, "Socialization: Some Basic Issues," *Journal of Communication* 27, no. 3 (Summer 1977): 154-59; Jack R. Griffin, "TV Kidnaps Sports," *Nation,* Mar. 29, 1965, pp. 336-38; Richard Harmond, "Sugar Daddy or Ogre? The Impact of Commercial Television on Professional Sports," in *Screen and Society: The Impact of Television upon Aspects of Contemporary Civilization,* ed. F. J. Coppa (Chicago: Nelson Hall, 1979), pp. 81-105; Derek Morgan, "I Want My Bloody Game Back," *Sports Illustrated* 27, no. 9 (Aug. 28, 1967): 52-54; Donald Parente, "The Interdependence of Sport and Television," *Journal of Communication* 27, no. 3 (Summer 1977): 128-32; Robert H. Prisuta, "Televised Sports and Political Values," *Journal of Communication* 29, no. 1 (Winter 1979): 94-102; Brian R. Williams, "The Structure of Televised Football," *Journal of Communication* 27, no. 3 (Summer 1977): 133-39. Donald Parente also raises some of these issues in his dissertation, "A History of Television and Sports" (University of Illinois, 1974).

3. James Michener, *Sports in America* (Greenwich, Conn.: Fawcett Crest, 1976), p. 31.

4. Colin McArthur, "Setting the Scene: *Radio Times* and *TV Times,*" in *Football on Television,* ed. Edward Buscombe (London: British Film Institute, 1975), p. 8.

5. An excellent case study of this process is Roger Silverstone's *Framing Science: The Making of a BBC Documentary* (London: British Film Institute, 1985).

6. Powers suggests that the unpredictable nature of live sports was one of the reasons "TV's ruling elite" did not want to become involved with it in the mid-1950s. Powers, *Supertube,* p. 91.

7. Morgan, "I Want My Bloody Game Back"; Richard O'Connor, "The Game Fans Should See – and Don't," *TV Guide,* Feb. 6, 1982, pp. 13-16.

8. Williams, "Structure of Televised Football," p. 137.

9. Bruce Berman, "TV Sports Auteurs," *Film Comment* 12, no. 2 (Mar./Apr. 1976): 34-35, 64. See also Robert Riger, "What Television Network Covers Football Best?" *New York,* Nov. 27, 1972, pp. 40-44.

10. Williams, "Structure of Televised Football," p. 137.

11. Percy D. Haughton, *Football, and How to Watch It* (Boston: Marshall Jones Co., 1922), p. 26.

12. Tom Ryall, "Visual Style in 'Scotland and Yugoslavia,'" in Buscombe, *Football on Television,* p. 37.

13. Rudolf Arnheim, *Visual Thinking* (Berkeley: University of California Press, 1969), p. 107.

14. Paul Comisky, Jennings Bryant, and Dolf Zillmann, "Commentary as a Substitute for Action," *Journal of Communication* 27, no. 3 (Summer 1977): 150-53.

15. Bryant et al., "Drama in Sports Commentary."

16. Graham McNamee with Robert Gordon Anderson, *You're On the Air* (New York: Harper and Bros., 1926), pp. 52-55.

17. *The Miller Lite Report on American Attitudes toward Sports* was based on telephone interviews using a questionnaire. It is innocent of theory and must be used with caution. (Milwaukee: Miller Brewing Co., 1983), p. 90.

18. Rudolf Arnheim, *Film as Art* (Berkeley: University of California Press, 1957), p. 162.

19. Novak, *Joy of Sports,* p. 121. Novak discusses the seven seals on pp. 122-66.

20. Those who went to bed in disgust when the Cowboys were 3-23 at the end of the first half of their first 1983 season game did not see their 31-30 victory over the Redskins.

21. Charles Barr, "Comparing Styles: England v West Germany," in Buscombe, *Football on Television,* p. 48.

22. Novak, *Joy of Sports,* p. 143.

23. TV producers may, in fact, have gone too far in emphasizing the spectacle. Fifty-five percent of respondents among the general public in the *Miller Lite Report* agree that "sports events have become too much of a spectacle," and 59 percent agree that "the spirit of the game has been hurt by placing too much attention on entertainment and not enough on athletics." Forty-nine percent thought that professional sports on television are primarily entertainment rather than "true athletic competition." Miller Brewing Company, *Miller Lite Report,* pp. 82-84.

24. Ronald E. Frank and Marshall G. Greenberg, *The Public's View of Television: Who Watches and Why* (Beverly Hills: Sage Publications, 1980), p. 333. The *Miller Lite Report* makes little attempt to distinguish between watching sport on television and watching it in person. In the *Sports Fan Index,* "avid fans" were those who took the most part in seven activities including watching television, reading, and talking about sport. Using this index, only 8 percent of women were classified as avid sports fans while 30 percent of men were. The figures on "watching sports events on television" were not broken down by sex. Miller Brewing Company, *Miller Lite Report,* pp. 207, 19, 21.

25. Women professional athletes are still few and far between. The money-spinners, golf and tennis, are not team sports, and both have long traditions of amateur female play. The Women's Basketball League, although heavily promoted, died; it is difficult to see other women's team sports having any commercial success in the near future.

26. For an analysis of the flood of literature on the relationship between television and behavior see George Comstock's *Television and Human Behavior: The Key Studies* (Santa Monica: Rand Corporation, 1975). This contains a section on television and violence. However, what constitutes "violence" is a moot point. As Burton Paulu remarks, when "the American producer of the 'Starsky and Hutch' shows, carried by the BBC, stated during a BBC interview that because of 'enormous pressure' in the United States there would be less violence on that series in the future, many regular viewers of the series called to complain, saying that they found newscasts showing the killing of seal pups much more upsetting than the violence on the 'Starsky and Hutch' show." Burton Paulu, *Television and*

Radio in the United Kingdom (Minneapolis: University of Minnesota Press, 1981), p. 185.

27. Much investigation has been done of news programming. Among the more outspoken book-length criticisms in the United States are Edith Efron, *The News Twisters* (Los Angeles: Nash Publishing, 1971); E. J. Epstein, *News from Nowhere: Television and News* (New York: Random House, 1973); and David Altheide, *Creating Reality: How TV News Distorts* (Beverly Hills: Sage, 1974). In Britain, the Glasgow Media Group published with Routledge and Kegan Paul *Bad News* (1976), *More Bad News* (1980), and *Really Bad News* (1982).

28. Jacques Ellul, *The Technological Society* (New York: Alfred Knopf, 1970), pp. xxxii, 43, 97, 298, 382.

29. See F. R. Leavis and Denys Thompson, *Culture and Environment* (London: Chatto and Windus, 1937); Bernard Rosenberg and David M. White, eds., *Mass Culture: The Popular Arts in America* (Glencoe, Ill.: Free Press, 1957); Richard Hoggart, *The Uses of Literacy* (London: Penguin Books, 1958).

30. Erik Barnouw, *The Sponsor: Notes on a Modern Potentate* (New York: Oxford University Press, 1978), pp. 149-51.

31. R. K. Goldsen, *The Show and Tell Machine: How Television Works and Works You Over* (New York: Dial Press, 1977); Marie Winn, *The Plug-In Drug* (New York: Viking Press, 1977).

32. Gaye Tuchmann, ed., *The TV Establishment: Programming for Power and Profit* (Englewood Cliffs, N.J.: Prentice-Hall, 1974), p. 5.

33. Hamid Mowlana, in a review article on the relationship between the mass media of communication and culture, skillfully differentiates between three schools of thought. There are those who conceive of the problem in terms of "mass society, mass media and mass culture"; others think in terms of "technological determinism"; and still others believe that "the media of mass communications are not so much a cause of mass culture as a tool to shape it." Mowlana postulates the need for a new conceptual framework; his integrative theory suggests that "the mass media system is . . . a rather complex social system consisting of actions carried out within the context of external social conditions of the community and the society in which it operates." What I am suggesting here fits very well with this point of view. Hamid Mowlana, "Mass Media and Culture: Toward an Integrated Theory," in *Intercultural Communication Theory: Current Perspectives,* International and Intercultural Communication Annual 7, ed. William B. Gudykunst (Beverly Hills: Sage Publications, 1983), pp. 149, 150, 152, 154, 158. More than twenty years ago, some media theorists were moving away "from the tendency to regard mass communication as a necessary and sufficient cause of audience effects toward a view of the media as influences working amid other influences, in a total situation." J. T. Klapper, *The Effects of Mass Communication* (New York: Free Press, 1960), p. 5.

34. Herbert Gans, *Popular Culture and High Culture: An Analysis and Evaluation of Taste* (New York: Basic Books, 1974), p. xi.

35. Alan Swingewood, *The Myth of Mass Culture* (London: Macmillan, 1977), p. 113.

36. A. Szalai, ed., *The Use of Time: Daily Activities of Urban and Suburban Populations in Twelve Countries* (The Hague: Mouton and G., 1972).

37. R. B. Bechtel, C. Archelpohl, and R. Akers, "Correlates between Observed Behavior and Questionnaire Responses on Television Viewing," in *Television and Social Behavior,* ed. E. A. Rubenstein, G. A. Comstock, and J. P. Murray, vol. 4, *Television in Day to Day Life: Patterns of Use* (Washington, D.C.: Government Printing Office, 1972), p. 294.

Charles Allen reports much the same thing from a study done in Oklahoma (Stillwater and Tulsa) and Kansas (Wichita). For 19 percent of the time the set was on no one was in the room and for another 21 percent, no one was actually watching. Charles Allen, "Photographing the TV Audience," *Journal of Advertising Research* 5, no. 1 (1965): 2-8.

38. There can be no doubt that advertising on television is effective. Exactly how effective, and whether over the short or long term, must be a matter of conjecture. Les Brown wrote in 1971, "During the early sixties surveys indicated that sponsors were losing 15 to 18 percent of the audience during commercial breaks. The figure is now up to 50 percent." Les Brown, *Television: The Business behind the Box* (New York: Harcourt Brace Jovanovich, 1971), p. 68. During the Super Bowl commercials, municipal water services report a surge of activity; TV sets come equipped with a button to turn off the commercials. Car sales slumped dismally in 1982, in spite of constant TV advertising; sales picked up when the economy did, not as a result of bigger and better TV commercials. It is also quite impossible to disentangle the symbiotic relationship between print and TV; network shows are heavily promoted not only in print media such as *TV Times,* but in newspapers and on billboards. However, as long as advertisers put their faith in ratings, commercial television companies will continue to do so too, because their profits come from selling airtime to advertisers.

39. George Comstock, et al., *Television and Human Behavior* (New York: Columbia University Press, 1978), pp. 146-47.

40. James D. Halloran and Paul Croll, "Television Programs in Great Britain, Content and Control," in *Television and Growing Up: The Impact of Televised Violence,* Report to the Surgeon General, United States Public Health Service (Washington, D.C.: Government Printing Office, 1974), p. 486.

41. Fred W. Friendly, *Due to Circumstances beyond Our Control* (New York: Random House, 1969), p. 273.

42. The May ratings sweeps are extremely important to networks. Because the NBA did poorly in prime time in 1978, CBS did not broadcast the championships during the sweeps period. In 1982, the NBA put the season back a week, so that the championships would not coincide with the sweeps and thus would be televised. *Dallas Morning News,* June 4, 1982, p. B10.

43. Comstock et al., *Television and Human Behavior,* p. 113.

44. *Dallas Morning News,* Oct. 2, 1980, p. C15.

45. *Dallas Morning News,* Apr. 9, 1981, p. C12.

46. *Dallas Morning News,* Oct. 23, 1981, p. C7.

47. *Dallas Morning News,* Apr. 18, 1982, p. B2. These figures have not improved over the years. In 1986, many sports fans watch cable TV; the ratings for

network sporting events for the weekend of Aug. 9-10, 1986, ranged from the top 9.6 rating for "Sports Sunday," through 5.0 for "Sports Special" to 3.6 for "Wide World of Sports." *Dallas Morning News,* Aug. 15, 1986, p. B2. (The A. C. Nielsen Company uses devices that record what a sample of U.S. homes is watching. Each ratings point supposedly represents 1 percent of all U.S. homes that have TV sets.)

48. *Dallas Morning News,* Mar. 11, 1984, p. B7. In contrast, for the week ending Aug. 14, 1983, two preseason NFL games were among the five bottom shows in the ratings. *Dallas Morning News,* Aug. 19, 1983, p. C9.

49. *Dallas Morning News,* Aug. 14, 1981, p. B6.

50. *Dallas Morning News,* Jan. 29, 1982, p. B11.

51. *Dallas Morning News,* May 27, 1983, p. B14.

52. *Dallas Morning News,* Oct. 17, 1982, p. B25.

53. *Dallas Morning News,* Oct. 8, 1982, p. B14.

54. *Dallas Morning News,* Oct. 19, 1982, p. B3.

55. *Dallas Morning News,* May 13, 1983, p. B12.

56. What draws particular advertisers to particular programs is so complex a subject that it obviously cannot be discussed here. Among other factors involved are the demographic composition of the audience presumed to be attracted to particular programs, "prestige," and the prevailing tax structure.

57. The best review of the literature is Lloyd Reynolds Sloan's "The Function and Impact of Sports for Fans: A Review of Theory and Contemporary Research," in *Sports, Games and Play: Social and Psychological Viewpoints,* ed. Jeffrey H. Goldstein (Hillsdale, N.J.: Lawrence Erlbaum, 1979), pp. 219-62. See also Allen Guttmann's *Sports Spectators* (New York: Columbia University Press, 1986). For a discussion of the so-called passivity of spectators, see Allen Guttmann, "On the Alleged Dehumanization of the Sports Spectator," *Journal of Popular Culture* 14, no. 2 (Fall 1980): 275-82. The *Miller Lite Report* sheds very little light on this topic. The only study of which I am aware that specifically examines "motives for viewing televised sport" is limited, but suggests that sports programs are watched differently and for different reasons than "other entertainment programming." Walter Gantz, "An Exploration of Viewing Motives and Behavior Associated with Television Sports," *Job* 25, no. 3 (Summer 1981): 263-75.

58. Prisuta, using data from a survey of 600 Michigan high-school students, suggests that sport is a family affair, and that "watching sports on television is related to both participation and watching in person." Prisuta, "Televised Sports and Political Values," p. 99.

59. *Chronicle of Higher Education,* Sept. 29, 1982, p. 13.

60. *Chronicle of Higher Education,* Oct. 13, 1982, p. 17.

61. Nineteen percent of respondents to the Miller Lite survey reported that arguing or fighting athletes "*most* upset [their] enjoyment of the game"; this factor and apparent bias of officials tied for first place when respondents were asked to select only one thing that most detracted from their enjoyment. Another 14 percent stated they were most upset when "the game is too violent"; another 8 percent put first "disruptive behavior of fans." That is, what 41 percent of the respondents were most upset by was violence on the part of players or fans. Only 4 percent put first "the athletes are not aggressive enough." Yet apparently most

people do not really want to penalize offenders severely. The greatest number, 39 percent, thought fighting players should be warned but allowed to go on playing, the least severe choice offered; only 14 percent thought players should be fined and sent off the field. Again, while 44 percent said that arguments with officials lessened enjoyment of the game, 20 percent said it added enjoyment. What these figures suggest is that some viewers are likely to enjoy altercation, but that they are a minority. On this evidence, deliberately to encourage brawls would seem to be a self-defeating strategy for those who want to encourage people to watch sport, televised or otherwise. Miller Brewing Company, *Miller Lite Report,* pp. 98-99.

On the other hand, a study in which students rated carefully selected football plays for enjoyment indicates that for men, "enjoyment of plays was found to increase with the degree of the apparent roughness/violence." Jennings Bryant, Paul Comisky, and Dolf Zillmann, "The Appeal of Rough-and-Tumble Play in Televised Professional Football," *Communication Quarterly* 29, no. 4 (1981): 256-62.

62. Clifford Geertz, "Deep Play: Notes on the Balinese Cockfight," *Daedulus,* Winter 1972, pp. 1-37. The bigger the bet, the better the cocks put up to fight; when the very best cocks fight, their abilities will be as equal as it is possible to arrange.

63. Forty-seven percent of the respondents to the Miller Lite survey said that they usually paid "close attention to the sports commentator"; only 21 percent said they rarely or never did so. Fifty-one percent said commentators "added to [their] enjoyment of the game." Miller Brewing Company, *Miller Lite Report,* p. 90.

64. Work is still in progress on analysis of game tapes; for a preliminary report see J. Chandler: ' TV Sports Commentators: What Do They Say and Why?" (Paper given at North American Society for Sport History 1982 Conference, Manhattan, Kan.).

65. They can also pass on their own prejudices. See, for instance, Raymond E. Rainville and Edward McCormick, "Extent of Covert Racial Prejudices in Pro Football Announcers' Speech," in *Sport Sociology: Contemporary Themes,* 2d ed., ed. Andrew Yiannakis et al. (Dubuque: Kendall Publishing Co., 1979), pp. 175-80 (reprinted from *Journalism Quarterly,* Spring 1977).

Chapter 2

1. Albert G. Spalding, *America's National Game: Historic Facts Concerning the Beginning, Evolution, Development and Popularity of Baseball with Personal Reminiscences of Its Vicissitudes, Its Victories and Its Votaries* (New York: American Sports Publishing Co., 1911), p. 7.

2. Donald Elder, *Ring Lardner: A Biography* (New York: Doubleday, 1956), p. 120. Elder quotes from Virginia Woolf's essay "American Fiction" (1925).

3. R. S. Rait Kerr, *The Laws of Cricket: Their History and Growth* (London: Longmans, Green and Co., 1950), pp. 33-37.

4. Murray Chass, "Baseball's Illegal Pitches: An Interminable Whodunit," *Dallas Morning News,* July 14, 1979, pp. 3-4. In commentary on the 1981 World Series, Jim Palmer openly remarked that Tommy John had been known to alter the ball.

5. John Arlott, *Cricket on Trial: John Arlott's Cricket Journal – 3* (London: Heinemann, 1960), pp. 122-37.

6. Bill Shannon and George Kalinsky, *The Ballparks* (New York: Hawthorn Books, 1975), p. 17; *Dallas Morning News,* Dec. 14, 1980, pp. B1, B7.

7. Neville Cardus, *English Cricket* (London: Collins, 1945), p. 12.

8. *Dallas Morning News,* July 18, 1982, p. 7G; *Time,* Sept. 5, 1983, pp. 71-72; John Thorn and Peter Palmer with David Reuther, *The Hidden Game of Baseball: A Revolutionary Approach to Baseball and Its Statistics,* 2d ed. (New York: Doubleday, 1985).

9. Melvin Adelman, "Premature Modernization and the Failure of Cricket in America: the New York Experience, 1840-1865." Paper given at North American Society for Sport History Convention, Banff, Alberta, Canada, 1980, p. 11. Adelman quotes the *New York Clipper,* May 19, 1857, p. 19.

10. Ian Tyrell, "The Emergence of Modern American Baseball c. 1850-80," in *Sport in History: The Making of Modern Sporting History,* ed. Richard Cashman and Michael McKernan (St. Lucia, Australia: University of Queensland Press, 1979), pp. 207-8.

11. Harold Seymour, *Baseball,* vol. 1, *The Early Years* (New York: Oxford University Press, 1960), pp. 15, 19.

12. Adelman, "Premature Modernization," p. 23. Adelman develops his views on cricket's failure as an American sport in *A Sporting Time: New York City and the Rise of Modern Athletics, 1820-70* (Urbana: University of Illinois Press, 1986), pp. 97-119.

13. Arlott, *Cricket on Trial,* pp. 63-64.

14. Ian Tyrell, "Emergence of Modern American Baseball," p. 211.

15. David Quentin Voigt, *American Baseball,* vol. 1, *From Gentleman's Sport to the Commissioner System* (Norman: University of Oklahoma Press, 1966), p. 13.

16. The "over" was increased from four to five balls in 1889, and to six in 1900. Kerr, *Laws of Cricket,* p. 83.

17. Douglass Wallop, *Baseball: An Informal History* (New York: W. Norton and Co., 1969), p. 72. Voigt, *American Baseball,* vol. 1, p. 206. In 1893 the distance from the mound to the batter became the present sixty feet six inches.

18. Voigt, *American Baseball,* vol. 1, pp. 207, 185.

19. Robert Allan Fitzgerald, *Wickets in the West; or, The Twelve in America* (London: Tinsley Brothers, 1873), p. 292.

20. Seymour, *Baseball,* vol. 1, p. 31.

21. Allen Guttmann, *From Ritual to Record: The Nature of Modern Sports* (New York: Columbia University Press, 1978), p. 100.

22. Seymour, *Baseball,* vol. 1, p. 35.

23. Ibid., p. 36.

24. Ibid., p. 45.

25. Tyrell differentiates between the professionalization of baseball, which involved players being paid, and the commercialization of baseball as an industry. By 1871 baseball was professionalized; in 1876 it was overtly commercialized. Before reading Tyrell's article, I had written what follows on Wright; I had not,

however, managed to articulate the distinction Tyrell makes so aptly. Ian Tyrell, "Money and Morality: The Professionalisation of American Baseball," in *Sport: Money, Morality and the Media,* ed. Richard Cashman and Michael McKernan (Kensington: New South Wales University Press, 1982), pp. 86-103.

26. Seymour, *Baseball,* vol. 1, p. 72.

27. Voigt, *American Baseball,* vol. 1, p. 59.

28. Seymour, *Baseball,* vol. 1, p. 80.

29. Wright did not, of course, accomplish baseball's reorganization. It was William Hulbert, president of the Chicago White Stockings, who engineered the coup that led to the foundation of the National League, and he had more powerful supporters than Wright, including Charles Fowle and Spalding. But Wright's career spanned the transition between baseball as an amateur and professional sport and the period during which professional players lost their autonomy.

30. Lee Lowenfish and Tony Lupien, *The Imperfect Diamond: The Story of Baseball's Reserve System and the Men Who Fought to Change It* (New York: Stein and Day, 1980), p. 18.

31. Voigt, *American Baseball,* vol. 1, pp. 173-74.

32. Seymour, *Baseball,* vol. 1, p. 83.

33. Tyrell, "Money and Morality," p. 91.

34. For a full account of this matter, see Eliot Asinof, *Eight Men Out: The Black Sox and the 1919 World Series* (New York: Holt, Rinehart and Winston, 1963).

35. Richard C. Crepeau, *Baseball: America's Diamond Mind 1919-1941* (Orlando: University of Central Florida, 1980), p. 42.

36. *Dallas Morning News,* Oct. 22, 1981, p. 4B.

37. Wallop, *Baseball,* pp. 142-43.

38. David Quentin Voigt, *American Baseball,* vol. 2, *From the Commissioners to Continental Expansion* (Norman: University of Oklahoma Press, 1970), pp. 50-51, 4.

39. Tyrell, "Money and Morality," p. 96.

40. Robert W. Creamer, *Babe: The Legend Comes to Life,* (New York: Penguin, 1983; 1st ed. 1974), pp. 217-19, 161, 201-2.

41. Ibid., pp. 106-7.

42. Elder, *Ring Lardner,* p. 170.

43. Seymour, *Baseball,* vol. 1, pp. 19-20. I have found no analysis of the changing rules of baseball; John D. Allen's M.S. thesis, "The History of Professional Baseball Rule Changes (1800-1970)" (University of Wisconsin, 1971), is not aptly named.

44. Creamer, *Babe,* p. 387.

45. Creamer devotes chapter 28 of his book to an analysis of Ruth's personality and also notes that from his earliest appearances he attracted attention whether he played well or not. Ibid., pp. 315-34, 19, 21.

46. Crepeau, *Baseball,* p. 180. Crepeau says Ruth signed for $62,000; I have taken Creamer's figure of $52,000 in *Babe,* p. 371.

47. Crepeau, *Baseball,* pp. 139-42. For players marketing themselves in the off-season, see Seymour, *Baseball,* vol. 1, pp. 117-19.

48. In 1934, the World Series was first commercially broadcast. Crepeau, *Baseball,* p. 187.

49. David Quentin Voigt, *America through Baseball* (Chicago: Nelson-Hall, 1976), p. 195.

50. Steven A. Riess, *Touching Base: Professional Baseball and American Culture in the Progressive Era* (Westport: Greenwood Press, 1980), pp. 85, 88, 91.

51. Shannon and Kalinsky, *Ballparks,* p. 11.

52. Reiss, *Touching Base,* pp. 94-95.

53. Voigt, *American Baseball,* vol. 1, p. 141; Shannon and Kalinsky, *Ballparks,* p. 10.

54. Riess, *Touching Base,* p. 103.

55. Voigt, *American Baseball,* vol. 1, p. 139.

56. Crepeau, *Baseball,* p. 112.

57. Ibid., p. 113.

58. Ibid., p. 188.

59. "Thumbs Down on Night Baseball," *Literary Digest* 38 (June 8, 1935): 38.

60. Crepeau, *Baseball,* pp. 191-92.

61. It may also be that sportswriters believed they had to do something other than report on the game. As major-league baseball was seen on television, readers no longer depended on newspapers to recreate games for them.

62. Donn Rogosin, *Invisible Men: Life in Baseball's Negro Leagues* (New York: Atheneum, 1983).

63. James B. Dworkin, *Owners versus Players: Baseball and Collective Bargaining* (Boston: Auburn House Publishing Co., 1981), p. 55.

64. Ibid., pp. 11-17.

65. Ibid., pp. 11-12, 15, 18-19, 26-27, 29.

66. Ibid., pp. 62-66. For Curt Flood's own views on the reserve clause, see his autobiography, *The Way It Is* (New York: Trident Press, 1971).

67. Dworkin, *Owners versus Players,* pp. 71-82, 45. Ward is quoted from U.S., Congress, House, *Organized Baseball: Report of the Subcommittee on the Study of Monopoly Power of the Committee on the Judiciary,* 82d Cong., 2d sess., 1952, H. Rept. 2002, p. 32.

68. Michael Novak, *The Joy of Sports: End Zones, Bases, Baskets, Balls and the Consecration of the American Spirit* (New York: Basic Books, 1976), p. 150.

69. *Dallas Morning News,* July 18, 1978, p. B7.

Chapter 3

1. William W. Roper, *Football, Today and Tomorrow* (New York: Duffield and Co., 1928), p. 147. Roper was a member of the 1902 class at Princeton and coached Princeton for seventeen seasons, retiring in 1930. Alexander Weyand, *The Saga of American Football* (New York: Macmillan, 1961), p. 158.

2. Roper, *Football,* p. 154.

3. Frank G. Menke, *The Encyclopedia of Sports,* 5th ed. rev. (New York: A. S. Barnes and Co., 1975), p. 405.

4. Spectators were charged admission fees, although Harvard apologized for doing so. Weyand, *Saga of American Football,* p. 11.

5. The true numbers of paying spectators present at these early games are difficult to ascertain. Lewis, for instance, states that 2,000 people were present at this game. Weyand puts the number at 1,200. Guy Maxton Lewis, "The American Intercollegiate Football Spectacle, 1869-1917" (Ph.D. diss., University of Maryland, 1965), p. 25; Weyand, *Saga of American Football,* p. 13.

6. Weyand, *Saga of American Football,* p. 16.

7. Ibid., pp. 55; Lewis, "American Intercollegiate Football Spectacle," p. 33.

8. Weyand, *Saga of American Football,* pp. 19-20.

9. Lewis, "American Intercollegiate Football Spectacle," p. 26.

10. Ibid., pp. 40, 46. Lewis points out that campus games did not attract anything like the same crowds; in 1882 Yale vs. Wesleyan drew 200; Yale vs. Harvard, 3,000; Yale vs. Columbia, 600; Harvard vs. Columbia, 600; Harvard vs. Princeton, 3,000 (p. 40).

11. Ibid., pp. 49, 55, 71. Lewis quotes the *New York Herald,* Nov. 28, 1889.

12. Weyand, *Saga of American Football,* p. 25.

13. Ibid., p. 26.

14. Alexander Johnston, "The American Game of Football," *Century Magazine,* Oct. 1887, p. 898.

15. Roper, *Football,* pp. 156-57.

16. Percy D. Haughton, *Football, and How to Watch It* (Boston: Marshall Jones Co., 1922), p. 67. Haughton played for Harvard as an undergraduate and was Harvard's professional coach from 1908-16.

17. Roper, *Football,* p. 155.

18. Weyand, *Saga of American Football,* p. 82.

19. Roper, *Football,* pp. 161, 165.

20. Weyand, *Saga of American Football,* p. 92.

21. Ibid., p. 104.

22. Ibid., p. 55, 123.

23. Ibid., p. 57.

24. Lewis, "American Intercollegiate Football Spectacle," pp. 134. Lewis quotes John F. Crowell, *Personal Recollections* (Durham, N.C.: Duke University Press, 1959), p. 229.

25. Lewis, "American Intercollegiate Football Spectacle," p. 142.

26. Ibid., p. 153, 150. Lewis quotes "The Stanford and California Football Teams at Their Practice," *San Francisco Examiner,* Dec. 11, 1892.

27. Lewis, "American Intercollegiate Football Spectacle," p. 101. Lewis quotes Francis A. March, *Athletics at Lafayette College* (Easton, Pa.: Lafayette College, 1926), p. 19.

28. Lewis, "American Intercollegiate Football Spectacle," pp. 207-8. Lewis quotes Ralph Chamberlain, ed., *The University of Utah* (Salt Lake City: University of Utah Press, 1960), p. 302.

29. Henry Beach Needham, "The College Athlete: How Commercialism is Making Him a Professional," *McClure's Magazine* 25, no. 2 (June 1905): 118. This practice of allowing itinerant players to stiffen a college team had been going on for years. See Lewis, "American Intercollegiate Football Spectacle," pp. 154, 194.

30. Lewis, "American Intercollegiate Football Spectacle," p. 261.

31. Lorin F. Deland, *At the Sign of the Dollar and Other Essays* (New York: Harper and Bros., 1917), pp. 37-39, 59. Deland worked in advertising, but was deeply interested in football, and coauthored a book with Walter Camp, *Football* (Cambridge, Mass.: Riverside Press, 1896), which was "published in the hope that it may aid in the development of American football, and more especially that it may encourage a scientific study of the game" (Preface).

32. Sack has suggested that Yale's athletic successes in the last quarter of the nineteenth century occurred because football, in particular, "functioned to reinforce the values of America's rising business class." Harvard during the same period clung to the "principle of amateurism." Allen L. Sack, "Yale 29-Harvard 4: The Professionalism of College Football," *Quest* 19 (Winter 1973): 24-34.

33. Lewis, "American Intercollegiate Football Spectacle," p. 270. Lewis quotes "Resignation of Abercrombie," *University of Alabama Bulletin,* 1911, p. 12.

34. Lewis, "American Intercollegiate Football Spectacle," pp. 44, 123-25.

35. Ibid., pp. 108, 111, 115, 170.

36. Howard J. Savage et al., *American College Athletics:* (New York: Carnegie Foundation, 1929) Bulletin no. 23, pp. viii, xxi.

37. Lewis, "American Intercollegiate Football Spectacle," pp. 278-79. Alonzo Stagg, coach at the University of Chicago, remarked ruefully that the new (1926) stadium holding 48,000 simply kept Chicago "in the rear rank of the Conference in accommodations." Stagg alleged that among others, Ohio State could seat 82,000, Illinois 69,000, and Minnesota 55,000. Amos Alonzo Stagg and Wesley Winians Stout, *Touchdown!* (New York: Longmans, Green and Co., 1927), p. 173.

38. Lewis, "American Intercollegiate Football Spectacle," pp. 95, 144, 146-47. Lewis quotes *Daily* (Lincoln) *Nebraska State Journal,* Nov. 1892.

39. Lewis, "American Intercollegiate Football Spectacle," pp. 148, 173, 182. Lewis quotes "Berkeley Item" *San Francisco Examiner,* Mar. 18, 1892.

40. John Rickards Betts, *America's Sporting Heritage: 1850-1950* (Reading, Mass.: Addison-Wesley Publishing Co., 1974), p. 129.

41. Ibid., p. 257.

42. Haughton, *Football,* p. 211.

43. Ibid., p. x.

44. Kyle Rote and Ray Siegener, *Pro Football for the Fan: How to Watch the Game the Way the Pros Do* (New York: Doubleday and Co., 1974), p. 16.

45. George Halas, with Gwen Morgan and Arthur Vesey, *Halas by Halas: The Autobiography of George Halas* (New York: McGraw-Hill, 1979), p. 87. Halas gives a good account of the shifts to which professional teams were put to survive in these early years. For a player's account, see Ernest L. Cuneo, "Present at the Creation: Professional Football in the Twenties," *American Scholar* 56 (Autumn 1987): 487-501.

46. Halas, *Halas by Halas,* pp. 108, 112.

47. Ibid., p. 147.

48. Ibid., pp. 161, 170.

49. Halas, *Halas by Halas,* p. 181. Colleges still had to take the ball back five yards from the scrimmage before passing, and were constrained by other rules.

50. Even the rules that were altered to make the game less dangerous were

changed with spectators in mind. If the game were banned because it was considered lethal, spectators obviously were not going to see it.

51. Bell became NFL commissioner in 1946. Gerald Newman, ed., *The Concise Encyclopedia of Sports,* 2d ed. rev. (New York: Franklin Watts, 1979), p. 74.

52. Halas, *Halas by Halas,* p. 152.

53. Hugh "Shorty" Ray, hired as a consultant, organized rules and officials to save seconds; he "increased the number of plays in the average game from 145 in 1936 to 174 in 1950." Ibid., p. 163.

54. Betts, *America's Sporting Heritage,* pp. 257-58.

55. For an account of one player's experience of college football, see Gary Shaw, *Meat on the Hoof: The Hidden World of Texas Football* (New York: St. Martin's Press, 1972).

56. Weyand, *Saga of American Football,* pp. 146, 149, 156. Criticism of football continued in the press, but it had no effect on the conduct of the game at the college level. For one contemporary discussion, see Reed Harris, *King Football: The Vulgarization of the American College* (New York: Vanguard Press, 1932).

57. Robert Leckie, *The Story of Football* (New York: Random House, 1965), p. 108.

58. Weyand, *Saga of American Football,* p. 159. It is interesting that women's college basketball players in 1984 started to use a smaller ball for precisely the same spectator-pleasing reasons.

59. Newman, *Concise Encyclopedia of Sports,* p. 74.

60. Clark Kerr, *The Uses of the University* (Cambridge, Mass.: Harvard University Press, 1963).

61. Savage, et al., *American College Athletics,* p. xii.

62. Colleges were much more stringent about substitutions. In 1941 players were allowed to substitute freely on alternate plays, but in 1953 the "platoon football" to which this gave rise was abolished, and players were allowed to enter only once a quarter. Not until 1965 were any number of players allowed to enter the game when a team lost possession of the ball, and two players allowed to substitute at any other time. John McCallum and Charles H. Pearson, *College Football U.S.A. 1869-1972: Official Book of the National Football Foundation* (New York: Hall of Fame Publishing, in cooperation with McGraw-Hill Book Co., 1972), p. 247.

63. Halas, *Halas by Halas,* pp. 246-49.

64. Howard Cosell, *Cosell* (Chicago: Playboy Press, 1973), p. 260.

65. Halas, *Halas by Halas,* p. 250. Halas is quite clear that he recognized the danger of TV money "enriching big-city clubs" at the expense of the rest, and therefore proposed equal revenue sharing. This is entirely consistent with previous NFL practice; but it runs counter to the accepted notion that Pete Rozelle initiated the whole process. Given Rozelle's original lack of status with the owners, and the speed with which the contracts were made and enabling legislation was pushed through Congress, I am inclined to accept Halas's account. Also, in 1960 Lamar Hunt's American Football League was using the idea NFL owners had mooted. The AFL sold its rights to ABC as a package.

66. *National Observer,* May 16, 1977, p. 1.

67. *Dallas Morning News,* Sept. 16, 1979, pp. F1, F3.

68. *Dallas Morning News,* Oct. 19, 1980, p. H1.

69. *Dallas Morning News,* Feb. 28, 1984, p. B2.

70. *Dallas Morning News,* July 8, 1983, pp. B1, 10; July 6, 1984, p. B12.

71. *Chronicle of Higher Education,* Dec. 1, 1982, p. 13.

72. I have been able to find no substantive accounts of the WFL's finances. USFL owners, however, made it clear that they had learned from the WFL promoters and were prepared for heavy losses. *Dallas Morning News,* July 15, 1984, p. B11; July 28, 1984, p. B13. What they did not learn from the WFL was that a TV contract does not automatically generate ratings. True, the WFL had only an independent network contract (TVS), but its ratings were weak from the start. Ron Powers, *Supertube: The Rise of Television Sport,* (New York, Coward-McCann, 1984), p. 235.

73. Harry Hurt III, *Texas Rich: The Hunt Dynasty from the Early Oil Days Through the Silver Crash* (New York: W. W. Norton, 1981), pp. 212-13, 269.

74. Robert Daly, "Super Pete," *Dallas Morning News, Weekend Sports,* Jan. 17-30, 1976, p. 35.

75. John Underwood suggests that the NFL could not afford to admit that goalposts were unsafe in their former position, and therefore played up the field-goal angle. Given the NFL's overt lack of concern for the physical safety of players on the field, the field-goal problem seems to have more weight than Underwood is prepared to give it. John Underwood, *The Death of an American Game: The Crisis in Football* (Boston: Little, Brown and Co., 1979), p. 48.

76. *Dallas Morning News,* Sept. 3, 1981, p. G27.

77. *Dallas Morning News,* May 16, 1978, p. B5. Rozelle stated his position on free agency very clearly in 1975. See Pete Rozelle, "Professional Sports: The View of the Owners," in *Sport in Contemporary Society: An Anthology,* ed. Stanley Eitzen (New York: St. Martins Press, 1979), pp. 304-12.

78. Halas, *Halas by Halas,* p. 151.

79. Bob Curran, *The $500,000 Quarterback; or, The League That Came in from the Cold* (New York: Macmillan Co., 1965), p. 31.

80. The NFL rules about reporting injuries are ostensibly designed to make sure that professional gamblers have no more useful information than amateurs. The Denver Broncos did not report that their quarterback, Craig Morton, had been hospitalized from Tuesday to Friday before the Sunday AFC championship game in 1978. As a *Washington Post* writer pointed out, had professional gamblers found out, and had Morton not played, the NFL's integrity would have been seriously damaged. *Dallas Morning News,* Jan. 4, 1978, pp. E1, 4. The writer was being somewhat naive; very little remains hidden from those whose fortunes depend on knowledge.

81. *Dallas Morning News,* Nov. 22, 1981, p. B26.

82. See n. 75.

83. Jack Tatum with Bill Kushner, *They Call Me Assassin* (New York: Everest House, 1979). Tatum discusses the rule changes that would cut down on violence on pp. 229-44.

84. Arnold J. Mandell, *The Nightmare Season* (New York: Random House,

1976). Far from trying to get to the root of the drug problem, the NFL had Mandell indicted by the state of California, on the grounds that he had prescribed drugs illegally.

85. *Dallas Morning News,* Nov. 26, 1977, p. C1; Mar. 19, 1978, pp. C1, 4; *Scene Magazine,* Mar. 28, 1982, pp. 6–12.

86. Based on data from the NFL Management Council, Glen Waggoner estimates that 58 percent of 1982 gross revenues came from TV. "Money Games," *Esquire* 97, no. 6 (June 1982): 53.

87. *Chronicle of Higher Education,* Oct. 12, 1983, pp. 27–28. In spite of its actions, the CFA has complained that its purposes have been misunderstood and that it has long been supporting tougher academic standards for student athletes. Yet at a special forum held in July 1987 at which the proposals presented by the NCAA commission of college presidents were considered, the CFA's executive director specifically rejected recommended cuts in football programs. Ibid., July 8, 1987, p. 32.

88. For a discussion of the problems of big-time college athletics, see John F. Rooney, *The Recruiting Game: Toward a New System of Intercollegiate Sports* (Lincoln: University of Nebraska Press, 1980); and James Frey, ed., *The Governance of Intercollegiate Athletics* (West Point: Leisure Press, 1982).

Star college players are now beginning to take care of their own futures. The NFL is in no legal position to stop players whom the NCAA will not allow to play from applying to be drafted, even if those players have not spent four years in college. College coaches may be outraged by the NFL's allowing Chris Carter to be placed in a supplemental draft after he had accepted money from an agent and been declared for college football (*Dallas Morning News,* Aug. 22, 1987, p. B8), but such coaches are still unwilling to admit they are running NFL farm teams. Players know better.

89. The notion of overexposure needs examination. We do not know whether anyone interested in football actually watches most games shown on TV or whether viewers are very much more selective. I suspect the latter; if so, the more games that can be shown, the better for the fans, since viewers can then watch their own teams.

90. In a game played between the Detroit Lions and New York Giants in November 1982, the score was shown seven times in the first half and eight times during the second half; the time was shown seven times in both first and second halves, mostly during the closing minutes of play; team statistics were shown eleven times during the first and twelve times during the second half.

91. Herbert Reed, *Football for Public and Player* (New York: Frederick A. Stokes Co., 1913), p. v.

92. Paul Zimmerman, *A Thinking Man's Guide to Pro Football* (New York: E. P. Dutton and Co., 1971).

93. See Graham McNamee with Robert G. Anderson, *You're On the Air* (New York: Harper and Bros., 1926).

94. See, for instance, David Meggyesy, *Out of Their League* (New York: Simon and Schuster, 1970); Bernie Parrish, *They Call It a Game* (New York: Dial Press, 1971).

95. See Gale Sayers with Al Silverman, *I Am Third* (New York: Viking Press, 1970); and Roger Staubach, *First Down: Lifetime to Go* (New York: Word Books, 1974).

96. For a review of some of this literature see Charles R. Kniker, "The Values of Athletics in Schools: A Continuing Debate," *Phi Delta Kappan* 56 (Oct. 1974): 116-20. See also Neil Admur, *The Fifth Down: Democracy and the Football Revolution* (New York: Delta, 1972); and John T. Talamini, "School Athletics: Public Policy Versus Practice," in *Sport and Society,* ed. John T. Talamini and Charles H. Page (Boston: Little, Brown and Co., 1973), pp. 163-82.

Chapter 4

1. Richard Brandt, *Hopi Ethics: A Theoretical Analysis* (Chicago: University of Chicago Press, 1954), p. 341.

2. It is clear that nations differ in their traditions, behavior, and aspirations, but it is extraordinarily difficult to discuss these differences in terms everyone finds acceptable. There is no agreed methodology for addressing the task; and because these differences are so often matters of perception, an anecdote may be nearer the mark than a survey result. Among the most insightful recent books that work on this broad canvas are Dennis W. Brogan, *The American Problem* (London: Hamish Hamilton, 1944); Geoffrey Gorer, *Exploring English Character* (New York: Criterion Press, 1955); David Potter, *People of Plenty: Economic Abundance and the American Character* (Chicago: University of Chicago Press, 1954); Anthony Sampson, *Anatomy of Britain* (New York: Harper and Row, 1962) and *The Changing Anatomy of Britain* (New York: Random House, 1982); Daniel Snowman, *Britain and America: An Interpretation of Their Culture 1945-1975* (New York: New York University Press, 1977). The inherent problems of discerning core values in any society are admirably discussed in Florence R. Kluckhohn and Fred L. Strodtbeck, *Variations in Value Orientations* (Evanston: Row, Peterson and Co., 1961).

3. As the first government-sponsored report into soccer hooliganism rather stuffily put it, "Football changed from a contest of violence and brute strength to a game of grace and skill. This was due largely to codification of the game that occurred in this country and the development of written and unwritten rules governing standards of discipline, sportsmanship and fair play. Britain taught the world not only how to play football but also the spirit in which it should be played, but there appears to have been a recent regression to older and long-forgotten patterns of behavior." Birmingham Research Group, *Soccer Hooliganism, A Preliminary Report to Mr. Dennis Howell, Minister of Sport* (Bristol: John Wright and Sons, 1968), p. 4.

4. Tony Mason, "Football and the Workers in England 1880-1914," in *Sport: Money, Morality and the Media,* ed. Richard Cashman and Michael McKernan (Kensington: New South Wales University Press, 1982), pp. 248-71. Mason describes the "major tenets" of Victorian England's "sportsmanship ethic" as, "first, playing for the side and not for self. Being modest and generous in victory and staunch and cheerful in defeat. Playing the game for the game's sake: there might be physical and moral benefits but there should be no other rewards and certainly

not prizes or money. No player should ever intentionally break the rules or stoop to underhand tactics. Hard but fair knocks should be taken and given, courageously and with good temper" (p. 249). Whether professional soccer players ever accepted these tenets it is impossible to know; but a 1970 cross-cultural study suggests that boys playing soccer in school had significantly higher standards of "fair play" than junior or senior professional soccer players. Peter McIntosh, *Fair Play: Ethics in Sport and Education* (London: Heinemann, 1979), pp. 128-35.

5. Ralph Turner, "Modes of Social Ascent through Education: Sponsored and Contest Mobility," in *Education, Economy, and Society: A Reader in the Sociology of Education,* ed. A. H. Halsey, Jean Floud, and C. Arnold Anderson (New York: Free Press of Glencoe, 1961), pp. 121-22.

6. As in the United States, there is confusion between equality of opportunity and equality of result. As British comprehensive schools are neighborhood schools, some offer much better opportunity than others. An interesting account of the experience and aspirations of the first comprehensive schools is to be found in National Union of Teachers, eds., *Inside the Comprehensive School* (London: Schoolmaster Publishing Co., 1958).

7. Sampson, *Anatomy of Britain,* pp. 57, 198, 163, 203.

8. Sampson, *Changing Anatomy of Britain,* p. 428. Excellent accounts of Eton and Winchester are Christopher Dilke's *Dr. Moberly's Mint-Mark: A Study of Winchester College* (London: Heinemann, 1965) and J. D. R. McConnell's *Eton: How It Works* (London: Faber and Faber, 1967).

9. Scholarship students in Britain have to work furiously hard to justify their selection. But they do not attain success by learning how to beat the system; they simply have to maintain a substantive standard of achievement richer or luckier children may not need to aim for. A readable and substantial academic study of working-class scholarship children is Brian Jackson and Dennis Marsden's *Education and the Working Class* (London: Routledge and Kegan Paul, 1962).

10. Chris Evert Lloyd with Neil Admur, *Chrissie: My Own Story* (New York: Simon and Schuster, 1982), p. 53.

11. Gerald Howat, *Village Cricket* (Newton Abbot: David and Charles, 1980), p. 42. Little League Baseball was founded in 1939; by 1978, about 20 million children aged six to sixteen were involved in organized sport. (Richard Magill et al., eds., *Children in Sport: A Contemporary Anthology* [Champaign: Human Kinetics Publishers, 1978], preface.) According to the *Miller Lite Report,* children of 62 percent of the respondents participated "in organized sports activities." Eighty-three percent of such activities were "competitive" in that they involved "scheduled meets, tournaments, games, races, etc." For a discussion of what many children are trained to do in such organized sports activities see James A. Michener, *Sports in America* (New York: Fawcett Crest, 1977; 1st ed., 1976), pp. 123-54; Andrew Yannakis et al., eds., *Sport Sociology: Contemporary Themes,* 2d ed., (Dubuque: Kendall/Hunt Company, 1979), pp. 122-64; D. Stanley Eitzen, ed., *Sport in Contemporary Society,* 2d ed., (New York: St. Martin's Press, 1984), pp. 122-66.

By no means all American parents put winning first, but the data in the *Miller*

Lite Report are confusing. Seventy-four percent of the respondents said that they "almost always" or "often" felt it would have been all right for a child to have lost an event he or she had won, but only 63 percent felt that it was "almost always" or "often" all right to lose when a child had in fact lost, and 40 percent "almost always" or "often" gave a winning child a special treat. Further, 49 percent of the "fans" who watched their children lose "almost always" or "often" "recommend ways that [they] can improve their skills," although only 11 percent of the "non-fans" did so. (Miller Brewing Company, *Miller Lite Report,* pp. 44, 52–53.) And whatever parents *say* they do, to attend a children's sporting event is often to be alarmed by the verbal abuse heaped by some parents on officials and children alike. British children largely escape this, if only because so few British adults systematically watch their children compete.

   12. John Bale, *Sport and Place: A Geography of Sport in England, Scotland and Wales* (London: C. Hurst and Co., 1982), p. 75.

   13. The Spanish International Network broadcast all fifty-two games of the 1982 World Cup Soccer matches; thirty-seven of the matches were rebroadcast (*Sports Illustrated,* July 26, 1982, p. 12). This network exists for the fans.

   14. *Dallas Morning News,* Oct. 17, 1982, p. B25.

   15. Letters from immigrants were not always joyful and hopeful; many make pitiful reading. Handlin chose the title of his book, *The Uprooted,* felicitously. Oscar Handlin, *The Uprooted: The Epic Story of the Great Migrations That Made the American People* (New York: Grosset and Dunlap, 1951). See also Charlotte Erickson, *Invisible Immigrants: The Adaptation of English and Scottish Immigrants in Nineteenth Century America* (Coral Gables: University of Miami Press, 1972). Pioneers traveling west suffered dislocation and hardship in spite of the "myth of the garden," which suggested that the trans-Mississippi West flowed with milk and honey. See Henry Nash Smith, *Virgin Land: The American West as Symbol and Myth* (New York: Alfred Knopf, 1950).

   16. Robert Dykstra's book *The Cattle Towns* (New York: Alfred Knopf, 1968) explores the means by which such boosting was carried on in five Kansas cattle towns between 1867 and 1885. The struggle to attract population has not ceased, nor is it confined to small towns. "Small is beautiful" has not yet drowned out the cry that "Bigger is better" in American municipalities, particularly as federally funded urban programs operate on a per capita basis.

   17. Isabella Bird, *A Lady's Life in the Rocky Mountains* (Norman: University of Oklahoma Press, 1960; 1st ed. 1879).

   18. Sinclair Lewis, *Babbitt* (New York: Harcourt, Brace and World, 1922), p. 119.

   19. Ian Tyrell, "Money and Morality: The Professionalisation of American Baseball," in *Sport,* ed. Cashman and McKernan, p. 89.

   20. Geoff Winningham and Al Reinert, *Rites of Fall: High School Football in Texas* (Austin: University of Texas Press, 1979), p. 9.

   21. International matches between youth teams are televised; but players here represent their country, not simply their home town, and victory is a national not a local event. In contrast, James Coleman wrote in 1961 that a visitor to an American high school might conclude "that the school was essentially organized

around athletic contests and that scholastic matters were of lesser importance to all involved." James S. Coleman, "Athletics in High School," *Annals of the American Academy of Political and Social Science* 338 (1961): 34.

22. *Sports Illustrated,* July 12, 1982, p. 13.

23. Edwin H. Cady, *The Big Game: College Sports and American Life* (Knoxville: University of Tennessee Press, 1978).

24. Red Smith, *Views of Sport* (New York: Alfred Knopf, 1954), p. 291.

25. We have forgotten the Ivy League recruiting scandals of the 1890s. For a brief discussion of them see Benjamin Rader, *American Sports: From the Age of Folk Games to the Age of Spectators* (Englewood Cliffs, N.J.: Prentice Hall, 1983), pp. 137f.

26. A similar desire for prestige led at least one boarding school in England to improve its sports facilities, so that games for gentlemen could be properly played. In the 1880s, Lancing sought to become integrated into the public school system by such means. J. A. Mangan, *Athleticism in the Victorian and Edwardian Public School: The Emergence and Consolidation of an Educational Ideology* (Cambridge: Cambridge University Press, 1981), pp. 37, 66.

27. This subsidy is distributed indirectly, through an independent committee set up for the purpose. British academics used to regard themselves as insulated from government pressure; Margaret Thatcher's budget-cutting measures have awakened them to the fact that when money is cut off at the source, the mechanism by which it is distributed indeed becomes a part of the political process. Attacks on tenure are now being made by the British government. *Chronicle of Higher of Education,* May 23, 1984, pp. 31-32.

28. See Richard Hofstadter, *Social Darwinism in American Thought,* rev. ed. (Boston: Beacon Press, 1955).

29. Martin J. Wiener, *English Culture and the Decline of the Industrial Spirit 1850-1980* (New York: Cambridge University Press, 1981), pp. 8, 10. Margaret Thatcher's policies have been directed toward reviving entrepreneurial enterprise.

30. Rodman W. Paul, *Mining Frontiers of the Far West 1848-1880* (New York: Holt, Rinehart and Winston, 1963), p. 26.

31. Frederick Jackson Turner, "The Significance of the Frontier in American History" (1893), in his *The Frontier in American History* (New York: Holt, Rinehart and Winston, 1962), pp. 1-38.

32. Harold Nicolson, *Diaries and Letters 1930-39,* ed. Nigel Nicolson (New York: Atheneum, 1966), p. 203.

33. Wiener, *English Culture,* p. 34. In his autobiography, Lawrence Olivier pointed out that he made sure his advertisement for Polaroid would not be shown in Great Britain. Europeans and Americans would understand his commercial acumen, he believed; the British would be offended. Lawrence Olivier, *Confessions of an Actor* (New York: Simon and Schuster, 1982), p. 298.

34. Sampson, *Changing Anatomy of Britain,* pp. 430-31.

35. *Chronicle of Higher Education,* May 9, 1984, pp. 31, 33. British university education was expanded as a result of the Robbins report (1963) but its elite, ivory-tower status was never in doubt. For details of the recommendations see

Higher Education Report, Cmnd. 2154 (London: Her Majesty's Stationery Office, 1963).

36. *Dallas Morning News,* May 14, 1984, p. D4.

37. *Chronicle of Higher Education,* June 12, 1985, p. 29.

38. It was officially acknowledged that the demand for souvenirs could not be overlooked, but distaste for "trade" led to a series of laughable regulations. Dish towels bearing a picture of the royal couple, for instance, were to be designated as "wall-hangings" lest someone sully the royal profiles with soapsuds.

39. Ian Tyrell, "Money and Morality," pp. 86, 101.

40. The string of reports concerning the failure of the American public-school system that were published in 1982 and 1983 all refer to America's dismal future as an industrial power if the schools are not put right. Other issues are, of course, addressed; but one function of public-school education is to keep American citizens competitive in world markets.

41. Ralph Turner, "Modes of Social Ascent," p. 123.

42. In the film *Absence of Malice,* the newspaper's lawyer has no concern at all for a story's truth or falsehood. His job is to ensure that the paper is not sued. Succinctly, he goes over the legal rules; provided the paper has conformed to them, however false and damaging a story may be to those named in it, to print it is "fair." Much later, when a reporter finally begins to realize what she has done and understands that she has the capacity to inflict damage on yet another human being, she is distressed because there are "no rules" to help her decide what she should do.

43. John Dizikes, *Sportsmen and Gamesmen* (Boston: Houghton Mifflin, 1981), p. 311.

44. R. S. Rait Kerr, *The Laws of Cricket: Their History and Growth* (London: Longmans, Green and Co., 1950), p. 58.

45. Court action forced American broadcasters in 1923 to pay fees for the use of copyright materials; in 1926, a court decision about the powers of the secretary of commerce led to the Radio Act of 1927. In 1948, the U.S. Supreme Court declared that eight film companies had acted to prevent competition through control over theaters and block booking; as a result, capital and people were suddenly released from contract and entered the TV industry. In 1951, the Supreme Court upheld the FCC's decision to accept the color system developed by RCA and favored by most manufacturers. In 1966 the U.S. Court of Appeals for the District of Columbia Circuit held that community organizations have the right to contest applications for license renewals; until that year, only those who had an economic stake in a case's outcome could intervene. No such court decisions have affected British radio and TV. (For details see Erick Barnouw, *Tube of Plenty: The Evolution of American Television,* rev. ed. (New York: Oxford University Press, 1982; 1st ed., 1975), pp. 41, 57, 115-16; Roscoe L. Barrow et al., "Development of Television: FCC Allocations and Standards," in *American Broadcasting: A Source Book on the History of Radio and Television,* ed. Lawrence W. Lichty and Malachi C. Topping (New York: Hastings House, 1975), p. 609; Erwin G. Krasnow and Lawrence D. Longley, *The Politics of Broadcast Regulation,* 2d ed. (New York: St. Martin's Press, 1978), pp. 43-44.

46. David Quentin Voigt, *American Baseball*, vol. 1, *From Gentleman's Sport to the Commissioner System* (Norman: University of Oklahoma Press, 1966), p. 316.

47. James B. Dworkin, *Owners versus Players: Baseball and Collective Bargaining* (Boston: Auburn House Publishing Co., 1981), p. 64. A short overview of the application of antitrust laws to sport is Steven R. Rivkin's "Sports Leagues and the Federal Antitrust Laws," in *Government and the Sports Business*, ed. Roger G. Noll (Washington, D.C.: Brookings Institution, 1974), pp. 387-410.

48. Ellul attributes the proliferation of laws and the separation of the idea of law from the idea of justice to the subordination of twentieth-century people to what he calls "technique." In Ellul's words, "Application of law no longer arises from popular adherence to it, but from the complex of mechanisms which, by means of artifice and reason, *adjust behavior to rule*" (italics added). Players of professional sport play strictly to the rules because, as Ellul puts it, "law ensures order instead of justice." Jacques Ellul, *The Technological Society* (New York: Alfred Knopf, 1970), pp. 293, 296.

49. George W. Keeton, *The Football Revolution: A Study of the Changing Pattern of Association Football* (Newton Abbot: David and Charles, 1972), p. 48.

50. Gentlemen played the game, but their behavior afterward was by no means genteel. As Kenneth Sheard and Eric Dunning point out, players celebrated by getting drunk, singing obscene songs, and even destroying property. But the social status of players helped them "flaunt [*sic*] social conventions without fear of punishment" (p. 295). Kenneth Sheard and Eric Dunning, "The Rugby Football Club as a Type of 'Male Preserve': Some Sociological Notes." In *Sport Sociology*, ed. Yiannakis, pp. 294-302.

51. For a discussion of the games ethos that ruled British public schools from 1860 to 1940, see Mangan, *Athleticism*. One index of a shift in emphasis is to be found in figures for public attendance at the Eton-versus-Harrow cricket match at Lord's. In 1939 there were 19,174 spectators, in 1948 there were 18,806, and in 1954 there were 14,845. In 1966, there were 7,219; and in 1972, only 2,466 (p. 145).

52. For selections of such articles and bibliography, see, in addition to the citations in n. 10, Robert Lipsyte, "Variety Syndrome: The Unkindest Cut"; Jonathan Brower, "The Professionalization of Youth Sports"; and Bruce Ogilvie, "The Child Athlete: Psychological Implications of Participation in Sports," *Annals of the American Academy of Political and Social Science* 445 (Sept. 1979): 15-23, 39-46, 47-58; Jay A. Coakley, *Sport in Society: Issues and Controversies*, 2d ed. (St. Louis: C. V. Mosby Co., 1982), pp. 82-135.

53. Voigt, *American Baseball*, vol. 1, p. 38.

54. See Richard Hofstadter, *Anti-Intellectualism in American Life* (New York: Alfred Knopf, 1963).

55. Alistair Cooke, "Teeing Off on Golf Announcers," *TV Guide*, June 16, 1979, pp. 17-18.

56. H. A. Harris, *Sport in Britain: Its Origins and Development* (London: Stanley Paul, 1975), p. 193.

57. See George A. Lundberg, "The Content of Radio Programs," in *American Broadcasting*, ed. Lichty and Topping, pp. 322-23. For descriptions of some of

these early shows see Hubbell Robinson and Ted Patrick, "Jack Benny"; Bernard Lucich, "The Lux Radio Theater"; and Martin J. Maloney, "The Radio Mystery Program," ibid., pp. 333-37, 391-94, 394-99.

58. David T. MacFarland, "Up From Middle America: The Development of Top 40," in *American Broadcasting,* ed. Lichty and Topping, pp. 402-3.

59. Lorin F. Deland, *At the Sign of the Dollar and Other Essays,* (New York: Harper and Bros., 1917), p. 72.

60. Leo Marx, *The Machine in the Garden: Technology and the Pastoral Ideal in America* (New York: Oxford University Press, 1964).

Chapter 5

1. Erik Barnouw, *Tube of Plenty: The Evolution of American Television,* rev. ed. (New York: Oxford University Press, 1982), pp. 33-34.

2. Leslie J. Page, Jr., "The Nature of the Broadcast Receiver and Its Market in the United States from 1922 to 1927," in *American Broadcasting: A Source Book on the History of Radio and Television,* ed. Lawrence W. Lichty and Malachi C. Topping (New York: Hastings House, 1975), p. 469.

3. Barnouw, *Tube of Plenty,* p. 41.

4. See Lichty and Topping, eds., *American Broadcasting,* pp. 195-98.

5. Barnouw, *Tube of Plenty,* pp. 21, 49-54.

6. Ibid., p. 55.

7. Lichty and Topping, eds., *American Broadcasting,* p. 203.

8. George A. Lundberg, "The Content of Radio Programs," in *American Broadcasting,* ed. Lichty and Topping, p. 323.

9. John W. Spalding, "1928: Radio Becomes a Mass Advertising Medium," in *American Broadcasting,* ed. Lichty and Topping, pp. 219-28. (Spalding quotes from Roy Durstine, "Audible Advertising," an article to be found in *Radio and Its Future,* ed. Martin Codel [New York: Harper and Bros., 1930], p. 51.)

10. Barnouw, *Tube of Plenty,* pp. 57-59.

11. See Lawrence W. Lichty, "The Impact of the FRC and FCC Commissioners' Backgrounds on the Regulation of Broadcasting," in *American Broadcasting,* ed. Lichty and Topping, pp. 621-31.

12. Asa Briggs, *The History of Broadcasting in the United Kingdom,* vol. 2, *The Golden Age of Wireless* (London: Oxford University Press, 1965), p. 48.

13. Barnouw, *Tube of Plenty,* p. 76.

14. Ibid., pp. 63, 89-96.

15. Gaye Tuchmann, ed., *The TV Establishment: Programming for Power and Profit* (Englewood Cliffs, N.J.: Prentice Hall, 1974), p. 8.

16. For what follows, see Richard J. Meyer, "Reaction to the 'Blue Book,' " in *American Broadcasting,* ed. Lichty and Topping, pp. 589-602.

17. Robert Pepper, "The Pre-Freeze Television Stations," in *American Broadcasting,* ed. Lichty and Topping, p. 142.

18. The alternative system of broadcasting set up under the Public Broadcasting Act of 1967 is watched by so few people and has such slender financial resources, that it is true to say that American television is a commercial enterprise.

19. For prime-time programs, see Tim Brooks and Earle Marsh, *The Complete Directory to Prime Time Network TV Shows 1946-present,* rev. ed. (New York: Ballantine, 1981); and Harry Castleman and Walter J. Podrazik, *Watching TV: Four Decades of American Television* (New York: McGraw-Hill, 1982).

20. Castleman and Podrazik, *Watching TV,* p. 146.

21. For discussion of how programming was done in 1970 see Les Brown, *Television: The Business behind the Box* (New York: Harcourt Brace Jovanovich, 1971). For a discussion of programming in the 1970s by one man, see Sally Bedell, *Up the Tube: Prime-Time TV and the Silverman Years* (New York: Viking Press, 1981).

22. Lichty and Topping, eds., *American Broadcasting,* p. 527.

23. *Chronicle of Higher Education,* Jan. 13, 1982, p. 5.

24. Michael Novak has made the point that Americans expect America to be morally better than other nations of the world; *The Joy of Sports: End Zones, Bases, Baskets, Balls, and the Consecration of the American Spirit* (New York: Basic Books, 1976), p. 18. There is no tradition in Britain of published breast-beating, while Americans cheerfully buy books such as David Riesman, *The Lonely Crowd: A Study of the Changing American Character* (New Haven: Yale University Press, 1950); Vance Packard, *The Waste Makers* (New York: D. McKay Co., 1960); Christopher Lasch, *The Culture of Narcissism: American Life in an Age of Diminishing Expectations* (New York: W. W. Norton, 1979); Allan Bloom, *The Closing of the American Mind* (New York: Simon and Schuster, 1987).

25. Asa Briggs, *The History of Broadcasting in the United Kingdom,* vol. 1, *The Birth of Broadcasting* (London: Oxford University Press, 1961), pp. 48, 95, 99, 101-6, 116, 123, 164; Burton Paulu, *British Broadcasting: Radio and Television in the United Kingdom* (Minneapolis: University of Minnesota Press, 1956), pp. 8-10.

26. Briggs, *History of Broadcasting,* vol. 1, p. 8. Briggs quotes J. C. W. Reith, *Broadcast over Britain* (London: Hodder and Stoughton, 1925), p. 17.

27. Briggs, *History of Broadcasting,* vol. 1, p. 347. As Paulu points out, the BBC did not have a monopoly by law; de facto, however, it did. Paulu, *British Broadcasting,* p. 14.

28. Paulu, *British Broadcasting,* p. 36. Paulu quotes J. C. W. Reith, *Into the Wind* (London: Hodder and Stoughton, 1949), p. 133.

29. Giving evidence to the Sykes Committee in 1923, a Post Office representative made the point that no one there wanted in any way to "control" broadcast news. Briggs, *History of Broadcasting,* vol. 1, p. 101. Although Churchill wanted to commandeer it, during the general strike of 1926, the BBC remained independent, as it did during World War II; see Asa Briggs, *The History of Broadcasting in the United Kingdom,* vol. 3; *The War of Words* (London: Oxford University Press, 1970). During the Suez crisis, the BBC gave airtime to the Labour, as well as the Conservative, position; see Burton Paulu, *Television and Radio in the United Kingdom* (Minneapolis: University of Minnesota Press, 1981), pp. 33-39. During the Falkland Islands war, the Conservative government denounced the BBC for being too fair-minded. In 1985, BBC journalists walked out for twenty-four hours

because a documentary on Northern Ireland was canceled as a result, they alleged, of government pressure. *Dallas Morning News,* Aug. 7, 1985, p. A10.

30. Paulu, *British Broadcasting,* pp. 17-18. Paulu quotes Reith, *Into the Wind,* p. 99.

31. Briggs, *History of Broadcasting,* vol. 2, p. 47.

32. Ibid., p. 57. Briggs quotes the *Times,* Jan. 30, 1934.

33. Briggs, *History of Broadcasting,* vol. 2, p. 55. Briggs quotes *BBC Handbook* (London: British Broadcasting Corporation, 1928), p. 71.

34. Briggs, *History of Broadcasting,* vol. 2, p. 361.

35. Ibid., p. 44.

36. Ibid., p. 363.

37. "By 1935, 98 per cent of the population could listen...to one BBC programme, and 85 per cent could choose between two." Ibid., p. 253.

38. Ibid., p. 185. Briggs quotes J. C. W. Reith, *Listener,* Apr. 30, 1930.

39. There were only about 20,000 TV sets in the United Kingdom in 1939. Paulu, *British Broadcasting,* p. 247.

40. Briggs, *History of Broadcasting,* vol. 3, p. 719.

41. These programs were completely stratified in 1970, Radio 1 offering pop music, Radio 2 light entertainment, Radio 3 cultural programs, and Radio 4 a mixture as on the old Home Service.

42. Asa Briggs, *The History of Broadcasting in the United Kingdom,* vol. 4, *Sound and Vision* (London: Oxford University Press, 1979), pp. 76-77. Briggs quotes William Haley, Address to the General Advisory Council, Oct. 29, 1947.

43. Briggs, *History of Broadcasting,* vol. 4, p. 227.

44. Ibid., p. 162. Briggs quotes Sir William Haley, "The Place of Broadcasting," *Listener,* Nov. 20, 1947. American broadcasters know their work is not an end in itself, but to say so is to suggest lack of commitment. The point of view that has to be established by commercial networks is reflected in a May 1978 NBC memorandum discussing plans for saturation hype of the 1980 Olympic Games. The aim was to ensure that "anyone missing even so much as a half-hour of coverage will feel deprived. We will have turned the American people into a nation of Olympics addicts." Quoted from the *New York Times,* in Ron Powers, *Supertube: The Rise of Television Sports* (New York: Coward-McCann, 1984), p. 20.

45. Briggs, *History of Broadcasting,* vol. 4, p. 284. This tradition still, to some extent, holds. As Paulu points out, the BBC newsreaders are not "anchor persons," and do not command anything like the status or pay of their U.S. counterparts. Paulu, *Television and Radio,* p. 198.

46. Briggs, *History of Broadcasting,* vol. 4, pp. 31, 42-43. A letter to the *Times* has been the traditional British way of opening debate on public issues.

47. Ibid., pp. 344, 363.

48. Stephen Lambert, *Channel Four: Television with a Difference?* (London: British Film Institute, 1982), p. 8. For a full account of the origins of commercial TV, see Bernard Sendall, *Independent Television in Britain,* vol. 1, *Origin and Foundation 1946-62* (London: Macmillan, 1982).

49. Briggs, *History of Broadcasting,* vol. 4, pp. 132, 886.

50. Lambert, *Channel Four,* p. 9. Lambert quotes *Broadcasting: Memoran-*

dum on Television Policy (London: Her Majesty's Stationery Office, 1953), Cmnd. 9005, para. 17.

51. A full description of the organization and legal status of the Independent Television Authority (which became the Independent Broadcasting Authority in 1972 when some commercial radio was added to ITA's responsibilities) can be found in Paulu, *Television and Radio,* pp. 63-87. See also Paulu, *British Broadcasting,* pp. 51-59.

52. Just how similar, and how "establishment" these appointments have been is demonstrated by Paulu, *Television and Radio,* pp. 133-34.

53. For what follows, see Lambert, *Channel Four,* pp. 9-10.

54. Ibid., p. 10. Lambert quotes Sendall, *Independent Television,* p. 63.

55. Briggs, *History of Broadcasting,* vol. 4, p. 937.

56. *BBC Handbook,* (1979), pp. 34, 37.

57. Lambert, *Channel Four,* pp. 13, 15.

58. Ibid., p. 14. Paulu considers that competition from ITV was helpful to the BBC, because it finally freed young, creative people working in television from the domination of those who had worked in radio. ITV also forced the BBC to pay more attention to what the public really wanted to see, without necessarily abandoning its quest for quality productions. Paulu, *Television and Radio,* pp. 43-44.

59. Ibid., pp. 82-83.

60. Lambert, *Channel Four,* p. 17.

61. Ibid., pp. 18, 23.

62. Ibid., p. 93. Lambert quotes W. Whitelaw, speech at the RTS Convention, "Television in a Free Society," Sept. 14, 1979, Home Office news release, p. 3.

63. Lambert, *Channel Four,* pp. 108-10.

64. Ibid., p. 149.

65. As "minority" programs these may succeed; otherwise, apart from American football, they would seem to have no future. See chapter 2, and Joan Chandler, "American Pro Football in Britain?" *Journal of Popular Culture* 12, no. 1 (Summer 1978): 146-55.

66. British Broadcasting Corporation, *Annual Review of BBC Broadcasting Research Findings,* no. 7, 1980 (London: British Broadcasting Corporation, 1981), p. 91: tables 8.1 and 8.2, pp. 93-94. (Table 8-3, p. 95, does not match the data given in tables 8.1 and 8.2.) Data from a 1977 general household survey in table 8.4a showed that 10 percent or more of respondents reported participating in only darts, swimming, snooker, and soccer of the sports considered by the BBC researchers (pp. 95-96), so presumably for most respondents "interested in" meant "watching."

67. Miller Brewing Company, *The Miller Lite Report on American Attitudes toward Sports* (Milwaukee: Miller Brewing Co., 1983), p. 19 of "General Public Questionnaire," and table 6.4, p. 176.

68. BBC, *Annual Review,* pp. 93-94.

69. Miller Brewing Co., *Miller Lite Report,* tables 1.4, 1.5, 1.6, pp. 24-25.

70. Ibid., table 6.4, p. 176.

71. Ibid.; BBC, *Annual Review,* pp. 93-94. Fifty-four percent of men and 47 percent of women in the Miller Lite survey report participating once a month or

more in swimming. Miller Brewing Company, *Miller Lite Report,* table 6.3, p. 175.

72. BBC, *Annual Review,* tables 8.4a, b; pp. 96-97. Bale quotes 1970s figures from Inglis that indicate that British men and women prefer to watch different sports on TV, and that far fewer women than men watch televised sport of any kind. Inglis's figures, however, differ from those of the BBC in that soccer is by far the preferred TV sport of the men, while cricket is second (of eight sports named). Soccer is ranked third by the women and cricket seventh. These differences may be due to the dates when surveys were made, to variation in the questions asked, or other factors. John Bale, *Sport and Place: A Geography of Sport in England, Scotland and Wales* (London: C. Hurst and Co., 1982), p. 7. Table taken from F. Inglis, *The Name of the Game* (London: Heinemann, 1978).

73. Roland Bowen, *Cricket: A History of Its Growth and Development Throughout the World* (London: Eyre and Spottiswoode, 1970), p. 114.

74. Bale, *Sport and Place,* p. 78.

75. Ibid., pp. 81-82.

76. First-class counties began playing league cricket in 1969. "In League cricket it is more important to win than it is in County cricket where the game's the thing.

"County cricket, of course, needs money to keep going but nowhere is the financial aspect of the game given more emphasis than in League cricket where more points mean more spectators and more spectators mean more money." Maurice Golesworthy, *Encyclopaedia of Cricket,* 6th ed. (London: Robert Hale, 1977), p. 131.

77. Malcolm Musgrove, *Official Programme: Torquay United 74-75,* (n.p., n.d.), p. 3.

78. George Keeton, *The Football Revolution: A Study of the Changing Pattern of Association Football* (Newton Abbot: David and Charles, 1972), p. 49. This outline of club structure is taken from pp. 48-61.

79. Desmond Morris, *The Soccer Tribe* (London: Jonathan Cape, 1981), p. 219.

80. Ibid., p. 217.

81. British Broadcasting Corporation, *The Coverage of Sport on BBC Television: A Study for the BBC General Advisory Council* (London: British Broadcasting Corporation, 1974), p. 8.

82. Ibid., p. 6.

83. Ibid., p. 5.

84. Ibid., p. 10.

85. There is no precedent in Britain for TV companies deciding whether or not to allow political office seekers to buy advertising time, much less for announcing the results of an election before everyone has voted.

Chapter 6

1. Christopher Brookes, *English Cricket: The Game and Its Players through the Ages* (London: Weidenfeld and Nicolson, 1978), p. 2. "The Cricket Industry," *Political and Economic Planning* 22, no. 401 (1956): 3.

2. The MCC is the governing body of British cricket.

3. The number of books on the history of cricket is legion. A good many of them are antiquarian and anecdotal, but some are extremely useful, including H. A. Altham and E. W. Swanton, *A History of Cricket,* 3d ed., (London: George Allen and Unwin, 1947); Roland Bowen, *Cricket: A History of Its Growth and Development throughout the World* (London: Eyre and Spottiswoode, 1970); and Brookes's *English Cricket.* In what follows, I have drawn heavily on Brookes's conceptual outline. See also R. S. Rait Kerr, *The Laws of Cricket: Their History and Growth* (London: Longmans, Green and Co., 1950).

4. Altham and Swanton, *History of Cricket,* p. 22.

5. Brookes, *English Cricket,* p. 33.

6. Ibid., p. 36.

7. Ibid., p. 49-50.

8. Gerald Howat, *Village Cricket* (Newton Abbot: David and Charles, 1980), p. 70.

9. The third stump was added in 1777. Neville Cardus, *English Cricket* (London: Collins, 1945), p. 10. For illustrations of bats, balls, and games in progress, see Hugh Barty-King, *Quilt Winders and Pod Shavers; The History of Cricket Bat and Ball Manufacture* (London: Macdonald and Jane's, 1979). For a description of eighteenth-century practices, see Altham and Swanton *History of Cricket,* pp. 27f; for the nineteenth century, pp. 129f.

10. Kerr, *Laws of Cricket,* p. 13.

11. Ibid., pp. 21-22.

12. By 1900, pitches were as smooth as they are today; twentieth-century changes in law were therefore directed toward helping the bowler rather than the batsman. Ibid., pp. 46f.

13. Howat, *Village Cricket,* p. 11.

14. Kerr, *Laws of Cricket,* p. 41.

15. Brookes, *English Cricket,* pp. 77-79. For details of wagers and gambling, see Altham and Swanton, *History of Cricket,* pp. 39-40, 62-63; on gambling, John Arlott, *From Hambledon to Lords* (London: Christopher Johnson, Publishers, 1948), pp. 100-105; Kerr, *Laws of Cricket,* pp. 19-20.

16. Brookes, *English Cricket,* pp. 77.

17. Altham and Swanton, *History of Cricket,* pp. 55-56.

18. Brookes, *English Cricket,* pp. 90-91.

19. Howat, *Village Cricket,* p. 17.

20. Cardus, *English Cricket,* pp. 12-13.

21. Brookes, *English Cricket,* pp. 101f; Altham and Swanton, *History of Cricket,* pp. 88f.

22. Kerr, *Laws of Cricket,* p. 37.

23. Brookes, *English Cricket,* p. 114.

24. Ibid., pp. 114, 116-17. Brookes quotes from the *Times* in Aug. 1866; H. Silver, "Our Critic upon Cricket," *Once a Week,* June 1861, p. 665; and Anon., "The Siege of the Wicket," *Once a Week,* Aug. 1867, p. 225.

25. Altham and Swanton, *History of Cricket,* p. 177.

26. Brookes, *English Cricket,* p. 124. Brookes quotes Rev. R. S. Holmes, *The County Cricket Championship* (n.p., 1894), p. 32.

27. Wray Vamplew, "Playing for Pay: The Earnings of Professional Sportsmen in England 1870-1914," p. 109. Vamplew points out that professional cricketers faced competition from amateurs during this period, which kept their numbers relatively low. Their wages were also relatively poor, although winter pay was introduced in the 1890s. In *Sport: Money, Morality and the Media,* ed. Richard Cashman and Michael McKernan (Kensington: New South Wales University Press, 1982), pp. 104-30.

28. Kerr, *Laws of Cricket,* p. 42.

29. Eric Dunning and Kenneth Sheard, *Barbarians, Gentlemen and Players: A Sociological Study of the Development of Rugby Football* (New York: New York University Press, 1974), p. 181.

30. The Imperial Cricket Conference was formed in 1909. Test matches between member counties are now played by England, Australia, India, New Zealand, Pakistan, Sri Lanka, and West Indies.

31. Martin J. Wiener, *English Culture and the Decline of the Industrial Spirit 1850-1980* (New York: Cambridge University Press, 1981), p. 47.

32. Because fans were quiet, it did not mean they were uninterested. In an 1882 test match against Australia, England were nine wickets down and needed ten runs to win. During the last half hour, "one spectator dropped down dead, and another, after all was over, was surprised to discover that he had bitten large and irreplaceable pieces out of his umbrella-handle"; Cardus, *English Cricket,* p. 32.

33. Altham and Swanton, *History of Cricket,* pp. 238, 445, 220.

34. Jim Laker, *One-Day Cricket* (London: B. T. Batsford, 1977), p. 11.

35. John Arlott discussed "Cricket's Severest Famine," players, in the *Guardian,* Feb. 15, 1975, p. 17.

36. Laker, *One-Day Cricket,* pp. 28f.

37. Bowen, *Cricket,* pp. 252, 251.

38. John Arlott, "There's No Substitute for Genius," *Overseas Guardian,* Sept. 23, 1972, p. 28.

39. Laker, *One-Day Cricket,* p. 17.

40. Ibid., p. 27.

41. John Arlott, *How to Watch Cricket* (London: Collins, 1983), pp. 12-17.

42. H. A. Harris, *Sport in Britain: Its Origins and Development* (London: Stanley Paul, 1975), p. 78.

43. Edward Buscombe, ed., *Football on Television* (London: British Film Institute, 1975), p. 6.

44. Laker, *One-Day Cricket,* pp. 12, 14, 43.

45. Ibid., p. 43.

46. The Packer affair was reported in detail in articles in three successive editions of *Wisden Cricketers' Almanac* (the British cricketers' bible), ed. Norman Preston (London: Queen Anne Press, Macdonald and Jane's Publishing Group). I have taken facts from there; the interpretation is my own. The articles, all by Gordon Ross and all entitled "The Packer Case," are in *Wisden,* 1978, pp. 123-28; 1979, pp. 88-95; 1980, pp. 121-29.

47. Fred Trueman, *Ball of Fire: An Autobiography* (St. Albans: Mayflower Books, 1977, first ed. 1976), p. 66.

48. Jim Laker, *Over to Me* (London: F. Muller, 1960).

49. John Arlott, *Cricket on Trial: John Arlott's Cricket Journal – 3* (London: Heinemann, 1960), pp. 47-48; 147-48.

50. Brian Stoddart, "Cricket's Imperial Crisis: the 1932-33 MCC Tour of Australia," in *Sport in History: The Making of Modern Sporting History,* ed. Richard Cashman and Michael McKernan (St. Lucia, Australia: University of Queensland Press, 1979), p. 134.

51. Michael McKernan, "Sport, War and Society: Australia 1914-18," in *Sport,* ed. Cashman and McKernan, p. 8.

52. Cashman and McKernan, *Sport,* p. 1.

53. Stoddart, "Cricket's Imperial Crisis," p. 126.

54. *Wisden,* 1980, p. 127.

55. Ibid., p. 123.

56. E. W. Swanton, *Cricketer International,* Aug. 1977, p. 6.

57. *Wisden,* 1980, p. 129.

58. *Punch* is the British equivalent of the *New Yorker.*

59. Altham and Swanton, *History of Cricket,* p. 181.

60. Arlott, *How to Watch Cricket,* p. 43.

61. In the first four overs of this match, only three runs were scored; but the commentators once allowed more than a minute to go by without saying a word; the average time between comments was thirty seconds. The commentary, however, varied, just as normal talking would have varied; a short comment might be followed by another, or by a longer discussion about a particularly good or puzzling play. Even in a limited-over match the commentators do not regard it as their job to keep the party going at all costs. On June 15, 1980, in a John Player League match, six balls produced two comments, and in four overs the average length of time between comments was again about thirty seconds.

62. Stephen Pile in The *Sunday Times,* London, June 26, 1983, p. 1.

63. E. Gerald French, *It's Not Cricket: An Analysis of the Game's Unwritten Laws, Its Moral Code, Customs and Etiquette* (Glasgow: William MacLellan, 1960), p. 14.

64. Richard Cashman, "Crisis in Contemporary Cricket" in *Sport,* ed., Cashman and McKernan, pp. 304-12.

65. Arlott, *How to Watch Cricket,* p. 18.

66. Denzil Batchelor, *The Game Goes On* (London: Eyre and Spottiswoode, 1947), p. 1.

Chapter 7

1. Brian Glanville, *Soccer: A History of the Game, Its Players and Its Strategy,* (New York: Crown Publishers, 1968), pp. 2-4. A great many books have been written on the history of British soccer, but few approach the quality of work available in cricket or baseball. Anecdote abounds; documentation is sparse or absent. Admittedly the task is herculean. As Mason remarks of the thirty-three current league clubs operating before 1914 that he approached, "Eighteen claimed

to have no records, seven had records but refused access, four clubs had a very small number of items which they were willing to show, and only two clubs . . . had incomplete . . . collections of materials." Two clubs did not reply. (Tony Mason, *Association Football and English Society 1863-1915* [Brighton: The Harvester Press, 1980], p. 6.) Nevertheless, Mason's book is a valuable historical account, as is the pioneer study of one of the long-lived clubs: Charles Korr, *West Ham United: The Making of a Football Club* (Urbana: University of Illinois Press, 1986).

Information about soccer's early history may be found in the following: Lionel Francis, *Seventy-Five Years of Southern League Football* (London: Pelham, 1969); Maurice Golesworthy, ed., *The Encyclopaedia of Association Football,* 11th ed. (London: Robert Hale, 1973); W. E. Greenland, *The History of the Amateur Football Alliance* (Harwich, Essex: Standard Printing and Publishing Co., 1966); James Walvin, *The People's Game: A Social History of British Football* (London: Allen Lane, 1975); and Percy Young, *A History of British Football* (London: Stanley Paul, 1968).

2. Walvin, *People's Game,* pp. 41-42.

3. Glanville, *Soccer,* p. 12; and Brian Glanville, *A Book of Soccer* (New York: Oxford University Press, 1979), p. 14.

4. Steven Tischler, *Footballers and Businessmen: The Origin of Professional Soccer in England* (New York: Holmes and Meier, 1981), pp. 32-33.

5. Ibid., pp. 52, 55.

6. Ibid., p. 54. Tischler quotes *Athletic News,* Oct. 25, 1882, p. 1.

7. Ibid., p. 43. Tischler quotes *Football* (London), Oct. 11, 1882, p. 10.

8. Ibid., pp. 51f.

9. George W. Keeton, *The Football Revolution: A Study of the Changing Pattern of Association Football* (Newton Abbot: David and Charles, 1972), p. 19.

10. Tischler, *Footballers and Businessmen,* p. 58. Tischler quotes the *Birmingham Daily Mail,* Aug. 31, 1888, p. 2. Mason, *Association Football,* pp. 44-49. Karr's discussion of West Ham's finances demonstrates that management of the club cost directors time and money. Korr, *West Ham United,* pp. 44-54, 60.

11. The class distinctions that lay behind the controversy over professionalism led men who wanted to play with their "equals" to change their game. Rugby Union clubs were all amateur (and remain so, to this day). Professional soccer matches were played in the early months of World War I, which led after the war to the misperception that rugby players were more patriotic. This, coupled with the boisterous postwar crowds, the gambling associated with soccer, and the clearly professional attitude of league clubs, made it hard to find in soccer "the old public school virtues of selflessness, independence and the amateur 'sporting' mentality, and much easier to find those qualities in Rugby Union" (Walvin, *People's Game,* p. 114). Increasingly, public schools played rugby rather than soccer. By the 1930s "good" schools played rugby; schools for the working class played soccer.

12. Tischler, *Footballers and Businessmen,* p. 62. Tischler quotes the *Athletic News,* May 6, 1895, p. 1.

13. *Dallas Morning News,* Sept. 3, 1982, p. B8.

14. Tischler, *Footballers and Businessmen,* p. 112. Tischler quotes the *Athletic News,* Aug. 9, 1909, p. 1.

15. *Dallas Morning News,* Sept. 12, 1982, p. B21; Oct. 15, 1982, p. B9.

16. Tischler, *Footballers and Businessmen,* p. 113. Tischler quotes the *Sports Argus,* Aug. 28, 1909, p. 1.

17. *Conservative Digest* 8, no. 8, (Aug. 1982): 21-24, 51.

18. Tischler, *Footballers and Businessmen,* p. 113.

19. *Dallas Morning News,* Sept. 29, 1982, p. B5; Oct. 21, 1982, p. B9; Oct. 24, 1982, p. B14.

20. Tischler, *Footballers and Businessmen,* p. 115. Tischler quotes *Cricket and Football Field,* Aug. 21, 1909, p. 1.

21. Ibid., p. 116.

22. *Denver Post,* July 28, 1982, p. F1.

23. Tischler, *Footballers and Businessmen,* p. 117. Tischler quotes the *Athletic News,* Aug. 2, 1909, p. 1; *Cricket and Football Field,* June 5, 1909, p. 9.

24. *Dallas Morning News,* Oct. 17, 1982, p. B25.

25. Tischler, *Footballers and Businessmen,* p. 118. Tischler quotes the *Football and Sports Special,* July 3, 1909, p. 1.

26. Tischler, *Footballers and Businessmen,* p. 120.

27. In 1952 the maximum wage was fourteen pounds a week – then about fifty-six dollars. Norman Harris, *The Charlton Brothers* (London: Stanley Paul, 1971), p. 36. In 1957, the maximum wage had been increased to twenty pounds. Bob Wilson, *Bob Wilson: An Autobiography* (London: Pelham Books, 1971), p. 28. A maximum-wage scale was enforced until 1961.

28. Keeton, *Football Revolution,* p. 22.

29. The lowest teams in the Fourth Division must be reelected for the following season. Their claims are matched against the applications of teams that have applied for entry to the Football League. Normally, the threatened league team survives at least for a year or two, and its directors set frantically to work to hire a new manager, buy new players, and take whatever other measures they can to scramble up the division in the following season. Occasionally, teams will give up the ghost, as Accrington-Stanley did in 1962, which allowed another team to take its place.

30. In the 1949-50 season, 31,219 clubs were registered with the Football Association. Of these, roughly 500 employed about 7,000 professionals among them, but over 30,000 clubs employed no professionals at all. Walvin, *People's Game,* pp. 147-48.

31. For discussion of soccer spectators, see Mason, *Association Football,* pp. 138-73; Allen Guttmann, *Sports Spectators* (New York: Columbia University Press, 1986), pp. 105-9.

32. It is impossible to reproduce here the "maps" of players' movements I have drawn. It is a simple matter, however, to draw a player's movements for five minutes on a prepared plan of the field; the result shows conclusively how much ground a player covers, particularly in a hard-fought match.

33. A brief history of team strategies is to be found in Desmond Morris, *The Soccer Tribe* (London: Jonathan Cape, 1981), pp. 70-74. Morris identifies four-

teen "favoured formations" and points out that since the 1850s the number of players whose main job is to defend has steadily increased. Professional players and coaches differ in their view of "tactics," some believing in much more teamwork than others. For opposing viewpoints of players see George Best, *Best of Both Worlds* (London: Pelham, 1968), pp. 59-60, 73; and Ian Ure, *Ure's Truly* (London: Pelham, 1968), pp. 77-78.

34. Morris, *Soccer Tribe*, p. 317.

35. *Guardian*, Dec. 24, 1973, p. 16.

36. Young, *History of British Football*, p. 198.

37. Jeremy Bugler and David Jones, *Observer*, Jan. 4, 1976, p. 8.

38. Ibid.

39. Golesworthy, *Encyclopaedia of Association Football*, p. 193.

40. Jimmy Scoular, "Ban the Box," *League Football*, n.d. (1972-73 season).

41. John Bale, *Sport and Place: A Geography of Sport in England, Scotland and Wales* (London: C. Hurst and Co., 1982), pp. 31, 29, 43.

42. David Lacey, *Guardian*, Sept. 2, 1974, p. 16.

43. John Arlott, *Guardian*, Dec. 21, 1973. See also Hugh McIlvanney, *Observer*, Dec. 19, 1976, p. 16.

44. Christopher Brasher, *Observer*, Dec. 31, 1972.

45. *Guardian*, Sept. 23, 1972, p. 28; *Observer*, Aug. 18, 1974, p. 18; *Guardian*, Aug. 21, 1974; Aug. 25, 1974; Oct. 19, 1975, p. 27.

46. Marsh et al. have analyzed the behavior of young men who go to soccer matches bent on what the authors call "a ritualized expression of aggression." (Peter Marsh, Elizabeth Rosser, and Rom Harré, *The Rules of Disorder* [London: Routledge and Kegan Paul, 1978], p. 68.) Williams et al. have reported on the violent behavior of English fans who travel to matches in Europe. Some of them get too drunk beforehand to see the match they have ostensibly traveled to watch. (John Williams, Eric Dunning, and Patrick Murphy, *Hooligans Abroad: The Behavior and Control of English Fans in Continental Europe* [London: Routledge and Kegan Paul, 1984], pp. 83, 136.) Both sets of authors insist that violence occasioned by soccer, inside and outside the stadium, is a complex, multifaceted phenomenon, as do Roger Ingham et al. in *'Football Hooliganism': the Wider Context* (London: Inter-action Imprint, 1978).

47. Keeton makes detailed comparison of clubs' balance sheets for several seasons. In 1967-68, Manchester United, a First Division side that won the European Cup and had a good season in the league, had gate receipts of £530,800 and a year's surplus of £107,104. It therefore paid dividends on its shares, which cost it all of £481 4s. 1d. After tax, the club carried forward an accumulated balance of about £455,544. In contrast, Hull City, an aspiring Second Division club, had an accumulated loss in April 1969 of £161,606. Bury, a Third Division club, competing for fans with nearby larger towns, had an accumulated loss in 1971 of £47,443; Doncaster Rovers, a Fourth Division club, had a net loss in the 1968-69 season of £18,393. But no balance sheet is typical; as Keeton points out, "Balance sheets of the League clubs reveal the widest variation in modes of operation . . . the receipts and expenditures of one of the foremost clubs must seem to the less fortunate something of a fairy tale." The only common denomina-

tor is the reliance of clubs on gate receipts; if clubs want to embark on a spending program in the hope of raising attendance, they normally must rely on directors, or the supporters' club. Keeton, *Football Revolution,* pp. 61-76.

48. Richard Redden and Hugh Hebert, "Guardian Extra," *Guardian,* Dec. 19, 1975, p. 14.

49. The F.A. Cup is a knockout competition (see p. 137); any affiliated club, including amateur and semiprofessional sides, may enter. First Division clubs do not have to play in the early rounds, and it is rare for a team from a lower division to get very far. Brighton and Hove Albion had only just been relegated to the Second Division (the F.A. Cup is the last match of the season, after league games are over), and their supporters were overjoyed that despite the disgrace of relegation, the team was playing in the Cup Final.

50. Morris made a detailed study of chanting in the 1978-79 season. He found that in four First Division clubs, the number of chantings per match averaged 147. He then examined more thoroughly the chanting of Oxford United, a Third Division club. The average number here was 145 per game; between 49 and 86 different chants were used each game. Analyzing the fifteen home matches, Morris found there were 2,179 separate chantings and 251 different chants, which he divided into twelve different categories of such types as "confidence and optimism," "criticism of home club," "comments for the police," and "threats to the opponents." He noted that about 60 percent of Oxford United chants had nothing to do with action on the field but "belong to the separate world of the terrace culture." Morris, *Soccer Tribe,* pp. 306-15. Oxford United's matches are not a staple of "Match of the Day"; these fans are entertaining themselves, not a TV audience.

51. I do not know how much rehearsal camera crews were given before televising soccer games. British crews were trained by Americans before trying to translate the first NFL exhibition game at Wembley; and football, as I have pointed out, is a much more patterned although more complex game than soccer for cameras to follow.

52. Stadium crowds and TV ratings diminished after the 1982 strike was over; the season, like the 1981 baseball season, was perceived to be virtually meaningless. Fans and spectators had learned their lesson well; their appetite was not for football, but for football on the terms it had been sold to them.

53. A scholarly book on professional soccer in the United States has yet to be written. A useful introduction, *America's Soccer Heritage: A History of the Game,* by Sam Foulds and Paul Harris (Manhattan Beach, Calif.: Soccer for Americans, 1979) is undocumented, as is Chuck Cascio's *Soccer U.S.A.* (Washington: Robert B. Luce, 1975).

54. Kyle Rote, Jr., with Basil Kane, *Kyle Rote, Jr.'s Complete Book of Soccer* (New York: Simon and Schuster, 1978), p. 30.

55. Glanville, *Book of Soccer,* p. 135.

56. *Dallas Times Herald,* Mar. 26, 1978, p. C2; *Dallas Morning News,* Oct. 20, 1980, p. B10; May 22, 1983, p. H1.

57. *New York Times,* May 22, 1984, p. 24.

58. Rote, *Kyle Rote, Jr.'s Soccer,* p. 25.

59. Glanville, *Book of Soccer,* p. 146.
60. Rote, *Kyle Rote, Jr.'s Soccer,* p. 103.
61. *Dallas Morning News,* Sept. 27, 1981, p. B22.
62. Glanville, *Book of Soccer,* p. 150.
63. Indeed, the Fédération may have to accept changes. In 1976, the Football League was discussing point changes for goals scored. *Herald Express,* May 13, 1976, p. 14. The World Cup must still be played on grass; but Queen's Park Rangers soccer club now uses artificial turf. Other teams may follow. *Dallas Morning News,* July 3, 1983, p. B11.
64. *Dallas Morning News,* Apr. 27, 1978, p. B3; Apr. 2, 1981, p. B6.
65. Derek Morgan, "I Want My Bloody Game Back," *Sports Illustrated* 27, no. 9 (Aug. 28, 1967): 52-54.
66. Bale, *Sport and Place,* p. 51.

Chapter 8

1. Rod Laver with Bud Collins, *The Education of a Tennis Player* (New York: Simon and Schuster, 1971), pp. 210, 299.
2. *Dallas Morning News,* Jan. 17, 1982, p. B10.
3. The relationship between TV and sponsorship is not always direct. All TV advertising of cigarettes was banned in 1971. So, just as Gillette had hoped to secure indirect TV exposure by sponsoring one-day cricket, so Virginia Slims supported Gladys Heldman's group of touring women professionals to promote its brand of cigarettes for women. Shannon, *Official Encyclopedia,* p. 74.
4. Kramer goes so far as to suggest that Lamar Hunt would now be controlling international tennis had he been able to sign Arthur Ashe in 1968. Jack Kramer with Frank Deford, *The Game: My Forty Years in Tennis* (New York: G. P. Putnam's Sons, 1979), pp. 263, 266-68.
5. Innumerable books on tennis exist; however, I have found no single social or cultural history of the game. Short factual accounts are contained in Bill Shannon, ed., *Official Encyclopedia of Tennis,* rev. ed. (New York: Harper and Row, 1981) and Max Robertson, *Wimbledon: Centre Court of the Game* (London: British Broadcasting Corporation, 1977). Interesting diagrams of courts and equipment are to be found in Gianni Clerici, *The Ultimate Tennis Book* (Chicago: Follett Publishing Co., 1975), pp. 28-32.
6. Shannon, *Official Encyclopedia,* pp. 1-4; Clerici, *Tennis Book,* pp. 62-67. Further details on Wingfield's game may be found in George E. Alexander, *Lawn Tennis: Its Founders and Early Days* (Lynn: H. O. Zimman, 1974), pp. 7-51, 109-18.
7. Robertson, *Wimbledon,* p. 16. See also Alexander, *Lawn Tennis,* pp. 77-107.
8. Robertson, *Wimbledon,* p. 17.
9. Ibid., pp. 20, 23.
10. Shannon, *Official Encyclopedia,* pp. 7-10. See also Alexander, *Lawn Tennis,* pp. 53-71.
11. A commentator on the 1987 Wimbledon Women's Final remarked that although the grass looked nice on TV, by the server's position on the baseline, "it's sand." A closeup showed that indeed it was.

12. Shannon, *Official Encyclopedia,* pp. 394-95, 24.

13. Ibid., pp. 21-22, 25-26.

14. Ibid., pp. 26-27.

15. Frank G. Menke, *The Encyclopedia of Sports,* 5th ed. rev. (New York: A. S. Barnes and Co., 1975), pp. 966-67, 969-70.

16. Kramer, *Game,* pp. 190-91, 193, 203, 214-16.

17. Ibid., pp. 245, 252-54, 259-60.

18. Laver, *Tennis Player,* pp. 201-3.

19. Ibid., pp. 23, 168-70.

20. Ibid., p. 203.

21. I have drawn on Rich Koster's *The Tennis Bubble! Big Money Tennis: How It Grew and Where It's Going* (New York: Quadrangle, 1976) for much of the following information.

22. Ibid., p. 64.

23. John Arlott, ed., *The Oxford Companion to Sports and Games* (Oxford: Oxford University Press, 1975), p. 610.

24. Koster, *Tennis Bubble,* p. 6.

25. Margaret Smith Court with George McGann, *Court on Court: A Life in Tennis* (London: W. H. Allen, 1976).

26. Althea Gibson, the first black Wimbledon champion, turned professional after winning her second U.S. Open title, in 1958. She found purses too low, and became a professional golfer instead. Eugene Scott, *Tennis: Game of Motion* (New York: Crown, 1973), p. 79.

27. Asa Briggs, *The History of Broadcasting in the United Kingdom,* vol. 2, *The Golden Age of Wireless* (London: Oxford University Press, 1965), p. 611.

28. Arlott, *Oxford Companion,* p. 602.

29. Bobby Wilson with John Cottrell, *My Side of the Net* (London: Stanley Paul, 1964), p. 19.

30. *Dallas Morning News,* May 13, 1977, p. B1.

31. The court surface in Moody Coliseum on the Southern Methodist University campus was deliberately made faster for a professional tournament in 1976 to stop the killing of the women's services that had occurred in the mixed-doubles events in 1975.

32. *Dallas Morning News,* Sept. 6, 1982, p. B2. See also Bob Greene, "Final Days of Glory at Forest Hills," *Dallas Morning News,* Sept. 5, 1977, p. D3.

33. See, for instance, *New York Times,* June 28, 1981, p. 22, and *Dallas Morning News,* Oct. 4, 1981, p. B17. The Men's International Professional Tennis Council tightened the rules in 1987; McEnroe received a two-month suspension for accumulating fines. Cynics wonder whether McEnroe's appeal would have been allowed had he been playing better tennis at the time.

34. Several players in the 1987 U.S. Open Championships mentioned the difficulty of concentrating amid the crowd noise. Games were often slow to start because people were not in their seats. *Dallas Morning News,* Sept. 1, 1987, p. B7.

Tennis players require quiet because they must concentrate so intensely for so long. A baseball pitcher and batter certainly concentrate; but each has long rest periods during the course of a game and often have their strategy decided for them. Even in the gaps between games tennis players, particularly if they are losing, must think. No one intervenes for them to argue a bad call; no one else can pinpoint their opponents' weaknesses or tell them how to alter a losing game or suggest how to bring back a stroke that has suddenly deserted them. Noise and movement add distraction; players may blot them out but at the cost of added fatigue and self-control.

35. Laver, *Tennis Player,* pp. 220-21.

36. Koster, *Tennis Bubble,* p. 17.

37. *Dallas Morning News,* July 4, 1982, p. B12.

38. A new Dallas team tennis franchise, the Dallas Stars, played their opening game against Houston on July 7, 1982. Dallas is a tennis town; but only 300 spectators came. The event was well publicized; but the players' names were not known, and the event itself was meaningless for tennis fans. *Dallas Morning News,* July 8, 1982, p. B12.

39. Lawrence W. Lichty and Malachi C. Topping, eds., *American Broadcasting: A Source Book on the History of Radio and Television* (New York: Hastings House, 1975), p. 522.

40. In 1975 more than 21 million people paid $330 million for tennis equipment and $200 million for tennis clothing. *Dallas Morning News,* Apr. 16, 1976, p. D3. For comments on the trendy nature of tennis, see Ronald J. Stupak, "Tennis, Television and Affluent America: Fault and Double-Fault," *Intellect* 104 (Jan. 1976): 321-22. The tennis boom had reached such proportions by 1977 that the Braniff trade magazine, *Flying Colors,* included an article called "Tennis – No Place to Play?" In it, the author cited a 1975 survey by the National Sporting Goods Association showing that 42 percent of the families playing tennis had incomes over $20,000 a year, and that the husbands in 42.1 percent of the families polled were college graduates. *Flying Colors* 6, no. 5, pp. 33-34.

41. Koster, writing in 1976 and quoting Lamar Hunt, suggests that golf tournaments cost $100,000 to televise and tennis merely $30,000 to $40,000. Koster, *Tennis Bubble,* p. 71. Powers states that delayed-tape rights in the mid-1970s could cost as little as $15,000, while advertisers could be charged NFL rates. Ron Powers, *Supertube: The Rise of Television Sports,* (New York: Coward-McCann, 1984), p. 236.

42. The winner-take-all formula was susceptible to fraud. CBS announced that Connors was playing Ilie Nastase on March 5, 1977, in such a contest, but in fact both players had received guarantees. Bill Riordan later took responsibility for not telling viewers what they were seeing, but the matter was cause for comment in the "As We See It" column of *TV Guide,* May 21, 1977, p. A1.

43. McEnroe is rare among top-ranked tennis players in that he has played regularly in Davis Cup matches. Most good players are like Borg, who in 1981 refused to play against Japan and Australia; he told the Swedish Tennis Association he wished to focus on tournaments like Wimbledon and the U.S. Open. *Dallas Morning News,* June 11, 1981, p. B10.

44. Baseball and cricket statistics serve the purpose of differentiating between individual players and teams. Meaningless as they are, these statistics developed

out of the fans' desire to place players in some sort of relationship to one another, within and across seasons, because no one wins a baseball game or cricket match on his own. How do I know X is better than Y? How do I know X is now playing better or worse than he used to? Statistics purport to tell me.

Tennis players individually win or lose matches. They can thus be directly compared with each other and with their past performances. Further, professional players use their whole repertoire in every match; perhaps a first serve does not go in as frequently as it usually does, but the same player serves more aces and makes fewer unforced errors. A pitcher can't alter his ERA by batting in home runs; and if he were to show a propensity for the latter, like Babe Ruth he would soon cease to pitch.

45. It is one thing to place a viewer briefly at eye level directly behind a player; this may help the viewer remember exactly what it feels like to face an opponent. It is quite another to remain behind the receiver at ground level throughout the point as was done by the NBC camera in the sixth game of the first set of the 1986 French Open Men's Final. Even though the rallies on the clay court had been quite long, NBC had resisted the temptation to break up their pattern. But the last point of the game was very hard to follow, since the viewer saw it almost entirely from Michael Pernfors's vantage point. Similarly, it was impossible to see where Martina Navratilova's second serve landed on the third point of the second game in the first set of the 1987 Wimbledon Women's Singles Final; Steffi Graf missed it, so Navratilova's tentative court position did not affect the outcome – but a viewer could not have followed subsequent play if it had. This camera placement behind the receiver is common – and almost invariably distracting.

46. During the U.S. Open Men's Final, viewers were taken several times from the match to another court on which Martina Navratilova and her partner were playing the Mixed Doubles Final. There was only one camera on this court, so placed that viewers could see only part of the playing area, not even up to the net. The ball, if one glimpsed it at all, appeared from nowhere and disappeared again; but CBS evidently assumed we wanted to watch the moment at which Navratilova did or did not win all three titles at one tournament. Greater concern with result rather than process could scarcely have been demonstrated.

47. This tape is not idiosyncratic. Similar figures could be taken from two other tapes I have analyzed; the commentators on this particular tape talked the least.

48. Probably proportionally more American than British children play tennis, particularly in regions where the weather is good. But tennis is not understood in the U.S. as baseball and football are understood, because it has not been integrated into the formal educational system.

49. As David Miller wrote in the *Times* on the following day, "Anyone at Wimbledon yesterday could have been forgiven for supposing they were watching by mistake first round croquet matches at Budleigh Salterton, rather than the semi-finals of a grand slam tournament." July 1, 1983, p. 25.

50. From the days of radio some British sports promoters had feared competition from broadcasting. See Asa Briggs, *History of Broadcasting,* vol. 2, pp. 77,

120, 613; and Briggs, *A History of Broadcasting in the United Kingdom,* vol. 4, *Sound and Vision* (London: Oxford University Press, 1979), pp. 838f.

Chapter 9

1. Lawrence W. Lichty and Malachi C. Topping, eds., *American Broadcasting: A Source Book on the History of Radio and Television* (New York: Hastings House, 1975), p. 522; Central Statistical Office, *Annual Abstract of Statistics* (London: H.M.S.O.), 1960, no. 97, pp. 62, 207; 1970, no. 107, pp. 66, 241. These sets were not distributed evenly. There were more sets in the northeastern United States and in the south of England (historically, the centers of communication), and more in cities than rural areas in both countries.

2. Lichty and Topping, eds., *American Broadcasting,* p. 522; Central Statistical Office, *Annual Abstract,* 1976, no. 113, pp. 90, 293.

3. R. E. Davies, *Airlines of the United States Since 1914* (London: Putnam, 1972), pp. 85, 181, 329, 386.

4. Harvey H. Firestone, Jr., *Men on the Move: The Story of Transportation* (New York: G. P. Putnam's Sons, 1967), pp. 170-71, 178.

5. M. Reynolds, "Little Boxes," recorded by Pete Seeger, on *We Shall Overcome,* Columbia Records (C12101).

6. Roger Kahn, *The Boys of Summer* (New York: Harper and Row, 1971), p. xix.

7. Jesse W. Markham and Paul V. Teplitz, *Baseball Economics and Public Policy* (Lexington: D. C. Heath and Co., 1981), p. 61. The figures prior to 1955 include attendance in Mexico, which was then less than a million a year.

8. Ibid.

9. Ibid., p. 60.

10. Donald V. Harper, *Transportation in America: Users, Carriers, Government* (Englewood Cliffs, N.J.: Prentice-Hall, 1978), p. 214.

11. Firestone, *Men on the Move,* p. 191.

12. Davies, *Airlines,* pp. 451, 458, 462.

13. David Quentin Voigt, *American Baseball,* vol. 2, *From the Commissioners to Continental Expansion* (Norman: University of Oklahoma Press, 1970), pp. 65-66, 116-17.

14. O. J. Simpson with Pete Axthelm, *The Education of a Rich Rookie* (New York: Macmillan, 1970), p. 201. Jerry Kramer noted, "Rookies sure have more expensive tastes than they did when I was a rookie. My whole rookie season I only earned $7,750." Dick Schaap, ed., *Instant Replay: The Green Bay Diary of Jerry Kramer* (Cleveland: The New American Library, 1968), p. 224.

15. National Football League Players Association, *A Report to Members of the National Football League Players Association,* Sept. 1981, p. 4.

16. *Dallas Morning News,* Jan. 20, 1984, p. B7; July 28, 1984, p. B13. Dworkin points out that rivalry between the ABA and NBA increased salaries for basketball players. James B. Dworkin, *Owners versus Players: Baseball and Collective Bargaining,* (Boston: Auburn House, 1981), p. 236.

17. Voigt, *American Baseball,* vol. 2, p. 223.

18. Dworkin, *Owners versus Players,* pp. 95, 162.

19. Glenn Dickey, *The History of National League Baseball Since 1876,* (New York: Stein and Day, 1979), p. 200.

20. Robert W. Creamer, *Babe: The Legend Comes to Life* (New York: Penguin, 1983; 1st ed. 1974), p. 132. Creamer gives interesting details of other bonuses and salaries; see, for instance, pp. 110, 118, 134, 175, 188, 254, 346, 351, 356. Ruth's highest salary was probably equivalent now to $562,000 a year, tax free.

21. See for instance, Voigt, *American Baseball,* vol. 2, p. 225.

22. Miller Brewing Company, *The Miller Lite Report on American Attitudes toward Sport* (Milwaukee: Miller Brewing Co., 1983), pp. 75, 72.

23. Ring Lardner, *You Know Me Al* (New York: George H. Doran, 1916).

24. Kahn, *Boys of Summer,* pp. 98-99, 115.

25. Linda J. Waite, *U.S. Women at Work* (Washington, D.C.: Population Reference Bureau, May 1981), p. 5.

26. Fernando Valenzuela won his arbitration case with the Dodgers in 1983; among other things he claimed that when he pitched, the Dodgers' attendance increased by about 5,000. *Dallas Morning News,* Feb. 29, 1983, p. B15.

27. In 1982, gate receipts were estimated to account for 34 percent of NFL gross revenues, 54 percent of major-league baseball's gross revenues, and 63 percent of NBA gross revenues. Glen Waggoner, "Money Games," *Esquire* 97, no. 6 (June 1982): 53.

28. Roger Angell, *The Five Seasons: A Baseball Companion* (New York: Popular Library, 1978), pp. 406-9.

29. *Chronicle of Higher Education,* Jan. 4, 1984, p. 24.

30. Janet Lever, *Soccer Madness* (Chicago: University of Chicago Press, 1983), pp. 4-21.

31. As Rowland and Watkins point out, "effort" in television studies in the last decade "has come to emphasize the study of television in context, to see it in intimate relationship with all other principal institutions, expressive forms, and patterns of meaning in society." Willard D. Rowland, Jr. and Bruce Watkins, eds., *Interpreting Television: Current Research Perspectives* (Beverly Hills: Sage Publications, 1984), p. 27.

INDEX

233

Note on the Author

Joan Chandler was born in England; a Cambridge graduate, she has taught in universities on both sides of the Atlantic. Her first book was an American history text for British schools, written after she had spent a year at Bryn Mawr on an English Speaking Union fellowship. Her book of American historical documents for British students' use was published while she was completing her Ph.D. at the University of Texas. Having played amateur sports all her life, she was fascinated by the contrast between American and British traditions of college sport, and began to work on the cultural significance of sport while she was an anthropology faculty member at the University of Massachusetts. Now American Studies Program Head at the University of Texas at Dallas, she is currently working on sport and ritual.